WINNIPEG
WITHDRAWN
PUBLIC LIBRARY
D1026073

PRAISE FOR *A Girl Walks into a Book*

"I've been watching Miranda Pennington happen for some time. Her first book is all I could hope for, as a fan and a fellow Brontë girl: As doggedly funny and practical as its heroines, perpetually surprising, and containing perhaps the world's first impassioned defense of Anne. (Wait. Were we supposed to care about Anne?) Read it on its own, and take it as a guide on your next tour through the eternally useful Brontë works."

   —Sady Doyle, author of *Trainwreck: The Women
      We Love to Hate, Mock, and Fear . . . and Why*

"In Miranda Pennington's telling, her relationship with the Brontës and their work is an epic love story, as real, reciprocal, and life-altering as they come. Warm, smart, and very funny, *A Girl Walks into a Book* offers a version of the experience it describes: entry into a singular world and a lasting friendship."

   —Michelle Orange, author of *This Is Running for Your Life*

"Miranda Pennington's literary memoir is a necessary book. While there have been many books about the Brontë sisters, Pennington's is the first to define their influence on a new generation of young women. Whether writing about Charlotte Gainsbourg, romantic confusion, or visits to the moors, Pennington is a witty, charming, candid observer of female rebellion, past and present. *A Girl Walks into a Book* champions the strange, beautiful magic of the Brontës, while establishing Pennington herself as a daring,

   —Rebecca Godfrey, autho   *ridge*

WINNIPEG
WITHDRAWN

A GIRL WALKS INTO A BOOK

A GIRL
WALKS INTO
A BOOK

*What the Brontës Taught Me
about Life, Love, and Women's Work*

MIRANDA K. PENNINGTON

SEAL PRESS

Copyright © 2017 by Miranda K. Pennington

All rights reserved. No part of this book may be
reproduced or transmitted in any form without written
permission from the publisher, except by reviewers who may
quote brief excerpts in connection with a review.

ISBN: 978-1-5800-5657-1
ISBN: 978-1-5800-5658-8 (e-book)

Library of Congress Cataloging-in-Publication Data
for this book is available.

Published by Seal Press,
an imprint of Perseus Books, LLC,
a subsidiary of Hachette Book Group, Inc.
1700 Fourth Street, Berkeley, California 94710
sealpress.com

Cover Design: Faceout Studio
Interior Design: Trish Wilkinson

Printed in the United States of America
Distributed by Hachette Book Group

10 9 8 7 6 5 4 3 2 1

One may say of Currer Bell that her genius finds a fitting illustration in her heroes and heroines—her Rochesters and Jane Eyres. They are men and women of deep feelings, clear intellects, vehement tempers, bad manners, ungraceful, yet lovable persons. Their address is brusque, unpleasant, yet individual, direct, free from shams and conventions of all kinds. They outrage "good taste," yet they fascinate. You dislike them at first, yet you learn to love them. The power that is in them makes its vehement way right to your heart.

—G. H. Lewes, from an unsigned 1853 review, *Leader*

For my family

Contents

Illustrations

A Note on Textual References

I have reproduced all misspellings, odd grammar, and weird or missing punctuation used by the Brontës, their friends, and correspondents, following the lead of Juliet Barker and Margaret E. Smith. Where either of these exceptional scholars made conjectures on missing words or phrases, I have incorporated their text.

Walking into the Brontës

This is a love story. Charlotte Brontë and her sisters loved to write, and I fell in love with their words on the page, and I have been looking for that kind of love in and out of books ever since. And maybe you too have fallen in love with a Jane Eyre or a Paul Emanuel or, Heaven help you, a Heathcliff, and so you will know exactly what I mean.

Let me be clear, I am not a fairy-tale-magical-wedding-day happy-ever-after sort of person. My favorite fairy tales are the weird ones, where the girl who trod on a loaf gets sucked underground for her hubris, or one of the seven brothers straightens his hat and freezes the world, or dogs with dish-sized eyes wait for the soldier to strike the tinderbox, or the princess weaves coats of flax for her swan brothers. At the end of these stories, the heroine's just lucky not to be dancing herself to death in a pair of bewitched shoes. That spiky strangeness is what I like most about them. When it came to my own ever-after, perhaps my expectations were unconventional, but I had still wanted a storybook ending, one way or another. I had been ecstatic to find someone with a winning smile who laughed at my jokes and wanted me around. I thought we were building a life together. But after one too many disappointed expectations and undelivered promises I finally became suspicious that it wasn't going to happen. Whether I was unworthy, the person I had picked was too flawed, or the story I'd based my dreams on was a lie—something was broken.

As I got ready to leave the apartment that had finally started to feel like "ours," my battered and beloved copy of *Jane Eyre* was the last book I packed, in the last bag I lined up by the door. I was leaving, taking only what I had brought with me and could call my own. It was a dark, bitter moment with one flicker of solace: Charlotte Brontë would have approved.

When I first came to the Brontës, I was a child, naïve and unwary. The old-fashioned prose and thick spine of *Jane Eyre* were promising; lots of the books written for kids my age (ten or so) were like potato chips, gone in a flash and leaving nothing behind but a greasy residue. I waded into the opening pages, read about a young girl huddled in a window-seat reading Bewick's *History of British Birds*, and was intrigued. I'd spent my share of hours curled up reading while adults talked, and I found the notion of a window-sill hidden by curtains especially romantic. My "library" was under the fluorescent lights of a basement playroom where I escaped my toddler brother, who was too little to climb downstairs. Rather than the finely furnished halls of Gateshead that Jane Eyre longed to escape, I had a battered sleepaway couch, a plastic foosball table, a hot pink wooden toy box with a chalkboard, and an array of particleboard bookcases that groaned under the weight of Louisa May Alcott, Mark Twain, The Brothers Grimm, and Beverly Cleary. Despite these drastic differences in our circumstances, I related to Jane—there's no accounting for the affinity one lonely kid has for another.

Then, as I read on, Jane's villainous aunt sent her to a miserable boarding school, with horrible people, who didn't understand anything that mattered, much less Jane herself. I was appalled. I wrote off *Jane Eyre* as unpleasant and unfair, a dull story about a plain girl's awful life. That first time, I never made it to Thornfield or met Mr. Rochester. It's possible I never even survived the ignominious "Liar" incident in Chapter VII. I have since gathered this experience is not uncommon—people tend to love *Jane Eyre* immediately or hate it. High school students made to suffer through it rarely make a return visit, unfortunately, and even adults who encounter it too late in life struggle to connect. London critic Elizabeth Rigby gave it an infamously harsh review in 1848, saying, "A little more, and we should have flung the book aside."[1] After that first attempt, I actually *did* toss *Jane Eyre* to the floor and heard the pages skitter as they hit the linoleum.

But the book was so satisfyingly weighty. Even as I hurled it off the bed, it seemed like a book that should matter. I kept picking it back up. I stared down Mr. Brocklehurst. I endured the boarding school. I crossed my fingers when Jane dared to advertise for a new position. Eventually, I found that I liked it, despite its darkness, despite Jane's trials, which I took personally. To despise Jane was to despise *me*. By the time I finished it, I had come to love *Jane Eyre*. I was a chubby tomboy with a mushroom cut, who always talked too fast. I liked reading fantasy epics and singing along to show tunes in the car. But *Jane Eyre* took me somewhere new. Jane's pastimes were ladylike—drawing and sewing; her language was dense and archaic, and I occasionally had no idea what was happening, but she spoke to me. She opened that door that exists inside all devoted readers. She made my heart beat faster and my fingers turn the pages ever more eagerly, hungry to know more.

Charlotte Brontë writes children like the child she must have been—the thoughtful, imaginative kind, with mature powers of observation and broad depths of feeling. Though shy, young Jane was fearless when spurred by oppression or injustice, which we see when she loses her temper with her bullying cousin a few pages into the novel's opening. So what if she inevitably loses the fight and gets locked in her dead uncle's haunted bedroom, bleeding from the scalp— Jane throws herself, nails out, at John Reed's smug, hateful face and does her worst.

Often grown-up authors seem to assume that children's thoughts are as simple as the words they have at their disposal. *Jane Eyre* radically departs from this attitude. Young Jane had the same faculties of understanding and sensitivity her grown-up self would, the same resistance to wrongdoing and the same enviable strength of passion. We expect this in our heroines—Charlotte Brontë's contemporary readers did too—but giving this defiance to a kid in 1847 was terrifically subversive. Even at ten, I felt my mind was a morass of new and conflicting and imagined and hoped-for information I didn't quite understand, and it was gratifying to see this complexity acknowledged in print. Until Jane, I had to read grown-up books to be challenged, usually sacrificing the pleasure of someone to relate to in the process. I felt certain Jane would understand my overwhelming feelings, the tidal wave of contradictory thoughts and impulses that barreled through my brain on a given day.

Sometimes we read to find ourselves; sometimes we read to escape ourselves; sometimes we read to see ourselves more clearly. When I read *Jane Eyre*, the words arranged themselves to form pictures; I could hear the voices, feel the dank drafts whispering through poorly fastened casements. I could hear really old jokes! Charlotte Brontë had meant to be funny when she wrote that Jane had "not a whit" of faith in Mr. Rochester as he tried to propose to her, and I had understood her being funny, and thusly we had communicated. *Jane Eyre* pulled me inside of it. When I looked back at the clock, it seemed time had gone faster while I read, the cost of living two lives at once. It was almost as good as time travel. Anything outside those pages vanished until, all too soon, I reached the last page, the adventure ended, and I was back on my bed where I started. Learning to speak Brontë gave me a secret power that nobody else had. And *Jane Eyre* was the key—it's what put me on the path to living my life in sync with the Brontës' work. It inspired a quest to discover as much about Charlotte Brontë as I could. Each Brontë has in turn provided exactly the right illumination for my life, but only when read at the right time. Try a Brontë novel too early, and you'll find yourself scrabbling around the sides, wandering off mid-story distracted, even bored. But open the right book on the right day, and it'll strike a bell you didn't even know needed to be rung.

That's how it was for me, anyway. *Jane Eyre* moved me to try *Wuthering Heights*, which I hated, then *Villette*, which I abandoned for being slow and inscrutable. In my early twenties I turned to *Agnes Grey*, which gave me a window into the life of a twenty-something woman and a nudge to grow up. I eventually devoured *Shirley*, savoring its feminism, friendship, and history; Charlotte is *silly* when she wants to be. After that, I tackled *The Tenant of Wildfell Hall*, which tore my life apart, only to remake it better. By then I was finally ready for *Villette*, the story it took Charlotte so many tries to get right. These days I reread *Jane Eyre* once a year, and take doses of the others as necessary. Sometimes I consult them like an oracle or a Magic 8 Ball—I open to a random page and see what they have to say; it's an idiosyncratic art of bibliomancy, a kind of *sortes brontënae*.

I needed the Brontës to help me figure out how to function in the world around me, and their work is always up to the task. Even though their characters live, think, and speak in outdated and occasionally unwieldy prose, it still startles me to be reminded that they aren't real. It seems much more likely they exist in the ether somewhere, fully formed and waiting for a reader to bring them to life again. Believing that my favorite characters live outside their pages may be why I hear new messages with every read. I have such faith in *Jane Eyre* that it always seems entirely plausible that *this time*, the ending might come off differently. There might be a new character to meet. Jane might not have such a hard time after fleeing the grounds of Thornfield. Rochester might come clean at the very start of their romance, or never have married Bertha Mason in the first place. St. John Rivers could let himself live a little and declare his undying love for Rosamond Oliver. All of these potential revisions seem equally possible. But it always happens the same way, as it has to happen, to eventually secure the happy ending I can't live without.

When I'm in need of relationship lessons, the books are all about how partners should be equals. When I'm in need of motivation, I notice they contain an awful lot about women managing their own affairs and getting things done. When I need a boost of self-reliance, when I need to be taught about patience, when I need to rediscover an internal moral compass: whatever I need, it turns out that's what the Brontës wrote. These novels examine women's independence, employment, social values, education, mental illness, alcoholism, adultery, trials of the soul, morality, mythology, and love, *especially* love. When you're tuned to the right frequency, there's a medicinal power in Emily's stubbornness, Anne's perseverance, Charlotte's sarcasm, and even Branwell's self-destructive dissipation.

I thought I had come to the end of the Brontë shelf, but then I found their poetry, Charlotte's letters, and a plethora of biographies. I read them all and I started over. I read the Brontës' juvenilia and their schoolgirl essays, their novella fragments and forewords to revised editions, their unfinished scraps and diary papers. I examined the doodles in the margins, their illustrations and sketches, Charlotte's watercolors and Branwell's portraits of their neighbors. My life has unfolded alongside the words of the Brontës, sometimes been carried by them. This is the story of that journey—there are advantages to having a literary roadmap, and there are costs. Their lives and their writing and my life and my writing have all come together in an entwining of threads that seems both surprising and inevitable.

The Family

The Bells are of a hardy race. They do not lounge in drawing-rooms or boudoirs. The air they breathe is not that of the hot-house, or of perfumed apartments: but it whistles through the rugged thorns that shoot out their prickly arms on barren moors, or it ruffles the moss on the mountain tops. Rough characters, untamed by contact with towns or cities; wilful men, with the true stamp of the passions upon them; plain vigorous Saxon words, not spoiled nor weakened by bad French or school-boy Latin; rude habits; ancient residences—with Nature in her great loneliness all around;—these—with the gray skies or sunset glories above—are the elements of their stories, compounded and reduced to shape, in different moods and with different success.

—Unsigned review of *The Tenant of Wildfell Hall,*
The Examiner, 1848[1]

Had my father given me a different book in the spring of 1995, I might be writing an account of a lifelong obsession with Virginia Woolf or Mark Twain or even George Eliot (and I wouldn't be the first). But he gave me *Jane Eyre* and, unexpectedly, a mission. As I opened book after book, turned page after page, sought out source after source in my pursuit of the Brontës, I was trying to get as close as possible

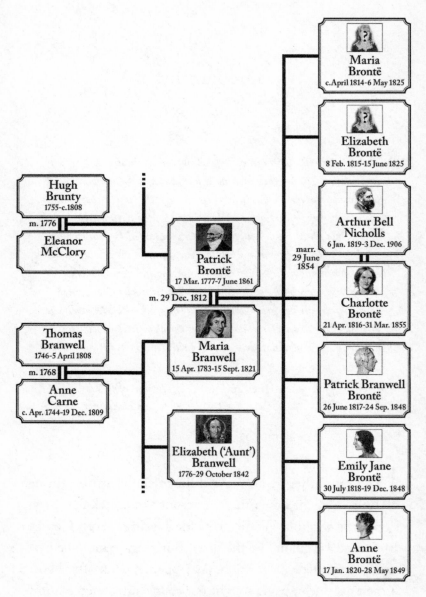

Figure 2.1: The Brontë family tree.
REPRODUCED BY PERMISSION FROM THE AUTHOR.

to them, to uncover who they were, how they lived, and why I felt like I knew them. I found myself asking questions. Are the characters inhabiting their fiction anything like them, or the people they knew? What do we have in common? What did they know about life that I need to understand in order to live mine? Though it often seems like the four Brontë children who survived to adulthood sprang, fully genius-ed, from their father's forehead, the truth is they began as scribbling children, writing to escape.

If you want a Lifetime Movie version of the Brontës, read Clement King Shorter's *Charlotte Brontë and Her Circle*; he's perpetually on the verge of histrionics. If you want an immaculately researched biography, read Juliet Barker's *The Brontës*.[2] If you want to know about every surviving scrap of paper in Charlotte's hand, seek out Margaret E. Smith's scrupulously edited volumes of her letters and juvenilia. They'll tell you what you need to know. But my mission is to uncover how the Brontës became the writers I connected with—and these are the breadcrumbs that led me there.

Early on, I came across the biography written by Elizabeth Gaskell, a novelist who befriended Charlotte after her literary career took off. Gaskell created the enduring—and inaccurate—perceptions of Charlotte and her sisters as pallid, isolated, otherworldly waifs. Gaskell had the benefit of actual contact with Charlotte and her closest friends, but the strikes against her include an annoyingly dreary oversimplification of the Brontës' lives, a misrepresentation of Charlotte's father, Patrick, as rageful and callous, and the omission of anything scandalous or exciting whenever possible. Charlotte was her focal point, to the detriment of Emily and Anne, and Gaskell managed to make Charlotte seem both incredibly intelligent and incredibly passive in establishing herself. Passive was the very last thing I could imagine the person who'd made *Jane Eyre* being. I kept digging.

THE essential facts are these: Patrick Brontë was a curate, the Anglican equivalent of a parish priest, in a small town in Yorkshire, in the northern part of England. He married a woman named Maria and they had six children, three of whom joined the ranks of the most famous Victorian novelists, one of whom never recovered from the fact that he did not. While I cannot hide the fact that Charlotte is my favorite, I am a stalwart Anne supporter as well. If it would establish Anne as the second-most-important Brontë, I would serve as her second in a duel. The historical neglect of her work is that appalling. We'll get to her later, I promise.

Maria was the daughter of a prosperous Penzance merchant family. She met Patrick Brontë in 1812 at school in Rawdon, Yorkshire. He was a thirty-five-year-old autodidact, a curate, a poet, and the author of a fairly moralizing novel, *The Maid of Killarny*. He had changed his name from variously spelled versions of "Branty" to "Brontë" after leaving Ireland to enroll in St. John's College in Cambridge in 1802. The shift camouflaged his Irishness, honored Lord Nelson, the Duke of Bronte, and looked better on paper. Patrick and Maria became engaged eight months after they met. Surviving letters from Maria reveal her to be a sweet and thoughtful woman, eager for Patrick's guidance and companionship. At twenty-nine, having lost her parents a few years earlier, Maria was accustomed to a certain amount of independence and freedom; when she decided to marry, it was because she had found a man she respected and loved enough to allow him to guide her. She even calls him "My dear saucy Pat," which is as embarrassing as any parental PDA.[3] They married in December of 1812, settled into Patrick's curacy in Hartshead, and proceeded to have six children.

Their daughters Maria and Elizabeth were born in 1813 and 1815 (the same years Jane Austen published *Pride and Prejudice* and *Emma*, respectively). Charlotte was born in 1816, followed by Branwell, the only son and family pet, in 1817. Emily, strong-minded and antisocial, was born in 1818, and finally, in 1820, came Anne, the quiet, opinionated, and oft-forgotten. Shortly after Anne's birth, the family moved to Haworth, a milltown near Keighley, where Patrick became the village curate. His responsibilities included giving sermons, performing ceremonies from baptisms to funerals, and generally maintaining the spiritual welfare of the populace. Haworth was small and industrial then, supported by weaving mills and those who worked in them. With the village church and graveyard at its highest point, the town spread down cobbled streets and narrow lanes lined with shops and houses into the Worth Valley. As a matter of fact it still does, though the mills are closed now and the Brontës are not merely residents, but the raison d'être of the town. It's surrounded on all sides by glorious moors filled with heather and tall grasses and lush green fields crisscrossed by picturesque stone walls. When the Brontës lived there, trees hadn't yet been planted near the church and the view was bleak in the gray autumn and winter, but a walk uphill in any direction would yield an incomparable view of the surrounding countryside.

Contrary to lore that surrounds the Brontës and their Parsonage in the popular imagination, they weren't in the middle of nowhere, their yard wasn't desolate and windswept all year round, and they didn't lack access to community resources. They attended local concerts, art exhibitions, and the Mechanics Institute, which hosted lectures and social events. True, the graveyard comes right up to the Parsonage garden, and 41 percent of children born in the village died before the age of six, but there was more to their lives than all-pervading death.[4] The sooty grayness that covered the yellow stone of the small houses and shops was due to smoke from the mills, not from some inherent regional depression.

Patrick was an astute, well-read, political thinker, and he embraced his children's active imaginations and vociferous opinions. He read them newspapers, brought history to life through storytelling, and hired art and music teachers as the children became old enough. They were allowed to read whatever they wanted, from Aesop's *Fables* and *Arabian Nights* to Edinburgh's *Blackwoods* literary magazines. Patrick Brontë's Gaskell-induced reputation as a hothead and a bully doesn't seem entirely merited (and in fact was based on the testimony of one disgruntled servant). The bond between Charlotte and her father sustained them both in the wake of the losses that awaited the family; she was always willing to place Patrick's welfare above her own.

But then again, it's possible he was harsh in his youth and mellowed with age—like my own father, who tended to explode with anger when frustrated by his children, his wife, or his work, but who also introduced me to much of the arts and culture that I still love as an adult. I could never stand up to his fury, but the happy times are unmatched. Maybe Patrick's anger didn't bother her as much. Maybe Charlotte's coping mechanisms were more developed than mine. Maybe reports were exaggerated. We'll never know.

After giving birth to Anne, her fifth daughter, Maria Brontë began suffering symptoms of uterine cancer. She died in 1821, when her eldest was eight and Anne was only a year old. Maria's unmarried sister, Elizabeth Branwell, came to live with the family and take care of the children. In July of 1824, the eldest Brontë daughters, Maria and Elizabeth, were sent to the Cowan Bridge School for Clergymen's Daughters for a more formal education; Charlotte followed in August and Emily in November. They were taught English grammar and literature, geography, history, arithmetic, some natural sciences, and needlework. Thanks to poor ventilation and an inhospitable climate, both Maria and Elizabeth contracted consumptive illnesses and were quickly brought back home, where they died in May and June of 1825. Emily and Charlotte were called home immediately afterward, where they were educated by Aunt Branwell and Patrick alongside their younger brother and sister. This all sounds like it happened fast—a quick trip to school, a tragic loss, and a brisk ride home again. But think of childhood's emotional calendar. The low moments seemed to last forever, and the bright moments flash like streetlamps outside a car window. Even if every other year of her life was full of curiosity and creativity, the trauma of losing two sisters soon after losing her mother must have intensely affected Charlotte, who was already so sensitive. She woke to find herself the eldest daughter instead of a sheltered third, responsible for her younger siblings as she'd never been before.

In good weather, the Brontë children went to the moors behind the Parsonage and spent days walking and climbing, studying plants and animals, and telling stories together. Of the few images we have of the sisters, most are drawings or paintings they made of one another—Branwell's grouping of the surviving four (which he later painted himself out of, leaving a chalky gray pillar in his place) is the most famous. I used to mock Branwell for the portrait's ungainliness, until I saw it in person—he does capture something exciting in Charlotte's eyes. By contrast, Charlotte's watercolors are expressive and delicate, especially her botanicals.

The storytelling "plays" that represent the Brontës' earliest surviving written work may have begun before the deaths of Maria and Elizabeth, but they developed into nearly full-time occupations afterward. The sheer volume of the Brontës' juvenilia proves the rumors of their sickly depressiveness as children must have been greatly exaggerated. They kept busy by creating richly layered imaginary worlds drawn from the books and magazines that filled the Parsonage. The impact of losing their mother shows up in their fiction, where the mothers are either missing, careless, reappearing after a long absence, or impossibly warm and generous.

The Brontës first began recording their imaginative storytelling on paper in 1829, when Charlotte set down *The History of the Year*. In it, she recounts how she and her siblings had adopted their favorite characters from history, inspired by a set of Branwell's toy soldiers they called The Twelve. Charlotte claimed the Duke of Wellington, Branwell took Napoleon Bonaparte, Emily chose "a very grave looking fellow" they called Gravey, and Anne's was "a queer little thing very like herself" dubbed "waiting Boy."[5] They conscripted their tiny subjects into adventures both mundane and supernatural. Maybe that sounds weird, but let ye who never enjoyed mutant turtles named after Renaissance artists cast the first stone. They traveled to an imaginary Africa, established their own pretend nation-states, fought for and against their rulers, conducted courtly intrigues, and dabbled in romance. Within their imaginary kingdom of Glass Town, the sisters and Branwell ruled as Chief Genii or Little Queens and a Little King, and each had their own country to manage. The young Brontës also imagined themselves in a school superintended by the Duke of Wellington, who became Charlotte's lifelong hero.

When she was fourteen, Charlotte made a list of her work thus far in a little document titled "Catalogue of my Books with the periods of their completion up to August 3, 1830." You can go visit it in person at the Morgan Library and Museum in New York. Should you make an appointment online, after you've been signed in and admitted, the librarian will bring it over on two large plush triangular cushions, with weighted ropes gently draped across the pages to keep them open. When you're ready to turn the page, you call for the librarian again, who brings over a small strip of paper with an angled point and generously allows you to turn the flimsy leaf yourself. The catalogue is the size of a half-sheet of paper, folded over again, with three of the four leaves filled by Charlotte's assertive handwriting. She must have pinned the page down between thumb and forefinger to write on it. Her "&" symbols look like the incomplete figure-eights children use to represent fish. Screened from the librarian's view by the book the catalogue was pasted into, you might dare to surreptitiously run your finger back and forth over Charlotte's childish signature. On one side of the paper, lurking somewhere behind her words, way back in 1830, is Charlotte. On the other, you—or at least, I—sit, delighted. And awash in something else, too—an uncanny sense of recognition.

When I was twelve or so, I would script elaborate military "missions" for my younger brother Thomas and I to act out. We'd mix our Ninja Turtles, our G.I. Joes, Barbies, Trolls, beanie babies, and Playmobil figures in kaleidoscopic undertakings that crossed space, time, and genre. But since he was only five, his limited literacy and inability to memorize elaborate orders left him wandering rudderless whenever I sent him off with maps and passwords. We switched to improvisation games, inspired by *Whose Line Is It Anyway?*, and sketch comedy from *The Kids in the Hall* and sanitized reruns of *Saturday Night Live*. The video evidence of this period that survives shows me brusquely coaching a kid who barely knew his alphabet through skits, tool-safety PSAs, mock ballroom dance competitions, and quiz shows (and frequently breaking the cardinal rule of responding with "yes, and . . ." to seize creative control). We made up songs on the walk home when I picked him up from school, and watched *Monty Python* and *Mystery Science Theater 3000* until we could quote entire episodes from memory. Though we both lacked the attention to detail and manual dexterity to create tiny publications of our own, we fully inhabited this world we invented together. We still feel its impact—and not just in our incessant lapses into catchphrases and cackling. He started a public speaking club as an undergraduate using many of the skills we practiced together in our living room and backyard. I briefly wrote for a comedy clips show, and those improv techniques come in handy when I teach children and college students about writing and voice.

There's a lot of discussion these days about the merits and dangers of childhood vulnerability and adolescent missteps being preserved online, but I almost wish the juvenile ramblings of all the writers I love were still available, like these tiny works of art the Brontës left behind. Juvenilia gives us an opportunity to watch writers try out ideas in first one medium, then another, before making their more ambitious attempts in adulthood. For example, Charlotte's *The Professor* developed out of a short story Branwell began as a teen, and *Jane Eyre*'s Edward Fairfax Rochester evolved from Charlotte's Duke of Zamorna; they have a shared intensity of personality and tend toward arrogance. Knowing Charlotte fantasized about the same kind of dynamic hero

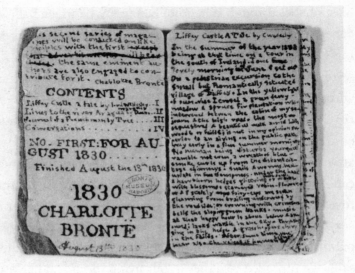

Figure 2.2: Cover page of Charlotte's *Young Men's Magazine*, August 1830.
PHOTO COURTESY OF THE BRONTË PARSONAGE MUSEUM.

from adolescence on unsettles the common perception that Rochester was entirely based on Constantin Heger, one of her teachers.

Branwell began writing a *Young Men's Magazine* in 1830, based heavily on *Blackwoods*, with the same short essays, satire, political debate, dispatches from around the empire, poetry, and installments of novels. Charlotte eventually took over the magazine and maintained Branwell's tiny bound-folio format for nearly two years. Her earliest surviving fiction reflects her interest in defying the constraints placed on her gender by society and literature—she frequently wrote as "Captain Tree" or "Charles Townshend," even into early adulthood. She rarely wrote about traditional "feminine" issues found in ladies' magazines. Instead she placed her characters in boisterous taverns, where they bickered about politics and demanded more venison. In the issues of *Blackwoods* she read as a child she would have encountered a constant barrage of sexism—"What if the Duke of Wellington were a Woman?" one essay asked before bemoaning the idea of pregnancy sabotaging the Battle of Waterloo; another scornfully derided the fledgling feminist efforts of "Bluestockings over the Border." Writing as a boy allowed Charlotte to take freedoms she didn't yet feel entitled to as an "authoress." The agency she took for herself as a girl is probably a large part of what made her mature fiction even possible—to write so

Figure 2.3: Charlotte's tiny books.
PHOTO COURTESY OF THE BRONTË PARSONAGE MUSEUM.

freely as an adult required years of practice in the grip of
Branwell's strong editorial style. Perhaps my brother has my
domineering director's approach to thank for the intensity
and integrity of his arguing style now.

The Brontë magazines that the Parsonage Museum keeps
today are two inches tall and an inch and a half wide, and
though the script is decipherable, it often requires a magnifying glass to make out. Charlotte continued Branwell's cun-
ning tradition of making the font look as much like typeface
as possible and imitating the composition of a *Blackwoods*
title page all the way down to the seller's information. They
are hilarious, both for the precociousness of the authors and
the straightforwardness of their delivery. My favorite "Conversation" dates from Charlotte's tenure as editor and features an argument between Captain Tree, the Marquis of
Douro (aka Lord Charles Wellesley), and "Stumps" during
an evening of squabbles and roast meat. Charlotte reveals
herself, irritable and funny, through her characters. Hearing
her "voice" on the page as a young girl makes her relatable—
not a refined, unreachable Author of Global Distinction and
Renown, but just Charlotte, writing stories for her imaginary
friends under made-up names, just like I did. Perhaps Charlotte never "became" a writer but just *was* one.

The Brontës and I all embellished our make-believe with
books we'd read and stories we'd heard, blurring the line between reality and art as we lived inside our creations even
off the page. My grandfather built me a dollhouse for my
fifth birthday, where I spent hours with the Williams family
(parented by Vivian and Vance, named after a misread title

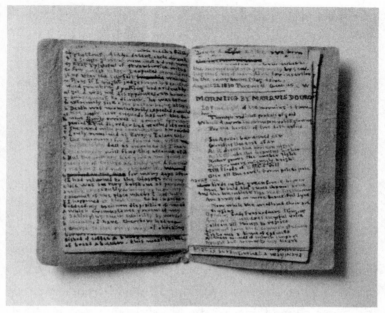

Figure 2.4: "Morning," from a *Young Men's Magazine*.
PHOTO COURTESY OF THE BRONTË PARSONAGE MUSEUM.

card from *I Love Lucy*) and their household concerns. I rarely played out loud, preferring to narrate in my head where nobody could eavesdrop. I played with the dollhouse well into adolescence, and occasionally wrote out the stories belonging to its inhabitants, with atrocious attempts at dialect inspired by *The Adventures of Huckleberry Finn,* and dramatic twists drawn from soap operas and Shakespeare. After I read Noel Streatfeild's *Thursday's Child,* I often acted out mock-flights with my neighborhood friends through imaginary canals and alleyways, dodging orphanage matrons and scullery maids. I even inadvertently followed in the Brontës' footsteps by curating a paper called *The Pennington Post*, assembled from articles and headlines clipped out of a fledgling local paper known as the *Washington Post*. I glued the newsprint excerpts onto ruled looseleaf, stapled them together, signed myself "editor-in-chief," and sold them for $1.50 to anyone who would buy them. Ultimately the Brontë sisters' debut collection of poems would outstrip my journalistic empire by just two copies. And they only sold two copies.

And what of Emily and Anne? We know from references in their few surviving letters and diary papers that Emily and Anne were just as involved in storytelling and writing as their older brother and sister, but almost none of their juvenilia survives. In her work, Charlotte is both affectionate and mocking when she refers to characters and events in Emily and Anne's kingdoms, as any older sister would be. Their realm was called Gondal, and all that remains of it are poems written in character and lists of inhabitants, though they continued writing tales of its adventures well into adulthood. In fact, it was the separation from the security of this imaginary world that made living away from home so painful when they traveled to school or to work as governesses outside Haworth. The fantasies were portable, of course, but away from home, the Brontës lost the opportunity to collaborate with one another, the intimacy of family language, and the luxury of unsupervised free time. Charlotte apparently destroyed the Gondal Chronicles after the deaths of Emily and Anne, along with any in-progress manuscripts they may have had. It's a tragedy for the Brontë voyeur who wants to read absolutely everything, especially since we can see such clear connections between the themes, characters, and style of the Brontë juvenilia and the more sophisticated prose of their adult work. But it's also a gesture of fierce loyalty, which perpetually characterizes Charlotte's stewardship of her sisters' work, and her friendships generally.

At fifteen, during her year at a Miss Wooler's school in Roe Head, Charlotte befriended fellow classmates Ellen Nussey and Mary Taylor; her relationships with them, as well as with Margaret Wooler herself, would endure for the rest of her life. What became a twenty-year correspondence began very simply, formally, and a little prudishly. Her letters to Ellen are affectionate, even clingy, as they ponder important questions like whether it's appropriate for boys and girls to dance together at village events, and how prominently love should figure in the decision to marry. Charlotte's lamentations about Haworth's isolation are another common theme. Notably missing is any hint that when Charlotte wasn't writing to Ellen or teaching Sunday School, she was sending her imagination on fantastical adventures around the globe. It's hard to believe this polite, conscientious student is the same mouthy teenage editor of *Young Men's Magazine*, so fearless when it came to orchestrating bar brawls and dangerous adventures in foreign lands. From the earliest days of their friendship, Charlotte kept an essential part of herself completely hidden from Ellen and everyone else outside the family circle. Oh how I relate.

We'd moved across the country for the fifth time when I was seven, leaving our extended family of grandparents and beloved aunts and cousins behind. Once school started again, my life at home was dolls and books and musical theater and documentaries on Friday nights, eating pizza with my whole family. My life at school was floundering to keep up with the pop culture references of my classmates who were allowed to watch TV on school nights and vain attempts to corral my innate lack of cool into something my peers might tolerate. As I made my way into middle school, I was always pudgy and awkward, never put-together or capable of doing things the right way. My journals from this period are so lonely and hapless I shudder to reread them: lists of makeup from *Seventeen* magazine I thought would help me fit in, frantic records of the minutiae of social interactions in search of encouraging subtext, and dramatic fantasy denunciations of the class bullies, who made fun of my chubbiness, my tendency to anger, my obvious crushes, my know-it-all pride.

In 1835, at the age of nineteen, Charlotte returned to Roe Head as a teacher, while Emily, seventeen, attended as a pupil. The fragmentary journals she kept there illustrate the frustration of being caught between Angria, the rich and vibrant imaginary world she had created at home, and the daily "cheerless" drudgery of life at school. One of Charlotte's journal pages from this time begins, "I'm just going to write because I cannot help it."[6] Emily's intense homesickness led her home in October. Anne took her place and remained for two more years.

This is a common pattern. Charlotte blazes a trail, Emily follows, Branwell strikes out in another direction. Then Emily quits, Branwell gets fired, and Anne steps up to put in a sustained, dedicated, unappreciated effort. Anne fell ill in 1837, prompting Charlotte to leave Roe Head with a good deal of resentment against Miss Wooler for not taking Anne's condition seriously. They eventually made up, and Charlotte returned to teach for an additional year in 1838. All together, the sisters only had seven years of structured education outside the home, which was enough to equip them for a career in the liminal space between guest and servant, practically the only respectable option for gently born young women. They became governesses. And unsurprisingly, so did many of their characters.

WE were living on Marquette Street when it all began, in a quiet Virginia suburb just outside of Washington, DC. I had a fort up on stilts in the backyard that I called a treehouse, though it was neither in a tree nor a properly enclosed house. I loved to smuggle pickles and cheese and a stack of books out there and lay under the trees for hours. I read alone a great deal—YA fantasy by Mercedes Lackey, vintage L. M. Montgomery, fairy tales and the D'Aulaires' books of mythology, stories from *American Girl* magazine written in the 1950s that advised young women how to let down their hair, be themselves, and *still* get taken to the sock hop.

That Easter, underneath the basket of candy and plastic grass the Easter Bunny (aka my mother) had left me, there was a stack of books contributed by my father. I picked up the heaviest one and looked at the cover. A young woman, with the faintly sad expression of someone who has never received a present, gazed calmly off into the middle distance. It sits in a place of honor at my desk now. The back cover has worn off; the glued spine is exposed. My name is written in my mother's neat handwriting on the title page, probably from when I took it to summer camp. Many pages are dog-eared; favorite passages are annotated in pencil and pen, exclamation points and underlinings and smiley faces and frowns. Makeshift bookmarks and receipts peek out between the pages, mementos from long-ago waiting rooms and car rides.

A round-trip Metro-North ticket from when I lived in Harlem and commuted to Connecticut every day for my first grown-up job. A stub from a performance of Henrik Ibsen's *Ghosts*. An empty white card-sized envelope. A fragment of paper with "Don't lose it!" written on it. Grains of sand fall out if I gently shake it, from trips to the beach. I've collected fancier editions at used book sales and sturdier editions for travel, and even a board book version illustrated with felt dolls that reduces the story to one word per page (*girl, red, stand, woman, fall, help, kiss, stairs, leave, cold, hot, care*), but this copy is still my favorite. This is what I think of, when I think of *Jane Eyre*.

Jane

I saw a girl sitting on a stone bench near; she had bent over a book, on the perusal of which she seemed intent: from where I stood I could see the title—it was "Rasselas;" a name that struck me as strange, and consequently attractive. In turning a leaf she happened to look up, and I said to her directly:—

"Is your book interesting?" I had already formed the intention of asking her to lend it to me some day.

"I like it," she answered, after a pause of a second or two, during which she examined me.

"What is it about?" I continued. I hardly know where I found the hardihood thus to open a conversation with a stranger; the step was contrary to my nature and habits: but I think her occupation touched a chord of sympathy somewhere; for I too liked reading, though of a frivolous and childish kind; I could not digest or comprehend anything serious or substantial.

—*Jane Eyre*, Chapter V

As self-conscious literature-loving girls love Anne Shirley, as tomboy writers love Jo March, as stubborn girls love Mary Lennox, as dramatic girls love Margaret Thursday, I, who am often anxious and awkward, love Jane. I love her fire. Her fire, and her isolation. Despite the reticence to talk to strangers, which I share, she is full of opinions, and she knows the value of having a place to go off to by herself.

The passage above is from Jane's first meeting with Helen Burns, a too-good-to-be-true character (based on Charlotte's sister Maria) who becomes Jane's best friend at Lowood. "Strange, and consequently attractive," encapsulates *Jane Eyre* almost perfectly. It may not have had any geniis or fairies or pictures, but it introduced me to the coming-of-age genre. Of the dozens of books I read as a child, only *Jane Eyre* met me where I was and took me with her as we grew up.

Without Jane's passion, *Jane Eyre* is basically a series of dismal British buildings populated by mostly unpleasant people with well-stocked libraries. Though technically her sister Anne beat her to it, Charlotte usually gets credit for the first plain, poor heroine in Victorian literature. Jane has neither wealth nor beauty to recommend her, only her own indefatigable moral code and a sharp sense of humor. After being sent to school, where she chafes under the cruelty and deprivation of the administrators, she buries her rage, loses her only friend to consumption, becomes a top student, and finally emerges as a teacher, trained to educate the children of wealthy families.

In the early days of my relationship with *Jane Eyre*, I identified first with young Jane and later with her pupil, Adele. I had already been the new kid in school twice when we arrived in Virginia the summer before third grade. At the magnet school where I was enrolled, many kids had attended neighborhood schools together for years. I knew nobody and lacked the social confidence to connect with new people easily. After I struggled bravely through the first few days in Mrs. McEllhatton's class (I believe what I actually did was cry at my desk), she assigned me a friend, a fellow bookish type who liked to sing, and whose guinea pig had recently given birth to an unexpected litter. That would cheer anybody up. Betsy and I spent weekends under her kitchen table in "Fort Guinea" eating pizza and talking, taking occasional breaks for Nintendo or to dress our American Girl dolls. I also met neighborhood kids who were kind enough to ask why I was sitting on the curb crying in the middle of a Saturday afternoon. We spent that summer and several after that exploring the woods that bordered their backyards and throwing rocks in the creek—we kept busy, but they weren't what Anne of Green Gables would call "bosom companions." We mostly confined our conversation to Power Rangers, Sabina's new Sega, and which cushions protected us from lava and which from ice monsters. I joined local youth basketball and soccer leagues, competed on the swim team, played the viola in the school orchestra, sang in choruses, tried out for plays. I gravitated toward creative, funny people, and gradually found a social niche where I could relax a little.

Safe at home, when I wasn't dancing to Broadway soundtracks in the living room or practicing my jumpshot in the backyard, I spent entire days at Thornfield. One of the secrets I always kept was that I still played with dolls at home—and not just Barbies, which plenty of my peers would have sheepishly admitted to, but baby and toddler-sized dolls that I dressed up and carried with me through make-believe dramas. I pretended I was one of Jane's classmates, or imagined myself as a second ward of Mr. Rochester's, being taught alongside Adele. At school, even with a friend like Betsy to lean on, I felt like a freak, awkward, dorky, and out of place, always spoiling for a fight. But inside, in the pages of *Jane Eyre*, I found sanctuary. And even when something unpleasant happened, I consoled myself that it gave me something else in common with Jane.

I always lost myself in books on the way to and from school; one afternoon I borrowed the only class copy of *Flight 116 Is Down*, a YA thriller about a teenage girl who survives a plane crash, which the teacher was reading aloud to us. I borrowed it to finish on the bus because I couldn't take the suspense, and walked from the bus stop to my house without looking up. But then I was absent the next day, so the class had to wait through a long three-day weekend before they got to finish the story. The sixth-grade boys turned vicious, mocking me for being so weird I'd taken the book home in the first place and so stupid I'd forgotten to bring it back. When I appealed to the teacher for justice, all he said was, "I think you deserve it, Miranda, don't you?" The entire class laughed, and I knew there would be no protection from the sixth-grade boys that year.

And there wasn't. They wanted me to be sure I knew I was fat, my haircut was short and ugly, *I* was short and ugly. Nobody wanted to be on my team. They didn't like what I liked, or understand who I was. Every small injustice stung, but I would remember Jane Eyre and how she endured that insufferable Brocklehurst's accusation, grit my teeth, and stomp off. I may have eventually learned to fake being "normal" in short, controlled bursts, but I was never fully myself in "real life." I couldn't be. I wasn't free to make mistakes, or get excited; I couldn't count on a generous reception. Most friendships didn't last—the unlucky target of my friendship would tire of my drowning-girl's eagerness, and I'd feel alone again.

THE vivid imagination of my childhood was reborn as fanatical, hopeless romanticism when I reached adolescence. I was constantly falling in and out of love. The objects of my affection were remote, unreachable, disdainful, assuming they knew I existed at all. The patience I demonstrated as I waited to have my heart sufficiently broken may be the only patience I've ever shown in my entire life.

As I outgrew Disney movies and MGM musicals, I studied the romantic comedies of the 1990s like they were Homer and Virgil. I was eager to unlock the secret wisdom of *Clueless* and *Ten Things I Hate About You* and *She's All That* and *Get Over It* and *Boys and Girls* and any other movie where boy meets girl (lifelong best friendship optional), girl changes herself to appeal more to boy, boy finally falls for her, and they go to prom. One of my irrational regrets was being the only person in my family who didn't need glasses, as it robbed me of the opportunity to suddenly become more attractive by letting down my hair and removing them.

I imagined I had outgrown *Jane Eyre*, too—that is, until I discovered an entirely different book when I reread it in between romance novels at sixteen. Suddenly I understood that the really significant plot points did not involve young Jane reading books and resenting her relations, but teen Jane falling in love! It's a Gothic rom com! Suddenly aware that he was not just rude to Jane, he was *in love* with her, I fixated on Edward Fairfax Rochester like a lovelorn baby duck. Their meet-cute alone was enough to send me into raptures, lighting a torch I carry still, but that proposal? The devastation of a canceled wedding? Jane's heroic departure into an uncertain night? The sweet, teasing reunion that leads us to one of the most famous four-word phrases in literature?* How had I missed this?!

As a kid I would have been perfectly happy to follow Jane into some sort of wild fantasy adventure after she befriends the spectral beast called a Gytrash she thought she was about to meet on that misty country lane. But older and wiser, I was glad to find that the horse tramping out of the fog bore Mr. Rochester upon its back. When Rochester is thrown to the ground and Jane rushes to assist him, we get our first glimpse of the man himself:

> He had a dark face, with stern features and a heavy brow; his eyes and gathered eyebrows looked ireful and thwarted just now; he was past youth, but had not reached middle-age; perhaps he might be thirty-five. I felt no fear of him, and but little shyness. Had he been a handsome, heroic-looking young gentleman, I should not have dared to stand

---

*"Reader, I married him," the introductory phrase that has launched a thousand wedding thank-you notes.

thus questioning him against his will, and offering my services unasked.[1]

However unpolished his manners, Rochester was a very appealing alternative to the polar opposites that defined my world—he was neither too godlike to notice Jane (and by egocentric extension, me) nor too average to be enticing. And what a departure this was from the typical romance I'd been stuffing myself with—our hero is not handsome and this plain heroine confidently shrugs off any sense of insecurity because gorgeous, charismatic people have nothing to offer her anyway. Jane's first reaction to this legendary literary lover is, "Oh, he's rude. What a relief." She answers his questions frankly and honestly, unashamed by any disparity in their stations. She doesn't try to be anyone she's not. I have *still* never had a conversation with a stranger where I spoke unapologetically about myself, and I have been attempting to live my life asking "What Would Jane Eyre Do?" for *years*.

Rochester represented all the brusque, mature manliness that I had never encountered off of a stage or screen but dearly hoped awaited me in real life. He was John Wayne in *The Quiet Man*, Yul Brynner in *The King and I*, Christopher Plummer in *The Sound of Music*, Humphrey Bogart in everything. He was everything I imagined I wanted—older, world-wise, smart, curious, witty, and intensely interested in me (well, in Jane). I ignored the gruff surliness and the fact that he was clearly hiding a gigantic secret in his garret. I thought, as everyone who idolizes an enigmatic stranger thinks, "Oh, he'd never be that way with *me*." As Jane and

Rochester commence their *Beauty and the Beast*–style friendship, Rochester sees Jane for the diamond (well, perhaps a really well-formed pearl) in the rough that she is, and speaks to her like an equal. Jane is won by his intelligence, his humor, and the dark, twisty past for which she believes he can find redemption.

Rochester looms so large in my romantic pantheon that Mr. Darcy is positively bloodless by comparison. Romeo seems like a quitter, and Teddy "Laurie" Lawrence a mere child. When *Jane Eyre* was first published, critics found him equally compelling and alarming. The *North American Review* observed, "The hero, Mr. Rochester . . . became a great favorite in the boarding schools and in the worshipful society of governesses. That portion of Young America known as ladies' men began to swagger and swear in the presence of the gentler sex, and to allude darkly to events in their lives which excused impudence and profanity."[2]

Like most geeky, pudgy kids, I was well aware of the popular cream of the crop—they were shiny, they were poised, they were slender and well dressed and we had as little in common as the sea does with a plastic bag that floats in it. My dating pool consisted of dorky, polite guys who were already my friends, and, if I could have only realized it then, offbeat, funny girls who found my enthusiasm engaging instead of embarrassing. They were all sweet and respectful, with braces just like mine, but there was no mystery, no magnetism, no pulsating dark heart to uncover and tame. I related to Jane and Rochester in different ways, but it was their dynamic together that I admired most. Together, they were everything I aspired to and had no hope of having for *years.* Being as compelling and distant as Rochester would require age, maturity, and sustained emotional dysfunction. Becoming Jane would mean acquiring a sturdy backbone, a sense of self, inexorable personal discipline, and a naïveté that could survive even the most taxing adversity. At least the naïveté I had covered. Everything else was as mysterious as whatever was going on with Grace Poole in the attic at Thornfield.

Neither Jane nor I had ever been in love before, so when Rochester, already smitten, leads her to believe that he will marry a wealthy, shallow woman named Blanche Ingram, we were both convinced by his performance. Jealous and depressed, Jane decides to end the prolonged agony of living with someone she believes cannot love her, and find a new position. You might expect a poignant goodbye scene, full of unshed tears and unspoken feelings, in the proud British tradition of emotional understatement. Think of the scene in *Persuasion* when Captain Wentworth and Anne Eliot finally get their quiet moment to reconcile. Barely anyone *says* anything, but a hand is fervently pressed, and *voilà*, they are engaged. Here is what we get instead:

First Mr. Rochester solemnly agrees that Jane must leave Thornfield, that she cannot stay Adele's governess once his bride arrives. He mentions he has found her a place with some friends in Ireland (Jane is appalled), asks her what she thinks of his Blanche, who has shown herself to be selfish and cruel. Jane holds back her scorn, with difficulty. Rochester wonders, oh so nonchalantly, if Jane will perhaps be a little sad to leave, for any little old reason at all. Would she miss the company of the venerable Mrs. Fairfax? Think fondly of the architecture, or the landscaping, perhaps? Fed up with his trolling, Jane lets him have it:

> The vehemence of emotion, stirred by grief and love within me, was claiming mastery, and struggling for full sway, and asserting a right to predominate, to overcome, to live, rise, and reign at last: yes,—and to speak.
>
> "I grieve to leave Thornfield: I love Thornfield:—I love it, because I have lived in it a full and delightful life—momentarily at least. I have not been trampled on. I have not been petrified. I have not been buried with inferior minds, and excluded from every glimpse of communion with what is bright and energetic and high. I have talked, face to face, with what I reverence, with what I delight in—with an original, a vigorous, an expanded mind. I have known you, Mr. Rochester; and it strikes me with terror and anguish to feel I absolutely must be torn from you for ever. I see the necessity of departure; and it is like looking on the necessity of death."[3]

How Jane feels about Thornfield is how I feel about her entire book, especially the end. And then Rochester turns the whole scene on its ear:

> "Where do you see the necessity?" he asked suddenly.
>
> "Where? You, sir, have placed it before me."
>
> "In what shape?"
>
> "In the shape of Miss Ingram; a noble and beautiful woman,—your bride."
>
> "My bride! What bride? I have no bride!"

"But you will have."

"Yes;—I will!—I will!" He set his teeth.

"Then I must go:—you have said it yourself."

"No: you must stay! I swear it—and the oath shall be kept."

"I tell you I must go!" I retorted, roused to something like passion. "Do you think I can stay to become nothing to you? Do you think I am an automaton?—a machine without feelings? and can bear to have my morsel of bread snatched from my lips, and my drop of living water dashed from my cup? Do you think, because I am poor, obscure, plain, and little, I am soulless and heartless? You think wrong!—I have as much soul as you,—and full as much heart! And if God had gifted me with some beauty and much wealth, I should have made it as hard for you to leave me, as it is now for me to leave you. I am not talking to you now through the medium of custom, conventionalities, nor even of mortal flesh—it is my spirit that addresses your spirit; just as if both had passed through the grave, and we stood at God's feet, equal,—as we are!"

"As we are!" repeated Mr. Rochester—"so," he added, enclosing me in his arms. Gathering me to his breast, pressing his lips on my lips: "so, Jane!"[4]

Jane is no fainting flower, however swoony I am over her. She mocks her suitor until he finally wins her over, his "incivility" being his best proof of sincerity:

"Your will shall decide your destiny," he said: "I offer you my hand, my heart, and a share of all my possessions."

"You play a farce, which I merely laugh at."

"I ask you to pass through life at my side—to be my second self, and best earthly companion. . . .

"My bride is here," he said, again drawing me to him, "because my equal is here, and my likeness. Jane, will you marry me?"

Still I did not answer, and still I writhed myself from his grasp: for I was still incredulous.

"Do you doubt me, Jane?"

"Entirely."

"You have no faith in me?"

"Not a whit."[5]

But yes, yes, of course, my dear Edward, we will marry you. Yes we said we will yes. This scene is possibly the greatest in literature. Maybe even in the history of the printed word. I may be exaggerating slightly, but imagine the peace and prosperity that would have followed if whole religions had been founded on this moment instead of all the messiness that came after "Let there be light." Too much?

Fine. Blasphemy aside, it has everything I love—a smartmouthed heroine demanding her due, a previously aloof, suddenly impassioned hero speaking eloquently, a murky secret to add a foreboding air, and a storm whipping up in the background, as though all of nature were suddenly involved in the welfare of this unlikely pair. True, nature is thrashing about crying "noooooo," but still—nature is *invested*.

After initially being swept off my feet, in successive readings I became a literary detective. I scrutinized Rochester's every word from the moment they meet until the scene where he proposes, to see if it was possible to detect his burgeoning feelings for Jane. Through older and wiser eyes, it is, obviously. Charlotte Brontë repeatedly shows Rochester on the verge of speaking and then breaking off in a fit of repressed emotions, or unsubtly goading Jane's nascent jealousy, or glaring meaningfully into the fire. She cultivates an air of romantic tension so dense it seems like there should be a literary haze wafting through Thornfield. But then, I was distracted. We were so giddy, Jane and I, we missed the glaring red flag of Rochester's aside, mid-proposal, when he mutters that Jane, having no family to interfere with them, is "the best of it." Anyone who celebrates how penniless and alone you are while they are asking you to enter into a binding legal agreement is not to be trusted. But it flew directly over my head, because, to borrow a gesture: Reader, I loved him. I loved his sarcasm, I loved his schemes (heartless though they were). I was utterly convinced he was as miserable and repentant as he purported to be. Though I am puzzled by the tedious game of charades he played with his society guests and still have no idea how "Bridewell" is worth illustrating with three tableaux, I would give nearly anything to hear him sing. I imagine he sounds like Brian Stokes Mitchell and Ezio Pinza combined.

Alas, on the day of their wedding, the intervention of a Mr. Mason and his attorney brings to light the horrible truth: Rochester already *has* a wife, the notorious Bertha Mason, who rages in his attic. Her brother Richard has returned to Thornfield, even after that nasty biting incident, to see that justice is done. Since we're here, I should acknowledge that *Jane Eyre* is often criticized for Rochester's treatment of Bertha. However, his accommodation of her violent mental illness was much better than she'd have gotten in any mental health institution at the time: a private suite of rooms in his mansion and a full-time attendant (albeit one who tipples). What other options did he have? Divorce laws at the time were fairly draconian, she couldn't function independently, and at least he didn't abandon her in the Caribbean. I'm inclined not to hold the attic part against him as much as the whole "lying about his imprisoned wife to his unsuspecting fiancée" thing.

For those of you who feel strongly the opposite, I refer you to *Wide Sargasso Sea*, where your concerns will be addressed and accommodated by the incomparable Jean Rhys. *Wide Sargasso Sea* takes a maligned and misunderstood character and gives her not only a voice, but a whole world of her own. I think it's noble and exciting to take someone like Bertha Mason, who in *Jane Eyre* is primarily an obstacle and an agent of chaos, and re-center her within cultural and mental health contexts that treat her more justly. The complexity of *Sargasso* and the proliferation of other *Jane Eyre* reinterpretations are testaments to what Charlotte left us, and to how fruitful exploring her work can be (or how disturbing, in the case of lamentable erotica that imagines a BDSM Rochester and Jane, or worse still, the steamy *Wuthering Nights*). You can call me a traditionalist, but I still prefer my Jane straight from the source.

After the revelation at the altar and its humiliating aftermath, Rochester urges Jane to come away with him, promising that they'll live like brother and sister in his Mediterranean villa. I might have believed him,* but Jane does not, and her self-respect will not allow her to remain with a man who hoped to make her his mistress. She flees Thornfield in the middle of the night, leaving all the clothes and jewels that would have belonged to Jane Rochester behind.

This is the moment of *Jane Eyre* that has the most to teach impressionable love-struck young women: Self-Respect Must Triumph Over Self-Indulgence. It is also the moment most frequently disregarded as foolhardy and unnecessary garbage by impressionable love-struck young women. Particularly when Rochester, his mansion, and the promise of a life together may be all we've ever dreamt of. While my moral compass was, to put it charitably, still under construction, nearly every time I read it I thought, *Why doesn't she just stay?! Nobody has to find out!* What I didn't know was that it takes strength to walk away even when it's obvious that staying has become impossible. Years and several Brontë books later, I would finally understand. But even then, I would have to force myself to emulate Jane's self-discipline, and would do so imperfectly.

Jane is saved from perishing on the moors by the Rivers siblings, St. John, Diana, and Mary. It's refreshing to see Jane with her peers after being constantly at the mercy of rich people. After being a despised child, a capable teacher, a

---

*And by "might," I mean "would absolutely with no questions, hesitations, or second thoughts whatsoever, just please don't leave me. I'll send Adele a postcard from Monte Carlo."

devoted governess (or maybe she was terrible—Adele's education fades to the background after Jane and Rochester become an item), and a bride-to-be, Jane is finally just herself, and St. John sets her up as the instructor of a small village school.

When Jane has spent a year supporting herself in this quiet way, St. John discovers, through a series of educated guesses and literary coincidences, that his dutiful friend is actually a long-lost cousin to the Rivers family on her father's side.* Allow me to stop and unpack this family tree for a moment, because I have spent *hours* thinking about it and friends don't let friends obsess over backstory unattended:

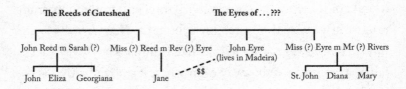

Figure 3.1: The Eyre family tree.

Long story short, St. John's mother and Jane's father were sister and brother, inexplicably never given first names. They had another brother, John, a wine merchant in Madeira, who has died and made Jane his Eyre. Sorry, *heir*. She promptly

---

*The incomparable 2005 BBC adaptation of *Jane Eyre* nonsensically describes Jane and St. John as "half-cousins." Maybe they hoped to make us all feel better about the idea of intermarriage, but it's very strange. What would it take to be "full cousins"? Both sets of parents being siblings?

shares her fortune with the Rivers family, creating the first happy home she's ever known (at least the first one not about to be destroyed by attempted bigamy). Then St. John ruins everything and proposes marriage to Jane—not out of romantic attachment, but out of an insistent belief that she will make a fit companion for his missionary's life in India. Despite her misgivings and St. John's utilitarian, truly horrible proposal, Jane is on the verge of accepting him when she hears Mr. Rochester's voice crying out to her on the wind: "Jane, Jane, Jane!"

I don't question this bit of magic intervention at all. It's never accounted for, never explained. It is perfect. My battered paperback practically falls open to it. I would not have been surprised or disappointed in the slightest to find out Mr. Rochester was secretly a wizard, and that the third act of the novel concluded with him revealing his hidden powers. No more skeptical of the supernatural than I, Jane hastens back to Thornfield to find it a broken ruin. An obliging passing shepherd fills her in on the necessary exposition—there was a fire, Bertha Rochester is dead, Mr. Rochester has been blinded and maimed, and he has exiled himself to a small manor house farther out in the country. That's a level of comeuppance not usually seen outside of Greek mythology. You've got to love an author who makes room for mysterious inciting incidents and epic twists of fate while cultivating an atmosphere of realism so vivid, many critics maintained an unshakable belief that *Jane Eyre* really *was* an autobiography.

Aspects of *Jane Eyre*'s Lowood school were so accurately depicted that her neighbors recognized the Cowan Bridge, the school on which it was based, which lent more credence to rumors of real-life "originals." When Charlotte dedicated the second edition to William Makepeace Thackeray, contemporary audiences began to suspect not only that "Currer Bell" was a woman, but that she was Thackeray's mistress. Unbeknownst to Charlotte (and the rest of fashionable London), Thackeray's wife actually *was* mentally ill and living in seclusion upstairs in his London home. Charlotte was mortified when word of this speculation reached her (but not so mortified as to refrain from basing her subsequent books on real-life people and places—in fact, she struck even closer to home with *Shirley*).

As a teenager, I embarked on a series of self-destructive infatuations with young men who had some of Mr. Rochester's poor manners but none of his redeeming qualities (aside from the occasionally compelling baritone), inspired by Jane's success in finding true and tender love in the heart of an outwardly rough and sarcastic man. I was always *so eager* and they were always *so indifferent* and together we were an absolute disaster—sometimes the explosive kind, sometimes the fizzling kind, but always the kind that leaves you wondering why you bothered. After yet another dismal dating interlude where I dumped a well-meaning sweet guy for an aloof one who unceremoniously abandoned me, I reread *Jane Eyre* and had an epiphany. All of my boyfriends were St. Johns. Every single one of them. Whether they expressed his anger or merely his tediousness, that's who they were. But being young and not a bit Jane-ish, I went along with them, because I so, so wanted to be in love.

At least I was able to realize, amidst my tribulations, that there was another explanation for always feeling different. Sometimes I wanted to swoon in the face of a swearing, swaggering dynamo; sometimes I wanted to stomp around with a snarl and romance the governess. I had overwhelming feelings for distant young men *and* engaging young women. A friend who came out as bisexual in middle school went through such an ordeal of teasing and humiliation that I decided to keep my realization to myself. Although I was attending a fairly progressive high school, "that's so gay" and worse slurs were still thrown around on a regular basis. I finally felt like I had faded into the background after the bullying gauntlet of middle school; I didn't need to revisit the experience.

Besides, I knew how to flirt with boys. I'd been practicing on my male classmates for years. It passed the time. But I'd never *knowingly* flirted with girls. I didn't have a script. I was intimidated by long hair and cosmetics prowess and cute sundresses. I assumed nobody was going to be attracted to me anyway. And forget about breaking it to my family—I thought they'd never understand. Though nobody is likely to be astonished when an androgynous bowl-cut-having child who turns into a basketball-jersey-wearing, dress-despising teenager then comes out as bisexual, I stayed in the closet until my twenties, pining for both Jane and Rochester without letting anybody be the wiser.

My first copy of *Jane Eyre* listed "Charlotte Brontë" as the author, so I didn't find out about "Currer Bell" or Charlotte's other pen names until I was older. I was fascinated by the way she used the freedom provided by male personas to tell stories the way she liked to tell them. When did she go from Charles Townshend, who brusquely dismissed his critics, to Miss Brontë, who desperately hoped to be taken seriously as a lady? As I'd later find out, the transformation must have begun in Brussels.

A Wish for Wings

Mary's letter spoke of some of the pictures & cathedrals she had seen—pictures the most exquisite—& cathedrals the most venerable—I hardly know what swelled to my throat as I read her letter—such a vehement impatience of restraint & steady work. such a strong wish for wings—wings such as wealth can furnish— such an urgent thirst to see—to know to learn—something internal seemed to expand boldly for a minute.

—Charlotte Brontë to Ellen Nussey, August 7, 1841[1]

In the summer of 1841, while working as a governess in her second and final position, Charlotte began planning to open a school with her sisters, despite the fact that none of them particularly cared for teaching or scheduling or structure or young people. They probably assumed that being able to organize things their own way would make up for the nuisance of having to admit pupils.

That September, Miss Wooler, Charlotte's former teacher and employer at Roe Head, wrote to say her sister had decided to give up her school at Dewsbury Moor, and offered the Brontës the chance to take it over.[2] It was an established institution in a familiar region, fully furnished; if they had actually *wanted* a school, it would have been a godsend. However, although Charlotte asked Aunt Branwell to loan them money for the undertaking, the scheme never quite took hold. This is as indicative of Charlotte's ambivalence about teaching as anything else. To buy some more time, Charlotte decided she and Emily should go study abroad to enhance their qualifications.

It's true, the credentials of a foreign institution and improvement in their French, German, and music would have made the Brontës' school more prestigious. But really, Charlotte had been bitten by wanderlust. Mary Taylor, one of her school friends, had been regaling her with stories as she traveled around Europe, and Charlotte was intrigued. In a letter to Emily, Charlotte even suggested she intended to seek employment and remain abroad rather than returning home. With the help of the Taylor family, the Brontës found a *pensionnat*—a school for locals and boarding pupils—in Brussels in the rue d'Isabelle. It was run by a married couple who taught German, French, and Italian, and would allow the sisters to give English lessons. Patrick, Emily, and Charlotte traveled through London, crossed the Channel, and arrived in Belgium in 1842. Charlotte was twenty-six, Emily was twenty-four. It was a pivotal moment in Charlotte's life; her experiences there would pervade her work until her very last novel.

WHEN I arrived at Ithaca College for my freshman year as a music major, I had lofty expectations of dazzling my teachers and classmates. I had coasted through chorus rehearsals and voice lessons for years, and I expected to find the formal, full-time study of music as easy as playing for my family in the living room. Unfortunately, I realized after a semester that I was definitely not cut out to be a professional musician.

Much like Charlotte valued education but hated teaching, I loved music but hated practicing. The solitary drudgery, the monotonous repetition—I had what Charlotte had called "a vehement impatience of restraint & steady work." No performance would ever be perfect, and nothing less would ever be good enough. Not for my ambition, not for my pride, not for the casting directors of the world, or the bright lights of old Broadway. The fact that there was no easy road in the direction I had always wanted to go turned me off the whole idea for good. This has been a bit of a lifetime problem.

To console myself for the disintegration of my dreams (and to distract myself from the fact that I was a spineless, inadequate quitter), I spent hours every afternoon and weekend in the library's A/V center watching rented DVDs on a tiny television, wearing scuzzy communal headphones. I watched film noir classics, went through a Woody Allen phase, saw every Shakespeare adaptation in the catalogue, and plowed through entire TV seasons with barely a break for meals. Looking back on it now, I realize I probably should have gotten screened for depression or anxiety or seasonal affective disorder or all three, but my denial was too strong. The numbing experience of staring at small screens in total isolation held comfort. By January I had abandoned every single aspiration that had brought me to Ithaca in the first place.

I knew I had to do *something* if I was going to stay, un-
willing to face the hassle of transferring schools and brav-
ing the unknown all over again. In the fall of my sophomore
year, when the information session for *The Ithacan*, the college newspaper, rolled around, I showed up to pitch a movie
review. Seeing my name in print a week later was thrilling.
And I hadn't needed to interact with another human being
to make it happen! More than that, my brain had actually
enjoyed the workout; the challenge of capturing the film
and evaluating how well it had been done shook me out of
my stupor. I'd gotten excited about something that wasn't a
weekend library *Welcome Back Kotter* marathon!

I took my first review and a paper on a Handel oratorio
that had been excoriated by my music history professor to
a meeting with Barbara Adams, an assistant professor and
local arts critic, to see if she'd let me take her Writer as Critic
course. I recently uncovered the note in which I asked for
the meeting, the first of many I would write to my personal
Miss Wooler. She proofread it for grammar and syntax, corrected my misuse of "hopefully," and wrote "Yes!" at the bottom. Over the course of the next few years I received Barb's
thorough (and sometimes painful) revisions, corrections, and
requests for more information, and our relationship shaped
me and my writing as nothing else has. With her support, I
would go on to graduate with a writing minor, become a TA
in academic writing, intern at a major book publisher, and
never again confuse "less" and "fewer."

Eventually, I became the go-to critic for campus theater productions and indie movies at the cinema downtown.
Writing didn't come easily, exactly, but the process was

satisfying and I was pleased with my work. My voice showed up on the page. Even if it didn't completely fill that void of anxiety, or assuage the fear that sent me scurrying away from every opportunity to forge human connection, it felt like a foothold. I still hid, and I still procrastinated, but writing would turn out to be one thing I was willing to work for.

BRUSSELS was not what Charlotte and Emily expected. It was strange for two sisters in their twenties to be schoolgirls again, especially when they'd had so little experience with formal schooling to begin with. Then, too, it was a dramatic shift from their insular Haworth village. The Flemish customs and pervasive Catholicism were strange and offensive to their deeply Protestant sensibilities. Charlotte and Emily kept to themselves at the *pensionnat* and struggled to communicate. As Charlotte's French improved, her opinion of Catholics worsened, and she began her acquaintance with the man on whom inveterate Brontë fans have hung their hopes for decades: Constantin Heger, teacher of French and literature. His wife, Zoë, monitored the day students and the twelve *pensionnaires* who boarded in the rue d'Isabelle. Charlotte described Heger as

> a man of power as to mind but very choleric & irritable in temperament—a little black, ugly being with a face that varies in expression, sometimes he borrows the lineaments of an insane Tom-cat—sometimes those of a delirious Hyena—occasionally—but very seldom, he discards these

perilous attractions and assumes an air not above a hundred degrees removed from what you would call mild & gentleman-like.[3]

Emily and Charlotte's schoolwork included French *devoirs*, or essays, many of which survive intact with Heger's comments and corrections. This was the first time someone outside the family had read their writing—the first time they'd even written with the intention of being read by an adult, much less an expectation of being challenged to improve and revise. Their imaginations had always held free rein at home; they'd invented collaboratively and spontaneously. Now they were confined to designated prompts and the strictures of correct spelling and grammar—in a foreign language, no less. It chafed.

Both Charlotte and Emily found ways to inject their characteristic wit and energy into what might have been tedious assignments, some of which Heger appreciated, some of which he appeared to find vexing.[4] While Charlotte thrived on the critiques, motivated by Heger's intensity and charisma, Emily resented the interference. In 1841, M. Heger gave the Brontës an "invitation and reply" assignment. Here is Emily's note from a music teacher to her student:

Dear Miss,

It would have been, in truth, a great pleasure for me had I been able to accept your invitation; but in a life like mine, our inclination cannot always be followed, and unfortunately the day of your party is, of all the days of my week, the busiest. . . .

But when I suffer a disappointment, I ordinarily seek some compensation in return; and at present, I console myself with the thought that if I am denied the opportunity to exhibit my small talent, at least, I will not undergo the mortification of witnessing the poor results of my work with you; because I have heard that you are to play a piece on this occasion, and forgive me if I advise you (out of pure friendship) to choose a time when everyone is occupied with something other than music, for a fear that your performance will be a little too remarkable. Still, I would not want to discourage you. Good day, and good luck with all my heart.[5]

The stealthy rudeness of the subtext here—"I may miss out on the concert, but at least I won't have to hear what a terrible musician you are"—makes it my favorite piece of writing by Emily Brontë. I've read some speculation that we can't know for sure whether the sass was intentional, but I would wager Jane's first kiss with Rochester against the ridiculous idea that Emily wasn't being deliberately snarky.

The *devoir* of Charlotte's that most touches me was one of the last she wrote in Brussels; she'd attempted to give her notice and return home but been talked out of it by M. Heger. She wrote this "Letter from a Poor Painter," in which she provides a snapshot of an oddball's life I deeply relate to. Writing in the character of a young artist to a wealthy patron, she says,

Milord, I lived for a long time with others without any thought of comparing myself with them; throughout my early youth, the difference that existed between myself and most of the people around me was, for me, an embarrassing enigma that I did not know how to resolve. I believed myself inferior to everyone, and it grieved me. I believed it my duty to follow the example set by the majority of my acquaintances . . . yet all the while I felt myself incapable of feeling and acting as they felt and acted. . . . People found me always clumsy, always boring. There was always excess in what I did; I was either too wrought up or too cast down; without meaning to, I showed everything that passed in my heart, and sometimes storms were passing through it.[6]

Me too, Charlotte, me too. "Incapable of feeling and acting" like other people might as well have been my high school yearbook quote. Brontë scholar Sue Lonoff, who undertook the vital task of transcribing not only the extant Belgian essays, but deciphering Heger's corrections, suggests this is clearly a heartsick Charlotte's attempt to get Heger's attention. Through the passion of her prose and the strength of this artist's sentiments, Charlotte is speaking from the heart. She was also entirely capturing the way I have always felt, ever since it dawned on me that I looked differently or played differently or spoke differently or even *read* differently than other people. Charlotte's description of self-transformation gives me hope. She continues,

Finally a day came (I was eighteen) when I opened my eyes and glimpsed a heaven in my own soul. Suddenly I realized that I had a force within that could serve as a substitute for that noble calm which I had so much admired. . . . I became a painter and a dreamer.

At twenty-one my dreams dissipated. I do not know what voice it was that cried in my ear, "Rouse yourself! Leave your world of phantoms, enter the real world, look for Work, confront Experience, struggle, and conquer." I arose, I wrenched myself away from that solitude, those dreams that I had loved, I left my country, and went abroad.[7]

I wish I had known these essays existed when I was younger; I would not have become a painter, but I might have been motivated by the way Charlotte embraced "a substitute for noble calm" (i.e., creativity), or her frank acceptance of the necessity of struggle in order to succeed. I am always looking for an easier, less turbulent path instead of sticking to my guns and, as she puts it, "tak[ing] my degree in the school of Adversity."[8]

JUST before graduating from high school, I had begun dating James, a sweet, daydreaming kid who liked to climb trees and work on his family's farm. He was more interesting than my usual romantic leads—he would debate the merits of fantasy novels and even agreed that they needed to be more feminist. He was silly, and he was kind. Unlike the brick walls at whom I'd thrown myself over the past four years, I could be assertive and independent with him. He wasn't threatened by me, but he also wasn't a pushover. I didn't have to feign (or hide) my excitement.

After a sunny and romantic summer, we decided to stay together as we faced our respective university and gap-year obligations. Plenty of people will tell you it's a bad idea to take your high school boyfriend along to college, that long-distance relationships rarely work out, that you're going to grow and change so much that it's doomed to failure. And you might as well explain astrophysics to a pet rock as get an eighteen-year-old in love to believe any of it. I packed the family car for upstate New York, he hopped on a plane. We spoke nightly when he was near a phone on his Colorado wilderness course. We wrote letters, we pined, we bickered, we broke up, and we got back together again.

By my junior year, things with James were both better and worse than they'd ever been. We'd shared a house during the previous summer on his family's farm—a bug-filled cottage, really—and found one another's domestic habits mutually off-putting. I was too controlling, he was too passive, nobody did the dishes. But we'd made it through, talking constantly about the future to take our minds off the unpalatable present. Moving to New York City had been my greatest ambition since I was nine; James liked to travel but didn't want to live so far from home after he graduated. To my mother's dismay, I repackaged my big-city hopes like they were just an idea I'd had one time. I would finish college and spend a year in New York; James would finish school the following spring and we'd get married and start a family. We thought we'd spend a semester studying abroad in London together, so we could finally be in the same place at the same time. That August, just when I should have started pulling together my application, I saw the flyer.

"Study Abroad in India," it said, and I stopped, transfixed. One of the best friends I'd made in my neighborhood was Indian, and I'd always been fascinated by her parents' home country. Later on, a friend of my dad's had introduced the whole family to Bollywood movies and their flashy exuberance—they are 1950s MGM on steroids, Busby Berkeley with unlimited leeway. Their maximalism would give Bob Fosse a stroke. Their stylized romance is unparalleled. I wanted to see the country that had created them, to be immersed in India's folktales, its food, its music, its artwork, but it had never seemed remotely possible. I didn't even have a passport—nobody in my family did.

That urgent thirst Charlotte felt when she read Mary Taylor's letters, I felt looking at this flyer.* I wanted Something Else, something that would light me up in a new and extraordinary way. The thing that would fulfill me the way falling in love was supposed to. That would come between me and whatever I was hiding from each weekend in the A/V department. I decided I would find that thing in India. James was surprised and disappointed, but said he understood and would see me when I got back. The Brontës went to Brussels for language and culture; I went to India with no coherent plan.

---

*I promise, we are not about to stumble into *Eat, Pray, Brontë*.

I stayed with a wonderful host family, who took me to neighborhood parties and did the best they could with a headstrong American who perplexed them by sleeping late and walking out in the midday heat. I made friends with roguish Indian men on motorcycles and danced in discotheques until unseemly hours with women in jeans and sari tops, smoked Gold Flake cigarettes, drank too much Kingfisher, discovered gin and tonics at rooftop bars. I bargained joyfully for bags and jewelry out of bus windows and even negotiated the price of a nose piercing in Udaipur.

The program that hosted me offered an anthropology overview and an intro to sociology course, along with practicums in the arts, from music to miniature painting. In the survey courses, I struggled to memorize names and dates from India's expansive history and failed to comprehend experiential research practices. The only class where I did well was Hindi, out of the sheer excitement of learning to think anew and the opportunity it gave me to speak more freely at my homestay and in the streets of Jaipur. If memorizing folktales recounted by my homestay hosts and their friends had been a class, I would have gotten better grades. I still felt awkward around my fellow American students, but despite my whiteness and my garish taste in *salwar khameez* color combinations, I felt at home in Jaipur. At least for the first couple of months. Maybe it was because for once in my life there was a perfectly valid explanation for feeling foreign: I was *very* foreign, and there was no way to camouflage it. But I also had my hosts, who gave me a comforting home base, something Charlotte never managed to find for herself in Brussels, or London, or anyplace other than Haworth, really.

I even wrote a column for my college newspaper, "Indian Immersions," documenting my embarrassing Western naïveté in five-hundred-word installments. Rereading those columns now is like hearing my younger self on tape—high-pitched and glib, thinking I had anything more than an entry-level perspective on India or the people I met there. I wonder if Charlotte felt the same way about those *devoirs*—she wrote with broad strokes, tackling big topics like Genius or The Philosophy of Life, despite her lack of worldliness. Most of these essays survived in Heger's effects, not hers, so maybe she wasn't terribly proud of them. But in her work (and a little in my own) I also hear something else: the foundation of the writer in progress.

Following their initial six-month stay as students, Emily and Charlotte were asked to stay on as teachers at the *pensionnat*—Charlotte to teach English, Emily to give music lessons. With some misgivings, since Emily was already homesick and Charlotte despised practically everyone, they agreed. A few months later, their Aunt Branwell died. The sisters raced home to Haworth and went into mourning. Constantin Heger sent a letter to Patrick Brontë in their wake, expressing his condolences and giving a report of the sisters' progress during their stay. He praised their accomplishments and their "love of work," and suggested he would be willing to offer one or both of them positions at the *pensionnat* if they returned to Brussels.[9] He sounds stuffy and a little pompous. I wish we had more evidence to bring Heger to life, outside of Charlotte's guarded letters to Ellen Nussey and Elizabeth Gaskell's underwhelmed reporting. I want to be persuaded of his charisma, to see what Charlotte saw.

After a respectable period, Charlotte traveled alone back to Brussels while Emily stayed at the Parsonage to run the household, remaining in Haworth for the rest of her life. Anne and Branwell returned to their posts as governess and tutor to the Robinson family at Thorp Green. Though Charlotte enjoyed teaching English to Heger and his brother, she had another compelling reason for staying. She had fallen in love. We have no hard evidence Heger was anything but sincere and teacherly to her, but I somehow doubt Charlotte was the type to bestow her heart without *some* kind of invitation. Charlotte's unrequited affection and contempt for the rest of the *pensionnat* exacerbated her discomfort in Brussels. She wrote to Branwell in May of 1843,

> As for me I am very well and wag on as usual, I perceive however that I grow exceedingly misanthropic and sour . . . the fact is people here are no go whatsoever. . . . I can discern only 1 or 2 who deserve anything like regard—This is not owing to foolish fastidiousness on my part—but to the absence of decent qualities on theirs—they have not intellect or politeness or good-nature or good-feeling—they are nothing—I don't hate them—hatred would be too warm a feeling. . . . The black Swan Mr Heger is the sole veritable exception to this rule . . . from time to time he shews his kind-heartedness by loading me with books—so that I am still indebted to him for all the pleasure or amusement I have.[10]

The characters and stories of Angria continued to provide her with an escape from what troubled her, as they did when she was despondent at Roe Head. I wish she could have tapped back into the sense of wonder and awe that sent her abroad. She had been so eager to experience the sights and sounds of the world, but she couldn't overcome the typical Brontë homesickness, which was made even worse by solitude.

I want to snap her out of it, to tell her she has only this chance to make a life for herself, far from home and its conventions and restrictions. Take a walk! Write something! Paint! Here are your wings! Fly! But then, my India journal is full of days where everything was strange and noisy and hot and difficult and I sound like a brat. My last month or so was basically a list of museums I would never get to visit and complaints about everything—no matter how much I wanted to revel in my adventurous life as a temporary ex-pat, I was lonely, overwhelmed, and disconnected. After I moved out of my homestay family's house for the independent study portion of the semester, often my only adventure was walking to the corner shop for chocolate and Diet Coke before retreating to the hotel. Even though I loved my teachers and was well aware this was the opportunity of a lifetime, I also felt the irresistible urge to hide and run out the clock. My time in Jaipur was full of contradictions—admiring the history and grandeur, loathing the street harassment and heat. I was caught between expectant ambition and debilitating anxiety. Wings, and the effortless flight they promise, aren't to be had just for the wishing.

I think it wasn't in Charlotte's nature to be happy away from home, surrounded by strangers and strange ways. But I imagine she would have been the first to recognize how beneficial her time at the *pensionnat* was for her future career. However disheartened we both became during our times abroad, we each gained necessary skills, a new appreciation for the comforts of home, and a more evolved ability to withstand criticism.* As my semester in Jaipur neared its conclusion, what I wrestled with most was the feeling I'd failed—and failed hard—at my first capital-R romance.

Charlotte went to Brussels and fell in love. I went to India and fell out of it. We had both picked the wrong men. The security of a high school sweetheart's affection couldn't compete with the intoxication of independence, or with those Indian men and their motorcycles. James and I were on opposite schedules, moving in different directions, and the long-distance phone calls that began as a treat had become an expensive chore. Plus, James's playfulness was also immaturity; he was still merrily climbing trees, barefoot in a bathrobe while I was confronting the future, whatever it held. His disregard for public opinion, which I had found so liberating after high school, wasn't so attractive to me as adulthood loomed on the horizon.

We broke up over the phone, which was tacky but unavoidable—the alternative was dragging it out for weeks. I sat on the rooftop of the guest house where I was staying and watched neighborhood kids play with kites in the dusty street below as I told him I wanted to stay friends and apologized

---

*I got an email from a reader complaining my column wasn't as reflective and leisurely as what her friend studying in Paris was writing. Charlotte learned to stand by her work in the face of Heger's critiques, which prepared her to face off with the critics who reviewed the Brontës' poetry and novels.

for his staggering phone bill. Later, I found out he launched into a new relationship immediately. When I heard about it, I left angry voicemails and petulantly asked for my tokens and letters back, despite having rebounded with a muscular man with tribal tattoos named Vivek who took me out in his Humvee to the remixed sounds of "Hotel California." A few years later, long after the dust settled, one unfortunate night my entire family and I ended up right next to James and his family at a play; his relatives were cordial to me, but he switched seats to get as far away from me as possible. A few days later I got a spiteful email in which he unleashed all the hurt and rage he must have been feeling months and months before; I responded with a mix of penitence and confusion—I was sorry, and had behaved badly, but we were both better off. I never heard from him again.

IN early October of 1843, Charlotte finally gave her notice. Afterward, she wrote to Ellen:

> Monsieur Heger—having heard of what was in agitation . . . pronounced with vehemence his decision that I should not leave—I could not at that time have persevered in my intention without exciting him to passion—so I promised to stay a while longer. . . .
>
> I have much to say Ellen—many odd little things queer and puzzling enough—which I do not like to trust to a letter, but which one day perhaps or rather one evening— if ever we should find ourselves again by the fireside at

Haworth or Brookroyd with our feet on the fender—curling our hair—I may communicate to you.[11]

Oh to be a fly on the wall by that fireside! I must be satisfied with the echoes of this moment in *Jane Eyre* and *Villette*, I suppose, though I feel so curious I can hardly contain myself. After three more months, Charlotte overrode Heger's objections and departed for Haworth and home. When she arrived, she wrote,

> Dear Ellen,
>   I cannot tell what occupies your thoughts and time— are you ill? is someone of your family ill? are you married? are you dead? if it be so you may as well write a word to let me know—for my part I am again—in old England. I shall tell you nothing further till you write to me.
>   C Brontë
>   Haworth 1844
>   Write to me directly that is a good girl . . . [12]

Years later, Heger's son donated four letters from Charlotte to Heger to the British Museum and suggested there must have been several more that have not survived. In the earliest extant one, from July of 1844, Charlotte apologizes for a previous letter that was "hardly rational, because sadness was wringing [her] heart."[13] She promises to be patient until he writes back to her, dancing on the line between eager and desperate. In the second letter, from October, Charlotte attempts to seem casual and disinterested, ostensibly writing merely to ascertain if her earlier letter had in fact been delivered. In the third letter, written in January of 1845, she loses her cool—

> Day and night I find neither rest nor peace—if I sleep I have tormenting dreams in which I see you always severe, always saturnine and angry with me. . . .
>
> I submit to all kinds of reproaches—all I know—is that I cannot—that I will not resign myself to the total loss of my master's friendship—I would rather undergo the greatest bodily pains than have my heart constantly lacerated by searing regrets. If my master withdraws his friendship from me entirely I shall be absolutely without hope—if he gives me a little friendship—a very little—I shall be content— happy, I would have a motive for living—for working.[14]

It's uncharacteristic for Charlotte to allow herself to be so vulnerable, at least on paper. Brontë scholar Juliet Barker suggests it was writing in French that freed Charlotte from the constraints of modesty and self-restraint she would ordinarily be under.[15] Charlotte comes to a close with, "I don't want to reread this letter—I am sending it as I have written it," which unconsciously imitates a letter written by her mother years earlier, who wrote to Patrick, "Enough of this; I must bring my pen to order, for if I were to suffer myself to revise what I have written I should be tempted to throw it in the fire, but I have determined that you shall see my whole heart."[16]

Charlotte's final letter, from November of 1845, makes reference to a lost letter to which Heger must have replied, for she says, "Your last letter has sustained me—has nourished me for six months."[17] Charlotte has regained some of her composure; while she still admits that thoughts of Heger intrude upon her every waking moment, she only asks for news of his children, his school, and himself. She also admits his extended silences leave her miserable.

Heger does not appear to have encouraged any future correspondence. In fact he tore Charlotte's letters up and discarded them—they were found and stitched back together by his wife, Zoë, somewhat inexplicably. Did she anticipate needing them as proof? Did she perceive some attachment on her husband's side, as Charlotte suspected? Or did she foresee Charlotte's writing career? Brontë biographer Elizabeth Gaskell was able to gain access to these letters (or rather, to hear Heger read them aloud) and discussed them in her biography. She attempted to downplay the evidence of a young woman clearly in love with her married teacher that they contained. She noted that Heger seemed to have appreciated Charlotte's talent, but she attributes the cooling off of the relationship between Charlotte and Zoë Heger to a difference of religion, delicately avoiding any further implications.[18]

As a love-struck teenager I *so* wanted to believe that Charlotte had a great love affair with a man she respected, although nothing on paper confirms Heger's feelings toward Charlotte were anything other than fatherly. The sad truth is Charlotte probably never experienced a love scene as good as the ones she wrote—though of course neither has anyone else I've known.

Shortly after Charlotte came home, Anne Brontë resigned her governess position—she'd been working for the

Robinson family for years. Branwell had been employed as the tutor to the family's young sons, but was soon after fired for "proceedings . . . bad beyond expression," which is the pre-Victorian euphemism for having an illicit affair with the mistress of the house.[19] It was a scandal that, though hushed up by the Robinsons themselves, has essentially become Branwell's legacy.

Home together again, the sisters once again discussed the possibility of opening their own school—this time planning to board pupils at the Parsonage. They even went so far as making advertisement cards and writing to their former employers to secure pupils. But by the end of the year the low response rate forced Charlotte and her sisters to realize the futility of their school plan—plus, let us not forget, *none of them actually liked teaching*. So, the sisters began to consider other ways of making money.

I'm genuinely sorry the Brontës' experiences with private households killed off their enthusiasm for running a school—I like to imagine myself in Charlotte's Roe Head classroom, or having a cup of tea together in the teachers' parlor, even still. It occurs to me as I think back on the Brontës' work that perhaps they did get their school. And they didn't even have to admit any boarders! They just had to write, and to live. Thousands of people have read their work, and dozens of those people became writers, inspired to create brave heroines, tell unconventional love stories, reign over imaginary nation-states, or simply to write, no matter what.

I let my enthusiasm for the Brontës spill into everything I do, but especially teaching. When I talk to my students, I like to point to the Brontës as evidence that sometimes your first effort ends in disappointment. Sometimes your second effort tanks too. And even your third one. You may have to try one avenue, then another and another before you find the one that satisfies and sustains you. Charlotte's desperation to forget Heger and take her mind off Branwell's failures was likely a major factor in her next attempt at self-sufficiency: publication of the writing she and her sisters had been doing all along.

Making the Rounds

*[In] dreary expectation of finding two hard hopeless lines . . .
instead he took out of the envelope a letter of two pages. He read
it trembling. It declined, indeed, to publish that tale, for business
reasons, but it discussed its merits and demerits so courteously . . .
that this very refusal cheered the author better than a vulgarly-
expressed acceptance would have done.*

—Charlotte Brontë, "Biographical Notice of
Ellis and Acton Bell," 1850[1]

After I returned to the States, I took refuge in New York for
the summer. Barb helped me get an internship with a book
publisher and I took to it immediately—reading fledgling
books out of the slush pile, sitting in on editorial meetings,
even ferrying paperwork back and forth from production to
marketing was thrilling. It was exciting to see how the literary
sausage got made. The editors I worked for had eclectic tastes
in projects, and I got to meet their authors and help with
their book parties, draft cover copy, and make art logs. I loved
hunting for new projects they'd like in the week's submissions,
reading their backlists, and hearing what it was like to spend
days between the pages of books nobody has read yet.

I lived with my aunt and uncle in White Plains, took the Metro-North train into Grand Central, and walked up Madison Avenue every day. I ate lunch next to a slab of the Berlin Wall where the Stork Club used to stand and passed St. Patrick's Cathedral and the Waldorf Astoria on my way home. I remember the first time I walked across the Brooklyn Bridge; I made myself go all the way to the middle, despite wearing flip-flops, before I turned around to take in the view. What can you say about the skyline up close that hasn't been said? It's dizzying and glittering and somehow still makes me think of the tiny colonial seaport that used to cluster at the water's edge. And then I turned to the left and saw the Statue of Liberty, who never fails to put a lump in my throat. The city made my still-painful breakup seem like an even better idea than it had been at the time. How could I ever have settled for only one year here?

I promptly developed a crush on a fellow intern named Bianca, a New York native who knew every bartender from the Upper West Side to the East Village. We wheedled garish happy-hour margaritas out of T.G.I. Fridays waiters, charmed bouncers into waving us in without checking ID, sipped gin and tonics at hookah bars in Alphabet City, and stumbled around laughing uproariously until the next day, when we'd commiserate over our hangovers via Gchat and hope our bosses couldn't smell alcohol through our pores. Bianca made me feel like I wasn't some socially remedial weirdo. I could be cool, casual, and vivacious too—liberated from my usual prison of self-consciousness, capable of anything. I would try to carry some of that confidence with me when I returned to Ithaca in the fall. Thanks to that internship, my post-graduation plan had gone from a vague notion of freelancing somewhere to "become New York publishing editorial prodigy."

I finished my final semester of college, spent a month publishing theater reviews in the local papers, and had a fling with a townie ten years my senior. I'd gone to Ithaca to become a musical theater ingenue and found myself a writer embarking on my own odyssey. I graduated with a folder of clips, a fairly high-profile editorial internship under my belt, and a desire to take my place as a star in the publishing firmament. It did not precisely unfold as I would have liked. The course of true love, the literal and the literary, never did run smooth.

COUNTER to the common legend that the Brontë sisters just so happened to be writing poems in 1845 in a magical confluence of chance and fate that catapulted them to stardom, Charlotte had been probing at the corners of a potential literary career for years (as had Branwell). In 1836 she sent some poems to the poet Robert Southey, who sent back an infuriating letter condescendingly explaining that women shouldn't worry about being literary, for some man would be along to marry them soon enough:

> You . . . so ardently desire "to be for ever known" as a poetess. . . .

The daydreams in [which] you habitually indulge are likely to induce a distempered state of mind. . . . Literature cannot be the business of a woman's life & it ought not to be. The more she is engaged in her proper duties, the less leisure will she have for it, even as an accomplishment & a recreation.[2]

This would not be the first time Charlotte heard such attitudes expressed—her own father's novel, *The Maid of Killarny*, contained similar sentiments. Charlotte replied to Southey so graciously I have to wonder if she was actually making fun of him:

I must thank you for the kind & wise advice you have condescended to give me. I had not ventured to hope for such a reply; so considerate in its tone, so noble in its spirit. . . . At the first perusal of your letter I felt only shame, and regret that I had ever ventured to trouble you with my crude rhapsody;—I felt a painful heat rise to my face, when I thought of the quires of paper I had covered with what once gave me so much delight, but which now was only a source of confusion; but, after I thought a little and read it again and again, the prospect seemed to clear. You do not forbid me to write; you do not say that what I write is utterly destitute of merit. You only warn me against the folly of neglecting real duties, for the sake of imaginative pleasures; of writing for the love of fame; for the selfish excitement of emulation.[3]

Every time I read Southey's letter I get livid. Firstly, the arrogance of some poet whose major contribution to literature was "Goldilocks and the Three Bears" making the author of *Jane Eyre* feel bad about writing poetry makes me *ill*. Secondly, why is she so polite? Then I started reading her response differently. Where at first I thought I heard sincerity in each line, I enjoy imagining every word dripping with sarcasm.

She wrote back once more to assure him her ambition was "cured." He replied again to urge her to "take care of over-excitement & endeavor to keep a quiet mind."[4] What could be less useful to a writer than a quiet mind?

So, did she believe him? Charlotte did keep Southey's letters and write "to be kept for ever" on the outside. But she also worked on at least five novels in the next ten years. In each one she spent time lambasting pompous blowhards who devalue the abilities of women as critical thinkers. She became a world-famous author and chose not to marry, despite several offers, until *after* she was well on her way to being "for ever known" so. She claimed the right for herself and her sisters to earn a living through their talents. She helped make a world where women can have a writing career *and* a respectable marriage. Maybe she thought of Southey the way I think of the classmate who read an autobiographical comic I had invested ink, tears, and months into and callously advised me to "stick to prose." I tell my students that story every year now, to motivate them to be thoughtful, constructive, and empathetic in their feedback with one another.

Maybe Charlotte had seen how Branwell's more confrontational tactics had failed and decided to try to catch literary flies with prosaic honey instead. His repeated letters to *Blackwoods* may have begun with humble compliments for the poetry of the Ettrick Shepherd, but by 1837 Branwell had become demanding and petulant. He had more success in reaching Hartley Coleridge, essayist, poet, and son of Samuel Taylor Coleridge. In 1840, Charlotte sent Coleridge a few chapters of her own novel in progress, *Ashworth*. It was a fairly Jane Austen–like tale of a French opera singer and her illegitimate daughter, presaging *Jane Eyre*'s Celine Varens and Adele. Coleridge told Charlotte her novel was unlikely to find a publisher. She wrote him a spectacularly strange letter back, in which she thanked him for writing and added that she was glad he couldn't tell if she were male or female:

> As to my handwriting, or the ladylike tricks you mention in my style and imagery—you must not draw any conclusion from those—Several young gentlemen curl their hair and wear corsets—Richardson and Rousseau—often write exactly like old women—and Bulwer and Cooper and Dickens and Warren like boarding-school misses. Seriously Sir, I am very much obliged to you for your kind and candid letter.[5]

Charlotte's voice in her letters is great—hearing it, I realize there is at least as much of Charlotte in Mr. Rochester as there is in Jane; they have the same ruthless wit and teasing sensibility. And for a twenty-four-year-old writer who'd never published anything she or her brother hadn't stitched together with their own hands, she has a lot of moxie running down Dickens and Rousseau! I imagine it was eye-opening for Charlotte to see that Miss Brontë, clergyman's daughter, got a sexist, dream-squashing reply from Southey, while the ambiguous "CT" received feedback on the quality of her *writing* and not her future family obligations. This version of the Brontës' literary beginning is not terribly exciting—it's practical. Charlotte consulted experts, learned to navigate rejection, built her confidence back up, revised her work, and then finally took the plunge: she began sending her work out to editors to solicit their opinions. It's how most writers get started. If they're lucky.

The myth she cultivated in place of this pragmatic reality sounds straight out of a legend: Arthur pulling the sword from the stone, Helen being born with a ship-launching face, Atalanta scooping up a golden apple without breaking stride.

In the autumn of 1845, the story goes, Charlotte discovered a notebook of Emily's poetry, and was struck by how much progress Emily had made since their evenings of reading to one another in the dining room as teenagers. She wondered if they could possibly publish them.* This prompted Anne to proffer up some poems as well, and Charlotte added some verses of her own to complete the collection. And suddenly, they were writers! Novels just happened to follow! With their names on them! Could have happened to anyone! In the forewords to reissued editions of her sisters' novels, Charlotte implied that they had occasionally thought of being authors as children but never expected anyone would want to read their work. I love Charlotte Brontë, but she was lying through her teeth. Charlotte had been soliciting feedback on

---

*I always imagine this with a Lifetime movie-level of bad acting, akin to Mickey Rooney and Judy Garland putting on a show in the ol' barn.

her writing for *six years* by the time she "stumbled across" the work that would become their debut publication! This spun-sugar origin story was designed to do two things: relieve the Brontës from the "unwomanly" stigma of ambition, and conceal the very deliberate effort they put into developing their skills.

It wasn't ladylike to want to be "for ever known," so the sisters decided to use pseudonyms (Currer, Ellis, and Acton, respectively) that would protect their identities and keep them from being dismissed as "women poets." They kept their endeavor secret from their father, their brother, servants, and everyone else in the village. Only the paper sellers in Haworth and nearby Keighley found the volume and frequency of their purchases suspicious, though it seems impossible that neither Patrick, nor Branwell, nor any of the Brontës' neighbors saw them correcting proofs or mailing large stacks of paper.

Charlotte undertook the role of literary agent for herself and her sisters, sending the little bundle of poems from publisher to publisher and coping with the disinterest and rejection that followed. Because of the secrecy Charlotte had promised Emily, there aren't any archives detailing this process, aside from the occasional submission or rejection letter. How I wish she had kept a journal, as she did at Roe Head!

Finally, Aylott & Jones accepted Charlotte's request to publish the work at the authors' expense. *Poems*, by Currer, Ellis, and Acton Bell, was paid for with 36 pounds, 10 shillings of Aunt Branwell's legacy. The first copies arrived on the Brontës' doorstep in May of 1846. Charlotte would come to look back on the earnest volumes with chagrin, and not just because they were a commercial failure. She thought the only verses worth reading were Emily's, dismissing Anne's as pleasant enough but lacking originality; Charlotte had never returned to poetry after leaving Brussels, so she felt like her contributions to *Poems* failed to reflect her maturation as a writer. Charlotte circulated review copies to a number of publications; W. A. Butler of *Dublin University Magazine* was one of the few who obliged with a review, saying, mildly, "Their verses are full of unobtrusive feeling; and their tone of thought seems unaffected and sincere," while also speculating whether there were really three Bells, as opposed to one prolific individual.[6]

Though *Poems* received a handful of other positive notices, only two copies were ever actually sold—one of the happy purchasers wrote to the Bells and asked for their autograph; in his estate, years later, was found the unique scrap of paper with the signatures of Currer, Ellis, and Acton Bell upon it. Today, you can buy a postcard facsimile at the Brontë Parsonage Museum and hang it by your desk and imagine you had the foresight to ask for it.

I know I said that I'd been touched by everything the Brontë sisters wrote in some way, but their poetry leaves me cold. Reading it feels like wading through knee-deep wet sand, though the nature descriptions are lovely. The restrained introspection of Emily Dickinson or the heat of Pablo Neruda are more my speed. The Brontë poetry lacks the sense of human immediacy that pervades their prose, and it's beset by the formal Victorian Englishness their novels are so notable for transcending. The acidic critic of *The Literary Gazette* who reviewed *Poems* called it "the kind of poetry which is not endured by gods, men, or bookstalls."[7] I hate to agree with any criticism formed in prudishness over what is "appropriate" in literature, but I think the broader success of the Brontës' narrative efforts speaks for itself. Once they escaped the stricture of verse, their careers took off.

WHILE *Poems* was still in production, Charlotte, Emily, and Anne were hard at work on novels. It may have been Emily's and Anne's first efforts at writing longer prose, but Charlotte had already set aside at least two novella drafts. Their plan was to each include a contribution to a three-volume novel. Charlotte sent *The Professor*, based on her time in Brussels, along with *Wuthering Heights*, Emily's Gothic tale of doomed love and passion run riot, and *Agnes Grey*, Anne's story of a quietly moral governess, off to seek their fortunes. Charlotte was aware of *The Professor*'s flaws—its overly sarcastic protagonist and emotionally distant narrative—and already planned to develop elements of her juvenile Zamorna stories into a more marketable work if this first effort didn't pan out. I'm not a big fan of *The Professor*. Nobody in it feels particularly real or compelling, and the narrator is terribly moody. It has yet to provoke any significant life alterations for me, but that may be just an issue of timing.

The novels were considered (and rejected) separately by various editors, rather than as a unit, possibly because *Wuthering Heights* was already double its intended length.

After sending them out a fifth time, in August of 1846, Charlotte accompanied Patrick Brontë to Manchester for a cataract operation. As she attended him during his recovery, she began *Jane Eyre*.

Finally, in July of 1847, an unscrupulous publisher named T. C. Newby agreed to publish *Wuthering Heights* and *Agnes Grey*. The terms were not very favorable—the authors were to advance the sum of £50 and be repaid from the novels' profits.

Discouraged but persistent, Charlotte crossed out the address of the previous publisher, wrote "Smith, Elder & Co." on the battered wrapping of *The Professor*, and gave it another go.

William Smith Williams, the head reader at Smith, Elder & Co., didn't care for *The Professor*, but he recognized the strength of its author. Along with the publisher, George Smith, he wrote Charlotte such a thoughtful and well-considered rejection letter that she wrote back, as Currer Bell, to thank them. She shrewdly suggested that *The Professor* might make up for its "want of varied interest" if it were "speedily followed up by another work from the same pen," mentioning another novel in three volumes that was nearly finished.[8] They accepted the new work (soon to be for ever known as *Jane Eyre*) two weeks later. Charlotte's elation at their acceptance was brief, as they also enclosed several suggestions for further revision (evidently they thought parts of the opening at Lowood too shocking for a contemporary audience). She promptly rejected their proposed revisions: "Perhaps too the first part of 'Jane Eyre' may suit the public taste better than you anticipate—for it is true and Truth has a severe charm of its own. Had I told all the truth, I might indeed have made it far more exquisitely painful."[9]

They must have decided to trust Currer Bell's instincts, because English literary society was introduced to Jane, Mr. Rochester, and the rest on October 19, 1847. Critics had varying responses—"The whole is unnatural, and only critically interesting," wrote *The Spectator*. "No woman could have penned 'The Autobiography of Jane Eyre.' . . . The apt, eloquent, elegant, and yet easy mode by which the writer engages you, is something altogether out of the common way," said *The Era*. My personal favorite is from *Atlas*: "It is a book to make the pulses gallop and the heart beat, and to fill the eyes with tears. . . . The action of the tale is sometimes unnatural—the passion is always true."[10]

William Makepeace Thackeray, author of *Vanity Fair*, loved it, writing to Williams,

> I wish you had not sent me Jane Eyre. It interested me so much that I have lost (or won if you like) a whole day in reading it at the busiest period, with the printers I know waiting for copy. . . . Some of the love passages made me cry—to the astonishment of John who came in with the coals. St. John the Missionary is a failure I think but a good failure there are parts excellent I don't know why I tell you this but that I have been exceedingly moved & pleased by Jane Eyre. It is a womans writing, but whose?[11]

The success of *Jane Eyre* laid the groundwork for *Wuthering Heights* and *Agnes Grey* when they were released a few months later, and eventually the sisters began receiving the occasional royalty check for their literary debuts. Perhaps even more important than the financial support, Charlotte had found a lifeline to the outside world in the form of letters and loaned books from her publishers. Though at first she was brisk and professional with Williams and Smith behind the mask of Currer Bell, gradually she became friendly, warming enough to write sarcastic letters about critics and reviews she found irritating and new novels she appreciated.

What's most inspiring to me about this part of the Brontë story is how *deliberate* their success was. I know she wanted us all to believe it was an accident, but Charlotte was an involved businesswoman—she gave printers and editors precise specifications for what sort of paper to use, how to spend their budget on distribution, and later on, what could and could not be reprinted. Having spent years making her own tiny bound books, it's natural she had strong opinions, though often tempered with a self-deprecating " . . . or whatever you think best." Even her decision to self-publish their volume of poetry shows moxie.

I've started to view *Poems* as more of a test balloon than a real first effort. It was material they already had so it didn't need more time for writing or revision; it gave them a chance to learn the publishing ropes; and following it promptly with novels gave critics and journalists a narrative to deploy in their coverage of the mysterious Bells. Were they three women? Were they one man? How could a man write women so well? How could three women be so coarse?

Charlotte was a hardy soul. After she became successful, her letters to her publishers included gems like, "It would take a great deal to crush me," in response to some critical notices, and, "The hard-wrung praise extorted reluctantly from a foe is the most precious praise of all—you are sure that this, at least, has no admixture of flattery," in response to some grudging admiration.[12] I have both of these quotes pinned up by my desk, and I look at them often.

My earnest efforts to join the editorial side of publishing might have been the initial steps I needed to take in order to find my feet as a writer. Writing may still be "that single absorbing exquisite gratification," as Charlotte wrote to Southey, but logistically, it's intimidating. It's a different world for writers now; we are often told to be happy with "exposure" for our essays and that we provide "content," rather than something so essential as storytelling. It would have required more self-assurance than I possessed (not to mention a source of independent wealth and something to *say*) to label myself a writer straight out of college. It was easier to believe myself an editor, eager to support the work of others, until I really found something of my own.

Wearying Heights

It should have been called Withering Heights, *for any thing from which the mind and body would more instinctively shrink, than the mansion and its tenants, cannot be easily imagined.*

—Unsigned notice, *New Monthly Magazine*[1]

The first time I read *Wuthering Heights* I was sixteen and full of a hearty dose of Jane Austen's persuasive sensibilities. Miss Austen (standing in for the Lintons) had shown me polite society and good breeding, and I wanted the gracious and civilized ending she had promised. Emily Brontë cares nothing for polite society, good breeding, or gracious and civilized *anything*, and neither does anyone (well, anyone remotely interesting) in her book. Everything is a mess and everyone is awful and I hate it.

Cathy Earnshaw: Anti-Heroine

Wuthering Heights *is a strange sort of book,—baffling all regular criticism; yet, it is impossible to begin and not finish it; and quite as impossible to lay it aside afterwards and say nothing about it.*
—Unsigned review, *Douglas Jerrold's Weekly Newspaper, 1848*[1]

Oh fine. When I initially read *Wuthering Heights* I was deep in my teen romance years, truly hoping to be swept away by a high-octane love affair. I'd taken the book with me on a trip to the mountains, where I curled up with it on the balcony overlooking rich forests and rolling hills. A romantic setting, I thought, for wild and sprawling love. But the book opens with Heathcliff setting his dogs on a stranger. The narrative then makes its way inside Cathy Earnshaw's diary, which the main character actually *nods off* while reading. The book is even bored by itself, and requires Nelly Dean's intervention to tell the story properly. I was similarly put off. But I did try. A few years later in college, again in my early twenties, and even in grad school, I looked for an anchor, a back door, or even so much as a toehold in *Wuthering Heights*. I would love to say that one of these rereadings finally gave me a revolutionary understanding of *Heights'* power and relevance, or provided a crucial insight that reshaped the rest of my life, or changed me for the better in some way. But it didn't. Or maybe it just hasn't, not yet.

Part of the problem is my track record of dating milquetoasts. Heathcliff is so *uncouth*. Difficult to take to the movies, or introduce to one's friends and relations. But, once you get past a healthy resistance to the inhuman and profane, *Wuthering Heights* is damnably entertaining—even hard to put down. I once recited the whole plot for high school students in a creative writing workshop I was teaching, and they reacted to each Gothic twist with *gasps* of disbelief. *Heights* is driven by strength of feeling; its unbridled, fiendish nature is clearly part of the appeal. Fans of *Wuthering Heights* possess a fervor even Cathy Earnshaw would have to approve of.

Heights is the story of a wild child of the moors, Catherine Earnshaw, and Heathcliff, an orphan gypsy child her father brings home from a business trip. Cathy and Heathcliff grow up together, never separated until Cathy runs afoul of their neighbors' watchdog and is kept at the Lintons' house to convalesce. For the first time, Cathy experiences the comforts of a well-bred household and the finer things in life—and she likes them. Mr. Earnshaw dies and Cathy's brother Hindley returns to Wuthering Heights, banishing Heathcliff to the barn. Though she loves Heathcliff as dearly as she loves herself, Cathy decides to marry Edgar Linton, who is wealthy and kind but weak-willed. She hopes to be better placed to help Heathcliff once she's married, but he takes her betrayal at face value and runs away to make his fortune.

When Heathcliff returns, financially secure and better dressed, he swindles the now drunken and disreputable

Hindley out of the Earnshaw fortune, takes over the estate, and marries Edgar Linton's sister Isabella to avenge
himself on Cathy. Some further unpleasantness ensues and
time passes, and about half the cast dies of suspicious natural causes and/or grief. We are left with Catherine's daughter (also named Cathy), raised by Edgar Linton; Heathcliff's
son Linton, initially raised by Isabella (who practically fled
Wuthering Heights on her honeymoon), but reclaimed by
Heathcliff when he reached adolescence; and Hindley's son
Hareton, who is abused by Heathcliff in retribution for the
sins of his father. Retelling it all is Nelly Dean, a maidservant
with an impeccable memory and the rare ability to survive for
the duration of the book.

This new generation of Heights inhabitants, Young
Cathy, Linton, and Hareton, manage to salvage some happiness from the ruins of their forebears' lives, after a fashion.
To make certain he will inherit the Linton estate, Heathcliff
forces Cathy to marry Linton, who is sickly and soon dies.
Young Cathy then forms an attachment to Hareton, who is
as rough as Heathcliff was as a boy, but with a gentler heart.
They live as happily ever after as a pair of borderline inbred
teenagers with seriously dysfunctional parents and an alarm-
ingly small social circle could be expected to. I don't think
there are more than a dozen people in the *Heights* universe.
Can you imagine this novel having either the intensity or the
impact if they'd lived in a slightly larger town?

Since *Jane Eyre*'s publication had made such a splash, the
appearance of two more novels from the Bell family prompted
numerous comparisons between the three. While *Agnes Grey*
was nearly ignored, *Wuthering Heights* scandalized even the

critics who had found something to approve of in *Jane Eyre*. The more charitable reviewers hoped for bigger and better things from Ellis Bell's pen, but few could refrain from clucking over the rude unfinishedness of his debut effort. The *Examiner* said, "This is a strange book. . . . [I]t is wild, confused, disjointed, and improbable; and the people who make up the drama, which is tragic enough in its consequences, are savages ruder than those who lived before the days of Homer."[2]

The anonymous critic of *Graham's Magazine* reacted even more strongly than I did—"How a human being could have attempted such a book as the present without committing suicide before he had finished a dozen chapters, is a mystery."[3] As you might imagine, the chorus of similarly vociferous reviews actually did more to drive sales than to warn off impressionable youth. Today, *Heights* competes with *Jane Eyre* for most-read novel in the Brontë canon.

But some of those readers—anyone who thinks *Heights* is just a thrilling epic love story, really—are clearly just skimming the CliffsNotes. *Heights* is a snake pit! The famous passages, where Cathy cries out that her soul and Heathcliff's are the same, and that her love for him resembles the eternal rocks? Those only come after Cathy announces she will marry Edgar because he's handsome and rich and loves her or whatever. Later, Edgar's sister Isabella develops a crush on Heathcliff, and Cathy reveals that she knows full well what Heathcliff is. He's not a sheep in wolf's clothing, tragically misunderstood, or in need of a friendly hand; he's a regular wolf in exactly the kind of wardrobe one expects on a lupine specimen. There is no mystique. There is no soft underbelly.

Heathcliff and Cathy's love is rude and unmannerly and untidy, and not in a good way. It doesn't enlarge or improve anybody, least of all the two of them. When Cathy is on her deathbed, Heathcliff sneaks in to see her, and even there she's not repentant or tender:

> Heathcliff had knelt on one knee to embrace her; he attempted to rise, but she seized his hair, and kept him down.
>
> "I wish I could hold you," she continued, bitterly, "till we were both dead! I shouldn't care what you suffered. I care nothing for your sufferings. Why shouldn't you suffer? I do! Will you forget me? Will you be happy when I am in the earth?"[4]

But they reconcile, sort of. As Nelly Dean watches with stunned detachment,

> an instant they held asunder, and then how they met I hardly saw, but Catherine made a spring, and he caught her, and they were locked in an embrace from which I thought my mistress would never be released alive: in fact, to my eyes, she seemed directly insensible. He flung himself into the nearest seat, and on my approaching hurriedly to ascertain if she had fainted, he gnashed at me, and foamed like a mad dog, and gathered her to him with greedy jealousy.[5]

What *is* that?! And I'm not even going to get into the scene where Heathcliff gets the sexton who's burying Edgar Linton to let him open Cathy's coffin in the cemetery. These two have hooks in one another that they use only for torment, in life and afterward. Never have I aspired less to a love than this one, forged in malice and spite. Sure, I found Rochester's rudeness appealing—but his version of being rude was asking impertinent questions of his governess, or neglecting to disclose the occasional spouse. Happens all the time. Heathcliff's rudeness is rage-induced callousness built on neglect.

If I met *Wuthering Heights* at a cocktail party, I would have literally nothing to say to it. "Sure, Cathy seems great, but what did you really accomplish by spite-marrying your neighbor, Mr. Heathcliff?" "What's that, Cathy? You're just too in love with Heathcliff to stop yourself from running shoeless out on the moors and catching a cold? Was this before or after he strangled your puppy just to make a point?" "Ah, Linton. Still no self-respect I see." Fortunately there wouldn't be much time for small talk, as the book and its denizens would be busy smashing ceramics and digging up landscaping and drinking everything in sight. It's the *Macbeth*, if not the *Titus Andronicus*, of the Brontë canon—it shows us evil, but teaches us nothing.[6] On the other hand, *Macbeth* and *Titus* still get produced on stages all over the world. People like a good train wreck, a bar fight, a PR meltdown, a bloodbath. And let's not overlook the timeline. Emily wrote *Heights* thirty years after Jane Austen's death; only thirty years to go from the Netherfield Ball to Heathcliff clutching Cathy's corpse, howling his agony to the sky. There were still forty years to go before *Dracula* would make the undead look good!

In modern literary criticism, *Wuthering Heights* is often celebrated for the exact same rough-edged quality that early critics found so dismaying; many a feminist booklover admires it for being so daring. Although I find much of *Heights* extremely unpleasant, I know there is major triumph in the idea that a female protagonist doesn't have to be "likable" to deserve to be heard, and that an anti-hero is merely a hero who has been very badly treated and takes a while to snap out of it.

I do enjoy the way Cathy acknowledges that Heathcliff isn't always a treat to be around—any more than she herself is—but she loves him anyway. It was news to me that such a thing was even possible, devoted as I was then to the idea of a perfect love that never made mistakes or crossed the line from supportive to demanding.

Virginia Woolf even called Emily Brontë's gifts "the rarest of all powers," and dubbed her a greater poet than Charlotte (fighting words!). Woolf said she observed "a struggle, half thwarted but of superb conviction, to say something through the mouths of her characters which is not merely 'I love' or 'I hate,' but 'we, the whole human race' and 'you, the eternal powers.'"[7] I think Woolf is overstating *Heights*' lofty ambitions a bit, and even missing the *fun* of it. There's a lot more dark humor in *Heights* than many people recognize—just as Jane Austen was both satirizing and celebrating the Gothic novel in *Northanger Abbey*, I think Emily Brontë was deliberate in her salaciousness. She was well versed in fiction that kept you coming back to see what horrible thing was about to happen. Why else would she write about a family so dysfunctional that Nelly Dean has to recite the entire saga in flashback to a visiting idiot whose name I can never remember?* Nobody else

---

*It's Lockwood, possibly the very dullest crayon in the box.

is qualified or stable enough to contain the narrative! Try to imagine another character whose head you could stand to be in for more than a chapter or two. Heathcliff would leave you homicidal, Cathy would leave you self-absorbed and flighty, poor Isabella probably has wuthering-related PTSD, Edgar Linton would put you to sleep, and Lockwood . . . well, let's just say if Bram Stoker got a hold of Lockwood, he'd be eating bugs within an hour.

The other element that explains the novel's appeal is her depiction of the moors, which *demand* to be populated with people as dramatic as they are. The steep hills, the mossy stones, the isolated cottages, the vast unfathomable sky, the constant wind that does nothing so much as "wuther" as it rips over and around the fields. If you go climb Penistone Hill, you can see why she loved it. You can see why she suffered so much after leaving it. You begin to understand the home it provided for her imagination. And maybe that's the kind of home *Wuthering Heights* provides for its fans—it gives you a place to be wild and antisocial and uncivilized and stubborn. If that's what you're into.

I'd like to say *Heights* inspired an out-of-character fling or encouraged me to follow my heart and damn the consequences, but it mostly made me feel like I needed a shower and some vitamin D. However, though I still feel like *Wuthering Heights* is almost alone among the Brontë literature in having almost nothing to offer by way of life advice,* I respect it, and Emily's audacity as a writer. If I knew more about her, I know I'd like her better. She didn't like very

---

*Maybe simply, "Do Not Marry For Spite."

many people, and neither do I, but she wasn't afraid to let them see it, which is a skill I have not yet acquired.

And you know, if I hadn't been so wrapped up in hating everything about it at the time, I might have noticed that *Wuthering Heights* actually serves as a cautionary tale for overzealous attachment to one's first love. It's a rare romance that acknowledges enduring love can have a painful tinge to it. *Heights* might have reminded me to let go when it's time, or not to hold a grudge, because it can ruin your life.* I do wish I could have filed away the most urgent lesson of *Wuthering Heights*: be honest with yourself if the person you want to marry is still obviously entangled with someone else. But that lesson would be a long time coming.

---

*Oh, and call your child something other than its mother's first or last name, just for clarity's sake.

Agnes Grey

The story of "Agnes Grey" was accused of extravagant over-colouring in those very parts that were carefully copied from the life, with a most scrupulous avoidance of all exaggeration.
    —Anne Brontë, Preface to *Tenant of Wildfell Hall*[1]

I came to *Agnes Grey* at something of a low point in my planned meteoric ascendance to fame—or at least rise to bill-paying self-sufficiency. Freshly graduated from college, I moved to New York City, teamed up with roommates, found a temp gig, and applied to every publishing job I could find. And then, after a few months, I actually got one! It was at a test-prep publisher, not a trade house, but I still went into it with starry-eyed expectations. I would be the best, most indispensable editorial assistant the test-prep publishing industry had ever seen. I would be beloved by my bosses. I would skip straight to the competent part of *The Devil Wears Prada*, minus the makeover. Eventually I'd find a foothold in trade publishing, I consoled myself, and get back on track. I made some significant progress, too—I acquired and edited an anthology inspired by my mom's experience as a lawyer, developed a few manuscripts, gained experience copywriting, and saw how a small trade program is built. Then I got to see how it's shuttered and dismantled, piece by piece. In April, I was laid off alongside a handful of colleagues.

The recession brought a lot of us thumping down to earth again, resolving not to be so misguidedly enthusiastic in the future. I searched for more publishing jobs and applied to administrative positions and assistant positions and clerical positions, but New York was awash in editorial assistants and it turned out precious little of my test-prep experience put me in the running for real trade publishing. I was beginning to contemplate moving home in disgrace when I was offered a place in a New York year-of-service program, which paid a stipend to volunteer coordinators who worked with nonprofit and city programs. I was assigned to an arts education organization where I would write grants, assist in classrooms, and help plan the annual benefit. I gathered the dregs of my idealistic vigor and went into my first day on the job like someone who had never been smacked in the face with the resistance of institutions to change.

When Charlotte Brontë was lonely and desperate in Brussels, she went to Confession despite her staunch Protestantism. So, despite being baptized and confirmed in the Church of *Jane Eyre*, when I was lonely and desperate in New York I decided to get to know her sister Anne. I could hardly have chosen a less worldly mentor. Compared to her sisters, we know the least about Anne as a person—though she's going through a bit of a renaissance at the moment, she isn't mentioned with the same reverence as Emily and Charlotte. Her work doesn't receive the same kind of breathless attention.

But the more I've gotten to know her, the more underrated she has seemed.

In the biographical notice that Charlotte added to Smith, Elder & Co.'s later editions of *Wuthering Heights* and *Agnes Grey*, she refers to Emily's poetry as "condensed and terse, vigorous and genuine"; having "a peculiar music—wild, melancholy, and elevating." Of Anne's poetry she says only, "I thought that these verses too had a sweet and sincere pathos of their own."[2] These pages that Anne handed Charlotte, after she'd "rediscovered" Emily's work, are bound in a small red leather volume at the Morgan Library and Museum, where I visited them one blustery January afternoon. Anne's handwriting is more assertive than Charlotte's, I noticed immediately. In addition to figuratively patting Anne's head with lukewarm praise, Charlotte had excised all traces that Anne's poetry resided in Gondal. This means that the poems are missing a huge part of their personality—their rooted origins in this vibrant imaginary kingdom! Without the names and places, there's no way to know Anne was writing *in character*, just as Emily was. Alongside the dominant personalities of Charlotte, Branwell, and Emily, no wonder Anne was "the quiet one." *Agnes Grey*, up against the wildness of *Wuthering Heights* and the intensity of *Jane Eyre*, seems even tamer by comparison than it actually is. Truly, it differs from an Austen novel mostly in having a heroine who actually works for her living. I'm very fond of Austen's wit and her social commentary, and I don't even have a problem with her repetitive marriage plots—it doesn't seem like there was much else to do besides play the piano forte, go for walks, and marry off daughters. But the Brontës broke away from those social conventions in their novels—Charlotte by giving Jane Eyre passion, Emily by unraveling the fabric of society, and Anne by telling the truth.

Anne, like her sisters, had several opportunities to earn a living away from home. She possessed the longest unbroken stretch of schooling (the two years at Miss Wooler's) and the most work experience. As governesses the Brontës offered instruction in reading, writing, natural sciences, geography, French, and sewing, and were also expected to help with laundry and other household chores. As usual, Anne's quiet, professional perseverance lasted the longest. Anne spent eight months with the Inghams of Blake Hall in Mirfield and three years with the Robinsons of Thorp Green (where Branwell was also employed as a tutor for a year or so). She found the behavior of her charges appalling, and in some cases their parents even worse. This is actually what makes me like *Agnes Grey* a little bit better than some of Austen's work: it lets us in on Agnes's inner monologue, which reflects, I imagine, Anne's perspective more directly. Anne was "the help"—she didn't need to stay a gloved-arm's-length away from the action. The social circles in which she was a governess were more than just absurd; she knew them to be actively harmful and even dangerous.

There is something very clear-eyed and pragmatic about *Agnes Grey* that I respond to. It depicts a capable young woman finding a job, losing it because her employers are horrible, finding another one, persevering despite the difficulties, opening her own business, and doing all this without worrying about her romantic relationship. *Agnes Grey* also has some strong commentary for the wealthy classes' treatment of their domestic employees and the horrid behavior of their children. When I came to it, I needed a novel that would reinforce the idea that my purpose in life involved self-sufficiency as much as it did *l'amour*. I read *Agnes Grey* in installments on the R train that took me from my apartment in not-quite-Park-Slope to my cramped desk in a minuscule Columbus Circle office.

Agnes arrived at her first governess post with the Bloomfields just as my position at the arts education nonprofit was beginning to feel thankless and hopeless. She found herself between a rock and a hard place—discipline the bratty, destructive children and find herself dressed down by her employers for not managing them more gently, or let them have their way, get abused by the children, and *then* be reprimanded by their unreasonable parents for not keeping them in better order. In addition to assistant-teaching in challenging classrooms, I was working with wealthy board members to solicit donations and plan the annual benefit. I had never felt so invisible—the board members ignored me in meetings, berated me over the phone, and talked down to me in emails while cc'ing my boss. The things I loved doing—volunteering in elementary school classrooms in the Bronx and leading an afterschool mosaic program in Harlem—nobody seemed to notice, even when I worked hard and did well. As my ideas were passed over and my projects micromanaged, my enthusiasm for everything except for the art classes waned. And even in those classes, all the flaws of any big city's public school system were alive and well. Too many students in a class, behavioral issues and no accessible accommodations, hardworking classroom teachers, and aides with inadequate administrative support. Instead of being given more responsibility or independence, I got less and less of either as my year at the nonprofit went on. I thought of Charlotte, Emily, and Anne and their litany of complaints about working in private houses, which would have been tolerable without the pupils, and agreed that nonprofits wouldn't be so bad if it weren't for their boards.

Unlike Agnes, I didn't work resolutely to improve. I dragged my feet. I frittered time in the office. I discovered Twitter. I got yelled at. I slacked off harder. Agnes was lucky enough to be fired by the Bloomfields for refusing to overlook the children's more egregious lapses in behavior. It all went down before her professionalism and good intentions had a chance to lapse. I had four more months on my contract by the time I hit bottom.

Refusing to be discouraged, Agnes set off again, this time to the Murray family at Horton Lodge. The Murrays were based on Anne's second employers, the Robinsons. She never spoke especially fondly of her charges, but the Robinson girls stayed in contact with her after she left their mother's employ, and even asked to be invited to visit the Parsonage once.*

---

*Charlotte was nonplussed at the prospect. "They threaten to pay us a visit," she wrote to Ellen Nussey, "they have written to ask if they can bring the carriage up to the house—we have told them 'yes', as we think if they bring it once through those breakneck turnings—they will not be in a hurry to try the experiment again." And if you'd ever navigated those turns clinging to the door handle of a cab, you'd be inclined to agree. In any case, the daughters never visited a second time.

Agnes's charges at Horton Lodge are considerably older than the Bloomfield children. She meets two young boys, who are sent off to school soon after she arrives; Rosalie, a ringleted marriage-minded beauty of sixteen, who seems borrowed directly from the supporting cast of *Sense and Sensibility*; and Matilda, a "strapping hoyden" of fourteen, who prefers swearing and running around with horses, dogs, and livestock to any of the more maidenly pursuits. She is one of my favorite Brontë characters. A pre-Victorian tomboy with a foul mouth—*finally* a Brontë character who could have spoken to my teenage self in her primary language!

Though they are less vexatious than her previous pupils, Agnes finds the Murrays irritating. They disregard her wishes, her schedule, her physical comfort, and most gallingly, her moral counsel. Agnes's tenure with the Murrays progresses from months to years, through Rosalie's coming out into society, Matilda's profane exultations over her new mare, and assorted shenanigans with local bachelors, until at last something interesting happens—the arrival of a new curate. Mr. Weston sees through (but is courteous to) silly, shallow Rosalie, he is admired by the less fortunate in the village surrounding Horton Lodge, and he becomes a fixation for our Miss Grey. When caught together in a timely rainstorm, Miss Grey and Mr. Weston develop a quiet rapport, so polite and respectful that nobody is sure of anybody's feelings for an impossibly long time.

After Rosalie's marriage to an unpleasant wealthy older man (over which Agnes shrugs: "There are, I suppose, some men as vain, as selfish, and as heartless as she is, and, perhaps, such women may be useful to punish them."[3]), Lady Murray's

attentions fall on her younger daughter, my tomboy heroine
Matilda. It was time for her to be civilized. No more traips-
ing through the stables. No more hunting with her dogs.
No more swearing. It seemed that maybe a similar transformation was in order for me. Perhaps it was time to actually
grow up, to stop slacking off. But rather than changing the
way I dressed or acted, or curbing my takeout habits, I still
believed the key to transitioning to adulthood was a serious
relationship.

I wouldn't say I had Rosalie Murray's cruelty in my dating
life—I didn't deliberately mislead my "suitors," laugh at them
behind their backs, or manipulate them into doing things
for me. But I definitely had some of her single-minded focus. That's how I found myself on dates with kind but boring
guys from OkCupid like Gordon, with friendly but uncouth
guys like Mike from choir, with wildly incompatible guys like
Max the Republican from New Jersey. I went for coffee with
Jess, who was immature but cute, and fun to make reading
lists with, and Maria, who was as alpha as she was feminine.
When I went out with Lauren, who was as awkward as I was,
we both brought our dogs as buffers. I dated terrible kissers
and compulsive phone checkers. Lesbians who sneered at my
bisexuality and straight men who thought being queer was a
party trick. I hid parts of myself altogether, feigning enthusiasm for whatever my date was into, no matter how esoteric.
I was tailoring myself in hopes they would like me, and as a
result I was neither genuinely happy nor genuinely appreciated. I wasn't ready to allow myself to be known.

The consequences of conformity would prove much worse
for Rosalie Murray, whose husband was a wealthy but not

particularly interesting man who, imagine the audacity, didn't even want her to flirt with other men on their bridal tour. But here's where Anne Brontë gets progressive (if a woman being libertine enough to flirt *on her bridal tour* isn't progressive enough for you). After Agnes's father dies, her mother suggests that the two of them open a day school together. Happy to leave everything at Horton behind, save Mr. Weston, Agnes agrees, and at first takes to the work with enthusiasm. Some time passes, and one day as Agnes enjoys a picturesque walk on the beach, who should she happen to see on the sand but Mr. Weston and a terrier named Snap. Mr. Weston has taken a living (that's curate-speak for "gotten a job") nearby and has "nothing but solitude to complain of, and nothing but a companion to wish for." One does not have to be a lovesick teenager to pick up on that subtle hint. He and Agnes have a lovely walk, during the course of which she takes his arm, "though not with the intention of using it for support."* The next day, and the next, he comes to call on her and her mother, and so on, and so forth. At last it comes to an end as tidily as even Miss Austen could have wished, with a proper seaside proposal and a marriage of equals.

I can't definitively assert that Patrick Brontë's colleague Mr. William Weightman was the inspiration for the impeccable Mr. Weston, but Charlotte did allude to a quiet sort of affection between Weightman and Anne Brontë in a letter to Ellen Nussey in 1842, two years after Weightman came to work with their father.[4] She teased Ellen about being in love with him too, though if the portrait Charlotte drew of

---

Hussy!

Weightman is any indication, she may have actually liked him for herself. Patrick looked on Weightman as a son, and he spent a lot of time at the Parsonage. Unfortunately, he died of cholera in September of 1842. A marble plaque dedicated to his memory still hangs on the wall of Haworth Church. It would have been fitting for Anne to right her personal and professional disappointments by awarding both marriage and school to her first heroine.

Agnes Grey closes her tale with "And now I think I have said sufficient." The prose doesn't crackle with passion or wit, and it's too moderate to really sustain much tension. But even where it is fictional it is true, which I felt even before I knew Anne herself had insisted it was so. This story reflects such an alert mind, so observant of a society she was permitted to live in, but not belong to, that I cannot help but like her. *Agnes Grey* also contains gems that give us little hints about Anne Brontë herself. She liked Shakespeare, for a start. When she first meets the Murray children, Agnes breaks the fourth wall to say, "As I cannot, like Dogberry, find it in my heart to bestow all my tediousness upon the reader . . . " to excuse moving forward more quickly.[5] Though Agnes is soft-spoken, she's not without humor: she "amuses [her]self with a hearty fit of crying" upon arrival at Horton Lodge, and later exclaims in exasperation, "Climax of horror! actually waiting for their governess!!!" in the face of her charges' impatience.[6]

Some Brontë scholars take offense at the suggestion the sisters wrote even a little autobiographically—they think the inference denigrates the imaginative talents or literary craft of the Brontës. As a writer of nonfiction, I would never suggest it demeans fiction to draw from life. Truth in fiction never makes it weaker, but anchors it, unlike lying in non-fiction, which is like robbing a tree of its roots. When we know so little about Anne, in particular, it's hard to resist connecting the dots between her home life and her literary one, no matter how light or faint the association may be. Plus, *come on.* In their juvenile adventures, when the Brontës went to school, their characters went to school. In their mature fiction, when the Brontës were teaching, their characters taught. The fact that these things happened in life and in literature is part of what gives them resonance. It's what allows the Brontës to capture detail and write so realistically. It's what makes them true.

AS my year with the service program drew to a close, alongside *Agnes Grey*, I considered what Agnes had said about wanting to work on her own after feeling "despised and trampled upon by old and young."[7] Nonprofits were not for me—too much pleading for money and trying to work miracles with no resources. I'd also realized that while I might look for more jobs in publishing, I still wanted to write. I had a blog—but then, everybody had a blog. I wanted to be spending serious time writing essays or reviews or maybe something bigger, something I hadn't even dreamt of yet. And I wanted to teach. With all the liberal arts options in the world open to me, funnily enough the ones I wanted to pursue the most were the same choices that had been open to the Brontës 160 years before.

The instability of the freelancer's life had always seemed too scary—the constant hustle, the financial insecurity, the unpredictability—but I took heart from Agnes's example that good things could come to those who took risks. When a friend passed along a job posting for writers on a pop-up-video-style sports clips television show, I dashed off a cover letter about my abiding love for sports and sarcasm, crossed my fingers, and submitted it. I hoped that being less comfortable on my own terms would pay off better in the long run than being in the employ of people who didn't even see me as useful.

I got an interview with the show's creator and head writers in a second-floor production studio near the Flatiron Building. I tried not to notice the life-size nude portrait of the producer on the wall behind him, ignored his insensitive jokes about teen girls and cutting when he heard where I was currently working, and agreed to write a test script. *This is the least my life has ever had in common with the Brontës*, I thought as I searched for obscure sports trivia and biographical information on Patrick Ewing.

After I got the job, I got to pitch jokes in the writers' room, spit-balling like a *Mystery Science Theater 3000* writer. I hunched over my laptop in coffee shops and bookstores. I stopped hesitantly introducing myself as unemployed and started calling myself a writer. I scrutinized grainy Madison Square Garden event clips until my eyes crossed, and was thrilled to see my jokes pop up, even in various degrees of rewrite, when the show aired on late-night cable. It wasn't Emmy-winning work, and the promise that it might lead to a full-time assistant position never materialized, but I was a professional writer. For a little while.

The show only ran for a single season, so I finished my final script just eight weeks after I began the first one. I channeled scrappy Matilda Murray and applied for any job I could find that would let me stay in New York. I ignored my mother's repeated assurances that I could always move home and help around the house. I spent a few months working retail in a store that sold fun dishes and glassware, and held my head up. I started actually taking care of my own apartment instead of letting my room reflect my mental state, cluttered and full of dirty laundry. *Agnes Grey* had helped me realize I could take my future into my own hands, without waiting for anyone or anything.

My newfound self-confidence was at last rewarded on a first date with a woman named Preeti, who I met on OkCupid. I knew we were clicking as soon as I walked up to the meeting place I'd suggested, near Brooklyn's Gowanus Canal. It had seemed like a good idea at the time—it was close to the train station and technically en route to the restaurant, but it was also pretty desolate after dark. I walked over to the only person I'd seen in about three blocks and said, "Hi, are you Preeti?" "Depends," she answered. "Are you here to murder me?" Dinner was a big success. No, seriously!

Preeti had two cats, knew how to cook, volunteered on a community farming co-op, and worked in a molecular biology lab. We'd spent about the same amount of time in India, where her parents were from, and both wanted to go back someday. Way cooler than me, and sure of herself in a way I

could only envy, Preeti was all the things I'd hoped for and
never imagined I could find in one person. And she *got me*.
I've never believed in love at first sight—largely because nobody has ever looked at me and fallen in love—but the spark
I felt with Preeti was instantaneous. I fell so hard I got dizzy.
I even called my parents and came out to them that same
night. My mom said, "You know we love you no matter
what. And I have to say, I'm not surprised. I mean . . . your
hair." (I had recently begun sporting an androgynous barber-
shop version of a pixie cut.) Her repeated emphasis on how
not-shocked she was made me slightly skeptical, but when
my dad paused for a long moment before saying, "OK, can I
go to bed now?" I knew everything would be fine. I raised a
toast to Matilda Murray and dug *Shirley* out of my bookcase.

Shirley and Caroline

The first chapter of Shirley *is enough to deter many a reader from advancing a step further than the threshold. It required all the remembered fascinations of* Jane Eyre *to keep down the feelings of dissatisfaction.* . . . Shirley *is better written than* Jane Eyre, *but there is less power in it.*

—Unsigned review, *Atlas*, 1849[1]

Shirley, first and foremost, is a story of female friendship. It is also about class distinctions, the Napoleonic War, Yorkshire politics, gender roles, the behavior of the clergy, the power of a female heiress, and "the condition of women question," i.e., should women earn a living and support themselves. It is some hybrid of Charles Dickens's thoroughness, Jane Austen's worldview, and Charlotte's own unique blend of Romanticism and candor. *Shirley* is the first Brontë novel to have a narrator who is not part of the action; the first time we hear the voice of someone who is neither composing a letter or scribbling in a diary nor making a private confession, but instead observing the local goings-on alongside us. Charlotte also stops to pivot downstage and give us her thoughts on youth, working-class morals, feminism, and whatever else comes to mind. It is surprising and odd and I love it.

Charlotte begins *Shirley* with four curates tediously bickering over theology at the dinner table. No joke, I tried to read *Shirley* four times before I got past the curates. One review compared the novel's opening to the monsters people put at their gates, or "ugly dogs to deter idle folk from entering."[2] My latest theory is that the curates are Charlotte's response to the male critics who seemed to want her books to be more like *men's* books. So she begins a book entirely about the interior lives of women with a bunch of tedious local clergymen, as if to say *Here, dudes, here are your men.*

Eventually, if we are stalwart and true, we meet the heroine, Caroline Helstone, a typical lighthearted romantic heroine. It's possible that Caroline is loosely, *loosely* based on Charlotte's best friend Ellen Nussey. She's a mild, well-behaved curate's niece, politely in love with her neighbor and distant cousin Robert Gerard Moore. She studies French and sewing with his sister, Hortense, and lives for the evenings when Robert joins them in the parlor to read aloud or chat. This mellow domestic sphere is disrupted when textile embargoes from Parliament force Robert to lay off his workers; Caroline's uncle forbids her to see Robert on the grounds that he's a presumed Flemish sympathizer. It's historically interesting (. . . ish) and lays the foundation for a conventional marriage plot with various temporary obstacles that will resolve as expected after the right people make the correct courtly gestures of affection and contrition at the appropriate times.

Caroline Helstone certainly *thinks* that's the kind of novel she's in—after an evening with Robert Moore during which he demonstrates basic human courtesy, she is luminous with hope and expectation. "When people love, the next step is they marry," she sighs, dopily.[3] I'm not saying Caroline was desperate, but she certainly went quickly from having no indication that Robert loved her to being sure they were about to become engaged. This is where my suspicions that Charlotte was mocking me began to develop. The next morning, all of Robert's lover-like manners from the night before are totally gone; Caroline is distraught. Charlotte The Narrator addresses the lovelorn flatly:

> Take the matter as you find it: ask no questions, utter no remonstrances; it is your best wisdom. You held out your hand for an egg, and fate put into it a scorpion. Show no consternation: close your fingers firmly upon the gift; let it sting through your palm. Never mind; in time, after your hand and arm have swelled and quivered long with torture, the squeezed scorpion will die, and you will have learned the great lesson how to endure without a sob.[4]

Yikes. I'm of several minds about the sudden onset of metaphoric martyrdom. Part of me thinks Charlotte is making fun of me for picking out nursery supplies before a second date and whining when it doesn't pan out. The other part of me is convinced that Charlotte crafts this restrictive, patriarchal world with all its ladylike confines and socially appropriate withholding of feelings so that Shirley Keeldar can kick the door open and let the sunshine in. A few pages later, Caroline's literally in the middle of conducting Old Maid research (Is it better to be the cheerful, saintly, helpful old maid everyone asks for favors, or the cranky, acerbic old maid people are afraid of?*) when her uncle drags her up to the local squire's estate, Fieldhead, to meet the new tenant. This is when we get to stop caring about all that thorough historical back-storying. In fact, the novel's entire historical foundation is about to stop being remotely compelling (even to Charlotte, who abandons the Luddite Rebellion plotline for chapters at a time—leaving me gasping, What about the *weaving machines*?!?!?).

The arrival of Shirley signals the end of this novel's resemblance to anything traditional. Twenty-one years old and the only child of parents who gave her the traditionally masculine name they would have given their male heir, this reincarnation of Rosalind, fresh from the Forest of Arden, strides in to flip on all the lights and crank up the volume. It's like we've been slogging through a despondent swamp and are yanked out by a claw machine.

Shirley has style, intelligence, an estate, a title, and oh best beloved Shirley, the panache to thoroughly enjoy all of it. Caroline is all naïveté and quiet resignation and faith in romance. Shirley is boisterous, funny, and confident, though not quite as self-assured as she initially seems. Charlotte wrote Shirley, she confessed to Elizabeth Gaskell later, as an homage to her sister Emily, had she been born "into health

---

*Door number two, obviously.

and prosperity."[5] Though there are other spitfires, other opinionated damsels, other protagonists with swagger, Shirley is unique among her contemporaries by also being thoroughly lovable, in ways your Becky Sharps or Emma Woodhouses are just not.

I was bowled over by Shirley's wit and charm; in Caroline and Shirley, I saw myself and Preeti. We were a matched set. The two of them, and the two of us, never ran out of things to say, and weren't afraid to tackle the big questions, like whether men and women are actually different or just socialized differently, or what exactly the producers hoped to improve on by remaking *The Parent Trap*. Our version of Shirley and Caroline's picnics was a constant Gchat conversation in which we debated the work of L. M. Montgomery, the upcoming season of *Mad Men*, the merits of various animals, kids, and vegetables. We could talk about the Bechdel test for hours, all day, every day, for weeks. After a million "oh my God you have to read _____" conversations, we formed a book club where we'd each read a new book and trade a YA book from our childhoods, which is how I discovered Cynthia Voigt's *Tillerman Cycle* novels and how Preeti met Margaret Thursday. I'd never cast myself as the quieter, inexperienced one before, but then I'd never been out with someone as warm and funny as Preeti, either.

Suddenly every bad date I'd ever suffered through with a bore or a jerk seemed like the price of admission I'd had to pay to have *this*, a girl I wanted to be my girlfriend, who was beautiful and funny and didn't want me to change or be less vocal, who liked lots of things I liked and knew many things

I didn't know. I gazed into the future and wondered which of us would get pregnant when it was time to start a family, or if we both would. We each had a brother, so the genetics wouldn't be a problem; I guessed it would depend on how our careers were going. This was after knowing her for eight days.

For our second date, I took Preeti to dinner at my favorite crepe place, and afterward we wandered the East Village; it was just as much fun as the first outing had been, though we again only parted with a friendly hug. I was confused, but figured I just needed to be more overt about the fact that I was attracted to her. On our third date, I upped my casual-arm-around-the-shoulders quota of the evening to four, and made sure we brushed hands every hour or so. Poor Preeti— she had to resort to dramatic gestures to let me know it wasn't going to happen. When we picked our seats in the empty movie theater, she sat down a seat away from me, plunked her bag down beside her, and took out her knitting.

I was crushed. I nursed my hurt feelings all through the (terrible) movie and said goodbye abruptly afterward. The next day when her name flashed up in a Gchat window, I didn't hurry to click to it. When I finally did, she was apologizing for not knowing how to say sooner that she only liked me platonically, but that she liked me *a lot*. What could I do? I'm sure I said something nonchalant and hid behind jokes about what a terrible couple we would have made, like *she* was the clueless one for thinking *I thought* it would work. I was grieving and simultaneously trying to act as if it hadn't occurred to me there was even anything to grieve over. I figured if I could stick around, eventually she might succumb to what I hoped was charm, and not just dogged neediness.

Nothing in our dynamic actually changed—we still chatted all day and cooked together, sat knee to knee on the couch, and planned road trips during movie marathons. If I hadn't known better, I would have thought we still *were* dating, just not particularly demonstrative. Meanwhile my heart was grumbling rebelliously from inside its carbonite prison.

What I most appreciated about *Shirley* (besides the Sapphic undertones and how glad Shirley and Caroline are to exclude men from their picnics) was Charlotte's sense of humor, delivered in sly asides to the reader and in the sillier plot devices. Mistaken identity and long-lost relatives have rarely been played so straight-facedly. This was also the first time I'd seen adult female friendship portrayed in any Brontë novel—Jane Eyre, Cathy Earnshaw, and Agnes Grey all have to make their own ways in the world, but Caroline and Shirley have one another to lean on. They get to socialize without chaperones or romantic prospects. They're not rivals or competitors (though a sketchy sort of love triangle does form around them, thanks to the inevitable intrusion of men); they're just *friends*, who read poetry and plan trips and sometimes sit quietly outdoors together, probably with one's head in the other's lap or casually holding hands or whatever. I'm not picky.

I think part of why I took Preeti's rejection so hard was that I find female friendship challenging generally. Not that I don't crave it, but that I don't often have the emotional currency to sustain it. Charlotte Brontë excelled at female friendship. She may have compartmentalized her friendships, or maintained them primarily through letter-writing, but they were profound nonetheless.

Charlotte's best friends included Ellen Nussey, Mary Taylor (who later moved to New Zealand), their teacher Miss Wooler, and eventually the novelist Elizabeth Gaskell. Though Charlotte initially attempted to indoctrinate Ellen into the Brontë literary lifestyle by inundating her with reading lists while they were at school together, she eventually gave up and found plenty to discuss with "almost the only, and certainly the dearest," friend she had outside her family circle.[6]

Her correspondence with Ellen is full of local nothings: how the journey was, whether the new cuffs were becoming, their health, the weather, traveling logistics. It's delightful to see her mind at play, but it also becomes strange as her homebody epistolary life began to coexist with her extraordinary literary one. Charlotte and Anne had made a pact with Emily that nobody should know the true identities of the Bells. However, Ellen was suspicious, having seen Charlotte correcting proofs of *Jane Eyre*. By mid-1848, she was even bold enough to ask Charlotte about her work in progress, which Charlotte pretended not to understand, replying, "Your naivety in gravely inquiring my opinion of the 'last new novel' amuses me: we do not subscribe to a circulating library at Haworth and consequently 'new novels' rarely indeed come in our way."[7] (In addition to the novel she was in the middle of writing, Charlotte was at that point regularly receiving whole boxes of books and periodicals from Smith, Elder & Co.) Resolute, Charlotte kept their secret from Ellen until Emily's death in December of that year.

Charlotte was one of the greatest literary artists in history, yet you would never know from most of her letters to school friends that she had ever even *thought* of writing—much less been writing constantly since childhood. In one letter Charlotte lectures her publisher on the best way to spend the funds the Brontës had set aside for publicity and printing costs; in another, written the same day, she thanks Ellen graciously for sending a bonnet, and updates her on the welfare of family servants and pets. She drops literary luminary Elizabeth Gaskell a line to commiserate about a critic who'd reviewed them both, and in her next note, nags Ellen about which train she'll be arriving on and complains of boredom.

Though Shirley was based on Emily Brontë, and Caroline (very loosely!) on Ellen, their friendship was likely derived from Charlotte and her friend Mary Taylor (whose family also served as inspiration for Caroline's neighbors, the Yorkes). Charlotte and Mary talked about politics, women's rights, and more intellectual subjects—including her books. Mary is funny and sharp, less fastidious-seeming than her contemporaries. After leaving Brussels, she worked as a tutor in Germany, then packed up and moved to New Zealand, where she opened a store, built herself a house, and stayed for nearly fifteen years. Her letters are distinguished both by their energetic nature and by the fact that she knew about Charlotte's publishing efforts much earlier than anyone else. After receiving a copy of *Jane Eyre*, she wrote,

> It seemed to me incredible that you had actually written a book. Such events did not happen while I was in England. I begin to believe in your existence much as I do in Mr. Rochester's. In a believing mood I don't doubt either of them. . . .

I will scold you well when I see you. . . .

I have lately met with a wonder of a man who thinks Jane Eyre would have done better marry Mr. Rivers! He gives no reasons—such people never do.[8]

Charlotte cheekily mentioned this letter to Margaret Wooler in August, saying, "I heard from Mary Taylor in June. . . . She expressed pity for my comparatively dull, uneventful, and unoccupied existence."[9] When Mary finally read *Shirley*, she wrote to Charlotte,

What a little lump of perfection you've made me! There is a strange feeling in reading it of hearing us all talking. Shirley is much more interesting than J. Eyre—who indeed never interests you at all until she has something to suffer. All through this last novel there is so much more life & stir that it leaves you far more to remember than the other.[10]

But here is why I'm really obsessed by Charlotte's friendships with Ellen, Mary Taylor, Miss Wooler, Laetitia Wheelwright, and her other intimate correspondents: these relationships, which she established as a young girl, sustained her for nearly thirty years.

In my own thirty years, I have retained *maybe* one friend from each stage of my life—middle school, high school, college—and that's it. Handfuls of acquaintances, with names and faces I recognize and would be happy to see again if I ran into them on the train, but the kinds of friends you keep informed of your daily activities? I could list them on an index card. I could tear the index card in half and share it with the hermit who lives in the Inwood Hill Park caves and gets his mail at Dunkin' Donuts. I socialize with neighbors at the dog park and am friendly with my coworkers, but I rarely join them for parties or meet up after hours. I don't seem to keep up with many people. Sometimes it just doesn't occur to me. Other times I'm deliberately cocooned inside my work or my own head and everyone else fades to the background. But then I feel sad, because when I resurface, I realize nobody tried to keep in touch with me either.

There are times when I totally understand Charlotte's feelings of being stuck, facing either isolation in a country home that she loved or the fatiguing overstimulation of the city's literary scene. And I understand her sense of inadequacy when her friends sent her boxes of books and magazines. She always wrote W. S. Williams and George Smith to say thank you and share her opinions of the contents, but she felt she had nothing to give them in return—not even an engaging account of rural life. What was a lecture at the Mechanics Institute going to offer the cosmopolitan literary gentlemen? What commentary could someone marooned in a tiny village offer on politics or current events?

My best friend, Sally, and I met in high school; she sends cards and care packages for every holiday you could possibly imagine, from St. Patrick's Day to Labor Day. Last time I saw her, I planned to make up for the unanswered pile of cards by treating her to dinner. Over dessert, she presented me with a bag of goodies and a card. Evidently it was Friendship Day. Sally and I often celebrate how easily we pick up where we left off when we finally do manage a visit or a late night of ice cream and TV bingeing, but it's bittersweet.

In college, I was part of a trio of best friends who thrived when we lived in the same building. But we barely even survived a semester of sharing an apartment—too much togetherness, rapid life changes, and mismatched habits sent us off the rails just after the winter break. After graduation, it took two years of living in the same city before I ran into one of them on the street and had the presence of mind to apologize for having been so passive-aggressive and distant.* She was gracious enough to forgive me, and we reestablished a warm, if occasional, friendship. She invited me to her wedding a few years later, and I was touched and happy to see her. But I noticed something else—she was surrounded by her bandmates and her family, friends from adulthood and childhood and everywhere in between. People loved her, and wanted to share her joy. When I thought about my future hypothetical wedding, I felt hard-pressed to name more than a handful of people I wanted there. Do I lack empathy? Is it that I just don't *like* many people? Am I too irascible? I feel deficient and wrong, but there it is.

The intimacy issues I'd never faced in a romantic relationship (because I was never honest or open enough to confront them) are all over the place in my platonic friendships. When you have no ability to navigate confrontation, you never work through the bumps and scrapes of daily close-knit acquaintance, so friendship is either superficial or drifts

---

*The other roommate I only recently got up the nerve to contact after ten years of radio silence; one of the morals of *Shirley* is it's never too late.

away over time. I did find a group of female friends in grad school, thanks to the closeness of workshops and the rigors of working in the department office. I hadn't experienced that kind of intimacy since high school theater productions. We stayed up late for program events, decorated for the winter ball like the prom committee I was never on, and I almost forgot to feel like an outsider. But then, after a year of being entertained and supported on a daily basis by these insightful, hilarious women, I let our once-daily text messages lapse into silence. I never vented my irritation over canceled brunch plans or being on our phones at dinner. I found myself becoming standoffish. Now I can see it as a defense mechanism; I didn't want to work through what was bothering me because that would mean *voicing* what was bothering me, which might mean they would reject me before I even had a chance to ghost out of their lives forever. Around the time we were all confronting the end of grad school and the beginning of the unknown, instead of huddling with them to face our uncertainties together, I was dismissive and brusque. I wanted no part of their fears about what was coming next, because then I would have to confront the terrifying fact that I had *no idea* what was coming next. Instead of commiserating, I belittled their uncertainty and kept them at arm's length. When my warmest, most openhearted friend moved out of state to start her next chapter, which she'd decided to do without telling me, I found that I was left behind. I miss her and her nurturing friendship every day.

Someday, I'd like to have the kind of friend—or be the kind of friend—who stays in touch regularly without finding it a burden. I am sometimes very afraid I will never be able to develop or maintain these kinds of bonds; that I am too gruff or judgmental or detached or arrogant. I'm often disinterested in the minutiae of people's lives, and I mask my feelings with humor when I should be sincere. Maybe I just lack the constancy to have the friendships I see other women having all around me in life and in literature. I love to see fictional characters be vulnerable—it's almost the fastest way to my heart—but I'm rarely able to achieve it myself. Maybe I don't deserve a Shirley. It's natural to grow apart from people, or to need new friends who meet us where we are, but I don't want to be incapable of putting down roots or letting my guard down. Were she able to read these words, Charlotte might say something like what she once wrote to W. S. Williams:

> We all—except the arrogant and self-confident—despise ourselves very thoroughly sometimes; objects of our own withering scorn, we have every one been on occasion. . . .
>
> A bad account—yet I believe there is hardly a human being breathes but might say as much.[11]

While *Shirley* seems to showcase that rare wide-open friendship that endures, despite conflict, disagreement, and romantic rivalry, Charlotte's epistolary friendships also help me see that close acquaintances can be maintained in small doses. And it bears remembering that she wrote *Shirley* as an homage to a beloved sister—there's no way to compete with those lifelong bonds. My mother is one of four sisters, and has always had the knack of making and keeping female friends. It's one of the many social skills she possesses that I envy, along with making small talk without screaming inside.

But back to *Shirley*. The second volume opens with a chapter titled "The Valley of the Shadow of Death" and an ominous proclamation: "The future sometimes seems to sob a low warning of the events it is bringing us."[12] Afterward, the cheery sunlit novel falters and dims; Caroline falls ill, Robert Moore is injured by the local rabble after a labor dispute boils over, and Shirley must suffer the arrival of unpleasant relatives. The halcyon days of social teas and local festivals and mocking idiotic curates are no more. Why the sudden shift?

Charlotte wrote *Shirley* between 1848 and 1849. When she began, she was flush with critical praise for *Jane Eyre*, and the generally positive reception to her sisters' work. But then, on the 24th of September, 1848, having suffered from advanced alcoholism and opium addiction since the Robinsons dismissed him, Branwell died in agony and despair. At his funeral, Emily caught a cold that weakened her never-strong constitution. Exasperating Charlotte and agonizing Patrick, she refused any medical treatment even as she worsened. Charlotte asked George Smith and W. S. Williams for advice, and even wrote a letter detailing Emily's case to a London doctor on their recommendation. But Emily wouldn't try the medicine he sent, or even describe her symptoms to her anxious sisters. On December 19, she died too. Her faithful dog, Keeper, followed the coffin to the church.

And though Charlotte imagined the worst was past, Anne soon began showing symptoms of the same consumptive illness. The water and the climate of Yorkshire was persistently inhospitable to the delicate Brontës—Patrick had been lobbying for years to get government officials to test the water quality, based on the infant and adult mortality rate of the village. Amid all of this loss and grief, Charlotte found herself quite unable to write. Her letters are short and full of symptoms and hope and dread, and she wrote far fewer of them than normal. When it looked like there might be hope for Anne's recovery, Charlotte sent the first volume of *Shirley* to Smith and Elder for them to review. Anne convinced Charlotte and Ellen Nussey to accompany her to Scarborough, on the advice of physicians who thought sea air was beneficial for consumptives. In April of 1849, in the last letter Anne posted before they set off on their journey, she wrote to Ellen,

> I have no horror of death: if I thought it inevitable I think I could quietly resign myself to the prospect. . . . But I wish it would please God to spare me not only for Papa's and Charlotte's sakes, but because I long to do some good in the world before I leave it. I have many schemes in my head for future practise—humble and limited indeed—but still I should not like them all to come to nothing, and myself to have lived to so little purpose.[13]

We haven't talked about *The Tenant of Wildfell Hall* yet, but I should assure you now that her life was *definitely* not lacking in purpose—or at least not in achievement. Anne died in Charlotte's arms on May 25, 1849, and was buried in Scarborough. According to Charlotte, with her last words

Anne urged Ellen to be a sister to Charlotte in her place, and assured them both that she was glad death had come so gently.

From September to the following May, Charlotte lost her entire family, except for her father. How was Charlotte to finish her wry, historical Yorkshire romp after such a year? How was Charlotte to take another breath or sit upright for more than a few moments at a time?! She stayed in Scarborough with Ellen for another week after Anne's death, then returned home to Haworth, where she was greeted by her father, the family servants, and Anne's and Emily's dogs. The dogs, she said, looked at her like her sisters must be following close behind.[14] Once she was back in the dining room that used to be full of her sisters' conversation, listening to the silence that had replaced it, she came to a realization. She wrote to W. S. Williams in June,

> Labour must be the cure, not sympathy—Labour is the only radical cure for rooted Sorrow—The society of a calm, serenely cheerful companion—such as Ellen—soothes pain like a soft opiate—but I find it does not probe or heal the wound—sharper more severe means are necessary to make a remedy. Total change might do much—where that cannot be obtained—work is the best substitute.[15]

Charlotte was never able to distance herself from the intensity of sorrow that interrupted the book's writing in order to revise the whole. It explains the jumping narrative, the tug-of-war between the political and personal, the abrupt transitions from serious philosophical rumination to goofy Restoration comedy shenanigans, the breaking of the fourth wall. After the dramatic opening of the second volume, Caroline contracts one of those literary illnesses that wastes one away, attributable to grief over her mistaken belief that Shirley is to marry her beloved Robert Moore. Caroline observes, "I believe grief is, and always has been, my worst ailment. I sometimes think if an abundant gush of happiness came on me I could revive yet," which prompts Shirley's governess, Mrs. Pryor, to reveal theatrically that she is Caroline's long-lost mother, Agnes Pryor, *née* Grey (Charlotte's quiet nod to Anne).[16] Agnes had been a governess before she married Caroline's father and then left him when he turned out to be cruel and abusive. In an era of impossible divorce law and prevalent social stigma, she actually *left*, even though it meant the whole village would think she was an unfit mother and Caroline would be raised by a stern uncle.

I like to imagine Charlotte was rewriting the story of losing her own mother with this plot twist. How wonderful would it have been for a caretaker to suddenly materialize from the next manor house over, someone who could have nursed Branwell, Emily, and Anne back to health, or helped Charlotte and Patrick bear the sadness of suddenly finding themselves alone in the Parsonage. *Of course* Charlotte wrote a *mater ex machina*—she was sorely in need of one herself. The least she could do was give one to Caroline. There are very few mothers and daughters in the Brontës' books— besides Agnes and her mother, Caroline is the only female character who even *gets* a mother she can talk to; Cathy

Earnshaw and Isabella Linton don't live long enough to get to know their own children.

The dose of happiness Caroline receives after being reunited with her mother is the beginning of her recovery. Soon she is well enough to resume her visits to Fieldhead, cheering up Shirley, who has become rather tired of the uncle, aunt, and cousins who have been visiting her (along with Robert Moore's brother, Louis, tutor to Shirley's cousin Henry). Next *Shirley*'s focus shifts from Shirley to Louis, the tutor. This annoys me, because there are no more picnics, no more feminist debates, and very little actually happens. He mostly skulks around the schoolroom waiting for Shirley to come back from parties. But maybe it was unthinkable for Charlotte to keep writing a character in her sister's strong, opinionated voice once that voice had been silenced.

I never thought anything would make me miss Heathcliff, but aloof, forbearing, never-laughing, seldom-smiling Louis makes me a little nostalgic for a man who at least knows how to plan a party. Why is Louis in this book, you may find yourself asking, since he is pretty clearly terrible? One afternoon, Shirley's cousin Henry, a conveniently placed Tiny-Tim-alike, is going through Louis's desk and finds a parcel of copybooks. Caroline opens one and discovers not only was Louis originally Shirley's teacher, too, but they'd been secretly in love for years. Gasp!

After letting Louis blather on in his diary far too long, Charlotte disposes of the curates and marries off Caroline and Robert. Shirley refuses to do any of her own wedding planning in order to force Louis to take up the reins of familial leadership (which frees her up to run her actual estate), and the book ends right as the power dynamics get interesting again. You'll be relieved, I'm sure, to learn that the Orders of Council are repealed, and the end of the Napoleonic War restores the wool market's stability within the community. Charlotte leaves *Shirley* by flashing forward to the narrator sitting at a kitchen table listening to her housekeeper retell the story of two local married couples, who married for love *and* companionship, and lived happily ever after. Conspiracy theorists may well wonder if this housekeeper is not *also* Nelly Dean, compelled to serve as perpetual neighborhood historian through some Faustian bargain.

The messages of *Shirley* are so much more complicated than what I get from most of the other Brontë novels. They reflect Charlotte's own evolving attitude toward marriage and attachment, no doubt; otherwise the characters would either marry or refuse to marry, and move on. Instead she expostulates at length about men and women and who must be dominant and why and whether they are truly equal and whether that's how it *should* be or merely how it *is*. In *Shirley* we are presented with nearly every option open to village-born women. We meet wives, old maids, chatty girls, withdrawn girls, girls who married well, girls who married poorly, servants, governesses, women who keep house for their bachelor relatives, a beautiful girl with a substantial dowry, and Caroline, a pretty girl just well-born enough to have few respectable employment options. The richest protagonist in the entire Brontë canon gets to manage her estate's affairs, not just passively wait to be married off while a male heir profits from the entailment. We get snapshots of unhappy families and happy families, marriages with children and marriages with no children, and are mostly left to sift through the data to draw our own conclusions.

In *Shirley*, Charlotte also contemplates whether women should work, disappointing Mary Taylor (who was rather radical on the subject for the time). *Of course women must work*, Mary thought. *The real controversy was how difficult it was to find any means of self-sufficiency at all.* As she grumbled to Ellen Nussey in 1849, "there are no means for a woman to live in England but by teaching, sewing or washing. The last is the best. The best paid is the least unhealthy & the most free. But it is not paid well enough to live by. Moreover it is impossible for any one not born to this position to take it up afterward. I don't know why but it is."[17] Later Mary would vent her frustrations in published work of her own, advocating financial responsibility and independence for women of every station and circumstance.

Unsurprisingly, *Shirley's* emphasis on women's options confirmed the suspicions of contemporary critics who already thought Currer Bell was a woman. Charlotte was chagrined—"I was sadly put out by the *Daily News.* . . . Why can they not be content to take Currer Bell for a man? I imagined, mistakenly, it now appears, that *Shirley* bore fewer traces of a female hand than *Jane Eyre*; that I have misjudged disappoints me a little, though I cannot exactly see where the error lies."[18] Oh Charlotte. Maybe it was something about the way the heroine goes around her village calling all the men stupid that gave you away.

The Mary Taylor philosophy, that women *must* be equipped to earn their own living, dovetails neatly with the values my mother instilled in me growing up. She comes from a line of women who had to shift for themselves after husbands and fathers died or left. She often reminded me, with some bitterness, that it would be up to me to provide for myself and my future children. My father, who recently retired from the US Securities and Exchange Commission after twenty-five years, usually finds it advisable to sit quietly when Mom's conversation takes on this theme. He had stuck around, but that didn't mean she hadn't been prepared.

And as for Shirley, for all she talks of wanting to submit to a masterful man, what she *really* likes is Louis undertaking to *make her* submit; whether she ever actually surrenders is debatable. It's all very *Taming of the Shrew*. She doesn't even let Louis have the last word when he asks her to marry him. After Louis proposes (or at least lectures himself to a standstill), Shirley counters with,

> Mr. Moore . . . I do not ask you to take off my shoulders all the cares and duties of property, but I ask you to share the burden, and to show me how to sustain my part well. Your judgment is well balanced, your heart is kind, your principles are sound. I know you are wise; I feel you are benevolent; I believe you are conscientious. Be my companion through life; be my guide where I am ignorant; be my master where I am faulty; be my friend always![19]

I like the collaborative but pragmatic note that Shirley strikes here—she's not making a whimsical leap; she's weighed the pros and cons and made her choice accordingly. If she would just leave out the "be my master" part, I could imagine using this in a proposal myself. The romantic teen-age Charlotte who once wrote to Ellen Nussey that only love could induce her to marry, and who gave Jane and Rochester the impetuous love of a lifetime, had by now acquired much more grown-up ideas about why two people might decide to enter into matrimony.

CHARLOTTE finished *Shirley* by September, and it was published in October. The critics didn't know what to make of it, really; it had elements of literature they recognized, but it was neither romance nor history, neither social critique nor a morality tale. It has Charlotte's signature dry humor, her luscious Romantic description, her keen observation of human foibles and pomposity, and, best of all, women searching for their places in the world. But all that most crit-ics could see were the signs of Currer Bell's presumed femi-ninity "clouding up his judgment." Their loss.

I read *Shirley* at a time when I needed the galvanizing energy of platonic female friendship in my life; I needed confidence in my own purpose, and an appreciation for non-romantic companionship. It might be a mess tonally, but *Shirley* has some of the funniest scenes Charlotte ever wrote, like when an idiotic curate comes to tea at Shirley's home and gets chased upstairs by the dog and locks himself into a guest room while another idiotic curate pounds on the door; it's practically a Victorian Bugs Bunny cartoon. Then there's the delightful hidden treasure of Mary Taylor's family as the Yorkes—the resemblance was so true to life that Mary observed dryly in a letter that Charlotte had put Robert Moore in the wrong back bedroom after he was wounded.

In many ways, *Shirley* has a lot more to say than *Jane Eyre*, though it does lack the power and electricity of its predecessor. Caroline has to confront her romantic notions and reconcile them with the real world while still protecting her poetry-loving heart. Mrs. Pryor sets an example of hard-won independence. Shirley gets to be confrontational and flamboyant and whistle and manage her estate and pick out a husband and go to the village fair. Role models all around.

Preeti and I maintained our high-intensity friendship for a few months, but then one afternoon, she told me she'd never thought we were "dating." Ever. I knew she'd decided she wasn't interested in a relationship after our first few dates, but I thought we had at least been on the same page up until then. I thought those had at least been dates. Puzzlingly platonic dates, yet still *dates*. But no. It had all been in my head. I was hurt more deeply by the idea that she'd never considered dating me than I had been by the fact that she didn't want to *continue* dating me. I signed off abruptly and later sent her a terse email: "I'm sorry, I just can't do the Preeti and Miranda show right now."

We would briefly reconnect a few months later, when it would turn out she almost *was* ready to date, but by then I'd moved on. Mostly. I think *Shirley* helped—Caroline's pathetic moping, Shirley's assertiveness, even Louis's manipulation all contributed to a list of dos and don'ts I could

work with. Don't be so waifish they can't tell you're interested. Don't go out of your way to pursue someone who's
clearly pursuing someone else. Don't put up with aloofness.
Don't put up with mercenaries. Don't conceal your identity
from your long-lost daughter. Be the kind of irascible old
maid people are afraid to bother. Be generous. Be bold. Find
someone who wants to be your partner in life. *Let them in.*

Taking Charlotte's "labour is the cure" maxim to heart,
I threw myself into my professional life instead of lingering
over my romantic misfortunes. I didn't want to work retail
forever, and I couldn't expect another professional writing
opportunity out of the blue, so I had to start thinking long
term. What would allow me to write, edit, and teach? Like
the voice from beyond that told Jane Eyre to advertise, I
heard a whisper from somewhere, *graduate school.** Where
would I find my living while I made that happen? I hadn't
lost touch with my old colleagues from my very first job in
educational publishing. In fact, after the layoffs I'd moved
to Brooklyn and into a three-bedroom apartment with Kate,
the editor who'd hired me, and a rotating series of third
roommates that included a drama queen, a food writer, an
aspiring singer who'd recently joined one of those "maximize
your life-meaning" cults, and a night owl obsessed with *Sleep
No More*, an immersive performance piece based on *Macbeth*
that had just begun its long run in an old hotel in Chelsea.

---

*The whisper came from Barb, my college mentor who had become
a confidante and occasional dinner-and-a-play companion whenever
she visited the city.

We'd recently adopted a dog named Gracie, a comforting presence who was supposed to sleep on the couch but snuck into my room every night to keep my feet warm.

I emailed around to see if anyone was hiring. Luckily, two of my former coworkers, Eric and Sheryl, had landed together at another educational publisher, and they had an opening for a production assistant. Without saying much about it to anyone, I also applied to a graduate program that would let me write and prepare me to teach. Since I was clearly en route to becoming an old maid, at least I would be employed and in pursuit of higher education at the ripe age of twenty-six. Sometimes in life, as in literature, the best route to the thing you're searching for is relatively uncharted.

Meeting Mr. Rochester

Then my sole relief was to walk along the corridor of the third storey, backwards and forwards, safe in the silence and solitude of the spot, and allow my mind's eye to dwell on whatever bright visions rose before it—and, certainly, they were many and glowing; to let my heart be heaved by the exultant movement, which, while it swelled it in trouble, expanded it with life; and, best of all, to open my inward ear to a tale that was never ended—a tale my imagination created, and narrated continuously; quickened with all of incident, life, fire, feeling, that I desired and had not in my actual existence.

—*Jane Eyre*, Chapter XII

As in every major life transition since middle school, starting a new job meant it was time to reread *Jane Eyre*. I paid special attention to the part where she pragmatically reassures herself that if she dislikes life at Thornfield, she can simply advertise again. I wasn't entirely sure I really *wanted* to be working back in publishing, especially another test-prep company with no trade books to play with, but when the worst-case scenario is "I'll do something else afterward," trying uncertain things becomes much less daunting. Plus, I like office work: maintaining files and answering phones, sticking to schedules and proofreading and proofreading and proofreading—being a competent person in a low-stakes job isn't a bad way to spend a year or two.

My new boss, Eric, had been an assistant editor at my last publishing company, and now he essentially ran the production department at LightBulb Publishing. In our first stint as coworkers, Eric was jovial and effortlessly social, one of the office's popular people. He'd also still been in a hard-partying phase of life and I was already on the verge of becoming Marian the Librarian. I had been eager to please at our old company, and stubbornly independent when it came to my work. His casual demeanor masked a detail-oriented mind with exacting standards. He was a tad micro-managey, and I was overconfident to the point of defiance. He found me annoying and bossy. I found his pug obsession weird and his management style aggravating. I once beat him in an office Scrabble tournament with the word "ratlines," and it took him two years to deliver the Chipotle burrito that he owed me. We were mismatched from the start.

But three jobs, two Brontë novels, and a few years later, I was more comfortable in my skin (and grateful to have a job) and he was more willing to trust my judgment, so we got along much better. He was funny, and exasperatingly precise. The longer we worked together, the more I found myself craving his approval, and even occasionally receiving it.

We worked side by side with a cubicle wall separating us, communicating mostly by Gchat since the office had an open floor plan. Sometimes we all had to listen while he argued over the phone with his live-in girlfriend. Our friendly professional relationship started to blur after about eight months. Gchat conversations that began with work-related questions devolved into terrible pun competitions and long, winding conversations punctuated by wisecracks and inside jokes. I would stifle laughter and listen for the sound of Eric's chuckle emanating from the other side of the flimsy wall. Every day around two o'clock, he and Sheryl and I would go down to the bodega in the lobby for soda and candy bars. We took long walks on our lunch hour, exploring Lower Manhattan in the September sunshine. Trinity Church, Battery Park, the East River Esplanade, where we debated whether the South Street Seaport's resurgence was the future or the demise of the city we both loved. He would ask me what I thought of a new "invention" of his—cupcakes, but bigger; or coffee but like, frozen; or a pie, but with chicken in it; or a feedbag for humans, and act astonished and confused when I laughed. Eric was prone to inventing the already extant, including cake, the Frappuccino, and chicken pot pie. Jury's still out on the feedbag.

Eric and I got into the habit of leaving notes and drawings for one another when we dropped off projects or paperwork at one another's desks. He made me a "gold star" out of a post-it to show my mom. I fashioned a medic alert bracelet out of paperclips and a file label (because of his advanced age, thirty-five) and left pretend messages from his mom when he was out of the office. "Eric, it's your mother, please call so we can discuss your inheritance. It's canceled." "Eric, this is mom, we just found out that either you or your twin brother was born evil. The test results are coming back today.

Call me." "Eric, we've just realized we live in Staten Island, send help."

I still thought my enthusiasm for seeing him at work every day was purely friendly until my annual reread of *Jane Eyre* over the holidays. As always, I was struck by Jane and Rochester's banter, but now I noticed something new.

> I was forgetting all his faults, for which I had once kept a sharp lookout. It had formerly been my endeavor to study all sides of character: to take the bad with the good; and from the just weighing of both, to form an equitable judgment. Now I saw no bad. The sarcasm that had repelled, the harshness that had startled me once, were only like keen condiments in a choice dish: their presence was pungent, but their absence would be felt as comparatively insipid.[1]

I was leaning against the headboard of the bed in my parents' guest room, and suddenly I found myself thinking of Eric. But why? I saw plenty of bad in Eric. He was the world's most annoying writing partner; it took us four hours to write a page of website copy because we fought over every word. Nobody was more critical of my writing than he was. We never agreed. He blamed the Internet for the world's ills, while I agreed with introverts everywhere that it is a lifesaver. And he was a *boy*. Since falling for Preeti, the only dates I'd gone on, even halfheartedly, had been with women, and I had begun to wonder if I was even into men anymore. I did have to admit he was generous, prone to nice gestures like buying me a soda on our walks or remembering to ask how my latest non-date with Preeti had gone. And he might be disturbingly fixated on his pug, but at least he lavished love and affection on her. But these questions were all academic—he was spoken for. And so I shrugged the thought of him away. I couldn't imagine what had even made me think about him in the first place. Then Charlotte Brontë tapped me on the shoulder.

> The ease of his manner freed me from painful restraint: the friendly frankness, as correct as cordial, with which he treated me, drew me to him. I felt at times as if he were my relation rather than my master: yet he was imperious sometimes still; but I did not mind that; I saw it was his way. So happy, so gratified did I become with this new interest added to life, that I ceased to pine after kindred: my thin crescent-destiny seemed to enlarge; the blanks of existence were filled up; my bodily health improved; I gathered flesh and strength.[2]

I told her to shut it. We squabbled constantly! He wasn't my type! I'd never even stopped to consider whether I found him attractive, which meant I probably didn't! She pressed on:

> And was Mr. Rochester now ugly in my eyes? No, reader: gratitude, and many associations, all pleasurable and genial, made his face the object I best liked to see; his presence in a room was more cheering than the brightest fire. Yet I had not forgotten his faults; indeed, I could not, for he brought

them frequently before me. He was proud, sardonic, harsh to inferiority of every description: in my secret soul I knew that his great kindness to me was balanced by unjust severity to many others. . . . But I believed that his moodiness, his harshness, and his former faults of morality (I say *former*, for now he seemed corrected of them) had their source in some cruel cross of fate. I believed he was naturally a man of better tendencies, higher principles, and purer tastes than such as circumstances had developed, education instilled, or destiny encouraged. I thought there were excellent materials in him; though for the present they hung together somewhat spoiled and tangled.[3]

Oh noooooo. For the first time in sixteen years I threw *Jane Eyre* off my bed and onto the floor, then turned out the light with a huff. That night I dreamed about passionately kissing Eric somewhere outside by a large body of water. I could feel his skin under my hands and his fingers in my hair. Abruptly I woke up and turned the light back on. "What is *happening,*" I said aloud. My copy of *Jane Eyre* was still on the floor. I picked it up and stuffed it into my suitcase. "Shenanigans," I said, flipping my pillow to the cool side and trying to go back to sleep.

Back at work the following Monday I gave Eric a wide berth. I clicked into the chat window with Preeti that was always peeking from the corner of my screen.

"I think I have an inappropriate work crush."

"That's great!" she wrote, undoubtedly relieved. "Who is she/he?"

She agreed about the red flags of the girlfriend, the age difference, and his general flirtatiousness (he was a world champion schmoozer). Plus he was my boss, though it was not a particularly formal office. Ironically, talking about Eric brought Preeti and me closer again, briefly. And I kept talking to Eric about Preeti to throw him off the scent, just in case he had any idea that I was leaning on his desk for any reason other than reviewing the latest production schedule. A month or so later, when Preeti shut the door to a potential "us" for good, I slumped down in the extra chair at Eric's desk to mope about it, and caught myself surreptitiously gauging his reaction for signs of relief.

Look, *Jane Eyre* did not prepare me to be rational about this! Charlotte Brontë made me believe it was entirely possible for a man with no earthly reason to be in love with me to be harboring a great and eternal passion without any external sign of it. Despite all my growth and maturity and life lessons and under-control laundry pile, I was still basically in seventh grade, confronted with the temptation to pass Eric a note with two boxes on it: "Do you like me? Check yes or no." Naturally, I was not up to the task of resistance or patience or any other rational response to ambiguous romantic feelings and very bad timing (quoth Jane Eyre, "I could not help it: the restlessness was in my nature"[4]).

I began to ask leading questions, like, "What would you do if you were seriously into someone who was in a relationship? If they really wanted to break up with the other person and be with you, they would have done it by now, right? Hypothetically?" I examined his "Not necessarily" response for signs that he had understood my meaning and was signaling me with a reply in code. He hadn't, and he wasn't. These are not proud moments in my life.

Somewhere in there, we actually got work done, and I enjoyed it more than ever. Even the tedious copywriting assignments we sparred through were pleasant. "Sometimes I think your curse is that only I'll ever know how funny you are," he said to me once. One afternoon I saw a card at The Strand with a picture of a pug in jail on the cover, and I snapped a picture and texted it to him. That was the beginning of us, really.

It was a simple start, but it soon became a constant stream of text-based conversation about everything and nothing. I felt guilty, but not so guilty I could stop myself from replying to "I'm going to Coney Island with my friend Bob to look for the Russian Mafia, pray for me" with "I'll light a candle to the patron saint of carnies for your safe return" and fishing for updates the rest of the day. Sometimes I swore off texting him for good and deleted his number, or changed his name to "Worst Idea Ever" in my phone. But he always made his way back in. *It's his responsibility to put a stop to it*, I rationalized. *He's the one with the girlfriend.* In April, I finally heard I'd been accepted to grad school. I was thrilled for two reasons—one, that I would have time to develop my writing and stay in the city, and two, I could put an end-date on yet another hopeless fixation. It backfired when I started planning an epic last-day-at-LightBulb scene for Eric and me. I'd walk him down to Battery Park where we'd have a Statue of Liberty view, and pour my heart out in a bold gesture before going bravely off to grad school and leaving him behind forever. That was my plan. Not for it to magically work out, but for it to explode dramatically, six months down the line. Girl Who Trod on the Loaf style.

But I have never been able to keep a secret; even someone as oblivious as Eric couldn't be blind to junior varsity flirting tactics forever. I was out of town at a cousin's wedding in June when I got a text from him.

"Can I ask you something crazy? Am I the person you've been talking about being into, the one who has a girlfriend?! Stop laughing!"

I wasn't laughing. My hands were shaking. I tried to imagine what someone who was capable of playing it cool would do.

". . . what makes you ask that?"

"I just had a *Usual Suspects* moment looking at all this stuff on my desk. Stop laughing!"

I briefly tried to distract him by admitting I'd never seen *The Usual Suspects* so he would get caught up in an over-reaction to my ignorance of movies released before my time, but he bounced back quickly, so I had to admit it was true. "Funnily enough, yeah. Sorry."

"Wow."

My family was in the middle of touring a nineteenth-century courthouse-turned-museum and I dawdled in the gift shop waiting for another response. Was he angry? Was he repulsed? Was he breaking up with his girlfriend? I decided to keep things light (and crib from *The Office*).

"I hope this will make things extremely awkward from now on."

"Haha," he replied.

Mortified, I texted our coworker Sheryl, who had been treated to a running play-by-play of my infatuation for months, "omg he knows," and was gratified by her rapid "!!!!!!!" response.

Somehow we got through the rest of the inevitable "let's stay friends" conversation; there was no windswept declaration of love. No lightning, no garden, no proposal. Apparently those only happen in books. Sometimes you really do have to take the job in Ireland (or in this case, graduate school in Morningside Heights) and not look back. But I was gratified to hear (or rather read) him drop the banter and say sincerely that he really liked me, that he thought we'd be good together, but he was with someone. "Of course, and I respect that," I assured him insincerely, "Just . . . you know . . . feelings." Eloquent, Pennington. Lord Byron is facepalming in his grave.

When Jane Eyre was disappointed in love, she painted an imagined portrait of the beautiful Miss Ingram, the woman Rochester was rumored to be in love with, then drew herself in stark charcoal, softening no harsh flaw and permitting no vain embellishments. I tried to do the same with words when I got home to my laptop—lecturing myself on my folly, my hubris, pointing out that whatever complaining Eric did at work, he still went home to someone else, who'd known him for years longer than I had, and in ways I didn't. I couldn't in good conscience vilify her, since I didn't even know her. I was totally in the wrong here. What right did I have to confess my feelings to him, anyway? But then, what right did he have to *ask* me about them?! You don't have to consider yourself a flirtatious person to know that constant daily

texting with a woman who is *not* your girlfriend is probably inappropriate—he had to be either more invested in "us"
than he was letting on, or less scrupulous than I had thought.
It wasn't the first or the last time that reconciling his words
and his actions would be a challenge.

I deleted his number from my phone (again), cleared our
conversation history (. . . again), removed him from my
Gchat list (. . . for probably the fifth time). I resolved to
be a more moral individual and an exemplary professional
at work. No more giggly lunchtime walks. No more mid-
afternoon trips to the bodega. I could buy my own soda. My
emails became formal and concise, and when he teased me
about my tone, I smiled enigmatically, a martyr of love. I sat
on the other side of Sheryl in our status meetings. I took the
elevator alone and went straight home after work instead of
lingering by reception so we could ride down together.

I was so eager to put the whole embarrassing revelation
behind me, I accepted a date with a guy I'd been talking to
on Twitter. That June, free pianos painted by New York artists were stationed in parks all over the city by a nonprofit
called Sing for Hope. Twitter guy and I tried and failed to
meet up at two different pianos (it turned out I'd been playing and singing at the one in Grand Army Plaza while he
waited patiently by the Prospect Park carousel). I felt bad
about wasting his time, so I agreed to go with him to a vegan
restaurant in Park Slope. His name was Alex, and he was a
very kind music critic and poet.

After our dinner and a walk through Prospect Park, my
feelings for him were lukewarm at best—he was on the rebound from his first marriage and a little too sincere. But the

next day at work, I Blanche-Ingramed the heck out of him for Eric's benefit. I inflated the "connection" we'd had and made it sound like a magical evening, something out of a Nicholas Sparks novel, but where nobody has to die. It turns out being Rochester is *way* easier than being Jane.

I saw Alex again, and again; too soon and too often. The next day he met me at the Bell House (an old factory turned music venue near the Gowanus Canal) for an Old 97's show, and the day after, we watched a movie on my couch. That weekend we went to a Brooklyn food fair, then took the East River Ferry to Governor's Island. We wandered around holding hands. I was surprised at how much I enjoyed myself, and knew I was playing with fire. I'm no Rules Girl, but two people fresh from failed relationships (even one-sided ones) have no business going all in on the first at-bat, to scramble a metaphor. Some guys give you relationship lip service ("I really see this going somewhere!") so they can fast-forward to the part where they get to sleep with you, then dump you immediately afterward (Thanks a lot, *Mike*); others, those rare taxi-in-the-rain express-train-on-time unicorns, are actually intent on having a relationship, and they don't let conventions like "we've only known each other a week" get in the way.

Things picked up momentum because Alex was a serial monogamist. He really liked having someone to be into and I was delighted to have someone who was actually interested in me after two rough forays in a row. Plus it was great to spend time with someone who didn't hate musicals, who knew he wanted kids (and in fact had two), and who wasn't already cynical about things a lifelong New Yorker takes for granted, the way Eric was. Poor Alex. He was a good guy; he deserved better.

Our fifth date in a week was a late-night walk on the Highline (an abandoned elevated train track in Chelsea, rehabilitated as a plant-filled walkway and park) under the full moon. It was Bastille Day, so there were fireworks. I was dressed up from ushering a play. He brought me a Gerbera daisy. Even a less romantic woman than I would have been disarmed by that setup. It was catnip presented to a domestic shorthair on a silver platter. So I did what I hadn't done since high school: I gave a convincing performance of enthusiasm for someone I was barely attracted to. He put his arms around me and we kissed in the moonlight, and suddenly I understood how all those people on dating reality shows wind up in the hot tub so fast. Things get away from you when the set is dressed just right. But then Alex went home and wrote a poem full of tender imagery and wonder and earnestness, which he emailed to me and posted on his blog. And linked to on Twitter and quoted on Facebook. We'd rushed into social networking the way we'd rushed into everything else, so there was no escaping his heartfelt posts and veiled references to his Very Romantic Experience. I saw them *everywhere,* and so did the mutual Internet friends we had. Even if I had been sincerely interested in him, I think I would have found the poem mortifying.

Eric was a private, offline sort of guy, which I had never appreciated as much as I did that day. I felt guilty, and my guilt made me uncomfortable, and my discomfort made me distant and abrupt. If he hadn't gotten so ahead of himself (if I hadn't let him), things with Alex might have progressed past that hasty honeymoon, maybe even blossomed into a misspent autumn in New York, before I was forced to confront my indifference (my inner Rosalie Murray). But now that free verse was involved, I had to shut it down.

It took some digging to place Alex in the Brontë pantheon. He's not St. John, because he at least thought he had genuine feelings for me. I suppose he could be cast from the Edgar Linton mold, but that would make me Cathy Earnshaw and that I could not bear. However, even better than a fictional incarnation, there were several corresponding gentlemen in Charlotte's actual love life who might fit the bill. She rejected four proposals of marriage (including Arthur Bell Nicholls's first one) before finally accepting Nicholls in 1854. First, the Reverend Henry Nussey, a brother of Charlotte's friend Ellen: Charlotte turned Henry down because she knew how much work being a clergyman's wife was, and wasn't willing to undertake it for less than genuine affection.

Then, in 1839, an Irish curate named David Pryce visited the Parsonage for a *day* and afterward sent Charlotte a letter declaring his attachment and asking for her hand in marriage. She laughingly wrote to Ellen, "Well thought I—I've heard of love at first sight but this beats all," and politely declined.[5] Charlotte's third proposal was from a Smith, Elder & Co. employee, James Taylor, who wanted Charlotte to accompany him to India, which is ironic when you consider how poorly St. John's whole plan went over. Surely any admirer who'd actually read *Jane Eyre* would have known its author was not likely to accompany a man she didn't ardently love on his quest to an inhospitable climate away from her friends.

Alex was most like David Pryce—our relationship was as unlikely to succeed and based on almost as little acquaintance. Mourn the lost art of letter writing anew, because it meant there had to be an excruciating break-up dinner. For those of you looking to set free the unwanted suitors in your lives, let me recommend you do it over *coffee* and *not* sushi, unless you're skilled at feigning genuine interest despite recently acquired revulsion for the person across from you. Or you know how to pick a fight and storm out dramatically. I am not so skilled; I'm terrible at covering up disdain. Before the miso soup even arrived he was asking why I didn't want to hold his hand (which there is no non-hurtful way to explain without having some kind of skin condition) and why I appeared to be searching for a trapdoor to crawl through. I clearly didn't want to be there. I had to explain that my feelings had changed, assure him there was nothing he could do to alter them, and, most painful of all, tell him I didn't want to stay friends either. And then we had to sit and wait for our bento boxes while he looked hurt and I looked anywhere else. You could ask me how many keys were in the collage on the locksmith's shop across the street and I bet I would know within fifty. As soon as I could extricate myself I fled down Hudson Street; I called Eric, needing to vent my wretchedness, and as I wandered the streets of Soho, we had our first phone conversation.

The next day I could tell Eric *was* relieved that I was no longer dating Alex. But instead of being gratified, I was angry. I had worked hard to give up on Eric. Really, I had. Why was he still over there harboring some kind of emotional response? After one last awkward talk where I asked point-blank if he was planning on being single in the near future (he hedged, tellingly), I finally reached the knot at the end of my tolerance-rope. In being an undemanding shoulder to lean on and a maintainer of secret inside jokes, I was settling for nothing because of how badly I wanted everything. I was an emotional airbag. It had to stop. Eric would neither make room for me nor let me go. Anyway, did I really want to be a person who broke up a long-term relationship? I wouldn't *mind* if they broke up, of course, but I didn't want to be the *reason*.

A friend of mine had been suggesting with increasing degrees of firmness that I should go to a ten-day silent meditation retreat in the Berkshires—not just because of my obsession with Eric, but also to learn some techniques for calming a noisy mind and managing anxiety. I couldn't let myself give in to the impulse to write desperate, confessional letters, like Charlotte had to M. Heger. At least she got to be miles away by the time he read them—I'd still be seeing Eric at the office for another month. Finally I decided to take her up on it. I was slightly afraid of discovering an internal void of unlovable toxicity, but I packed ten days' worth of flowy pants and loose t-shirts and turned off my phone for an Eric detox. There was going to be a lot of crying.

AFTER William S. Williams, the editor who stayed up all night reading the *Jane Eyre* manuscript after it arrived, George Smith was Charlotte's best literary friend—he appreciated her writing, fixed her spelling, and kept her supplied with novels, newspapers, and magazines despite her protestations that she didn't deserve the attention. Since Emily had made Charlotte promise not to disclose their identities as authors, Charlotte had only ever corresponded as Currer Bell or C. Brontë on the Bells' behalf. She had exchanged letters with Smith for about a year before finally deciding, in July of 1847, that she and Anne should go to London in person to put to rest some particularly pernicious gossip about the Bells and their novels.

Emily and Anne's publisher, T. C. Newby, had unscrupulously sold excerpts from *The Tenant of Wildfell Hall* to an American publisher, misrepresenting it as the latest work by Currer Bell. Newspapers had speculated for some time that either all three Bells were one person—Newby's announcement was an apparent confirmation that left Smith, Elder & Co. understandably rankled. Smith wrote to Charlotte to say that as her publishers, they were miffed that she'd evaded their right of first refusal; the only way to clear up the misunderstanding, Charlotte felt, was in person.

The account of Charlotte and Anne's first meeting with Smith and Williams is priceless. Charlotte wrote to her friend Mary Taylor, who was by then running a shop in New Zealand with her brother:

Somebody came up and said dubiously
"Did you wish to see me, Ma'am?" "Is it Mr. Smith?"
I said, looking up through my spectacles at a young, tall, gentlemanly man. "It is."

I then put his own letter into his hand directed to "Currer Bell." He looked at it—then at me—again—yet again—I laughed at his queer perplexity—a recognition took place—I gave my real name—"Miss Brontë"—We were both hurried from the shop into a little back room, ceiled with a great skylight and only large enough to hold 3 chairs and a desk—and there explanations were rapidly gone into—Mr. Newby being anathematized, I fear with undue vehemence. Smith hurried out and returned quickly with one whom he introduced as Mr Williams—a pale, mild, stooping man of fifty. . . . Another recognition—a long, nervous shaking of hands—then followed talk—talk— talk—Mr Williams being silent—Mr Smith loquacious—

"Allow me to introduce you to my mother & sisters— How long do you stay in Town? You must make the most of the time—tonight you must go to the Italian opera—you must see the Exhibition—Mr. Thackeray would be pleased to see you—if Mr Lewes* knew 'Currer Bell' was in town— he would have to be shut up—I will ask them both to din- ner at my house &c"[6]

Once the shock and excitement had calmed, Smith took the Misses Brontë to the opera, introducing them to as few people as possible as "the Misses Brown," to services at St. Stephens, to dinners that both impressed and exhausted the "quaintly dressed little ladies, pale-faced and anxious- looking." They returned home with friends for life. Shortly

---

*George Henry Lewes, longtime paramour of George Eliot, who had been corresponding with "Currer Bell" for months.

after, Charlotte received what surely was one of the last letters before she became so famous it would be absurd for someone to get her name wrong; Smith inadvertently addressed a bank letter to her as "Caroline." After she revealed her true identity, Charlotte's exchanges with Smith grew ever friendlier, though she is consistently overly self-deprecating—she insists he shouldn't trouble himself with the likes of her, he must have better things to do, she wouldn't want to intrude, etc. She and Williams corresponded like father and daughter, but George and Charlotte were, in an understated, heavy on the literary criticism sense, *totally* flirting.

In one of her letters, following a brief lapse in communication after another visit in London, Charlotte said, "Of course I was not at all pleased when the small problem was solved by the letter being brought—I never care for hearing from you the least in the world."[7] That sort of teasing banter doesn't occur in her correspondence with anyone else! "My dear sir I return the 'Times' and the 'Literary Gazette' with—Oh no! I forgot—not with thanks."[8] That "not with thanks" implies he told her to knock it off with the groveling.

The two of them went to a phrenologist together in London, under the names Mr. And Miss Fraser. According to Smith, Dr. Browne, the phrenologist, was so struck by the "imaginative power" of a lady he'd examined that he was talking about her days later to anyone who would listen. Since we don't have any of Smith's letters to Charlotte, we can't close-read them to assuage our curiosity about his feelings. We can tell, though, that Charlotte occasionally doubted her highhanded manner with him, but consistently

received reassurance: "Mr Fraser kindly understood me—
for which I beg to tell him—I am grateful—it is pleasant to
be understood."[9] And this bit of sweetness: "Forgive all the
nonsense of this letter—there is such a pleasure and relief
either in writing or talking a little nonsense sometimes to
anybody who is sensible enough to understand—and good
natured enough to pardon it."[10] That's what I'd always liked
about Eric—I didn't want to be dominated or overruled, but
I did want to be met halfway. To be challenged. To have my
volley returned. To have a little nonsense now and then.

I don't think George Smith was Constantin Heger 2.0;
Charlotte didn't look up to him as a teacher-god. They were
intellectual equals, even if their age and social standing was
uneven. Charlotte might *write* relationships that reflected
traditional gender roles, even as she queered them with tom-
boys and Captain Shirley Keeldar, but in real life she was attracted to men she could hold her own with. As much as she
liked his flippant correspondence, she carefully consigns her
most overt appreciation to the pen of Currer Bell, keeping
Charlotte Brontë at bay:

> But though Currer Bell cannot do this [write a serial for
> Smith, Elder & Co.]—you are still to think him your
> friend—and you are still to be his friend. You are to keep
> a fraction of yourself—if it be only the end of your little
> finger—for him, and that fraction he will neither let gen-
> tleman or lady—author or artist . . . take possession of—or
> so much as meddle with. He reduces his claim to a minute
> point—and that point he monopolizes.[11]

That is surely the sound of a woman in love who believes, rightly or wrongly, that she can make no larger claim on the object of her affection. But that pinkie finger is *hers*.

As much as George Smith appreciated Charlotte's friendship, admired her writing, and bantered with her through the mails, after her death he denied ever being in love with her. He even said he'd found her appearance insufficiently charming. This earns him a side-eye for shallowness. I also think his opinion of her was somewhat compromised by the well-meaning efforts of literary gossips like Elizabeth Gaskell and Harriet Martineau, who were prone to spreading reports of Charlotte's frailness and ill health even when Charlotte herself wasn't particularly sickly. She was irked enough—and perhaps aware that it was affecting his perception of her—to write to him about it:

> May I be so egotistical as to say a word or two about my health. Two ladies—neither of them unknown to Fame—whom I reverence for their talents and love for their amiability, but of whom I would beg the small favour of being allowed to remain in tolerable health—seem determined between them that I shall be a sort of invalid; . . . If I do not answer the letters of these ladies by return of post . . . flying rumours presently reach me derogatory to my physical condition. . . .
>
> Why may not I be well like other people? I think I am reasonably well; not strong or capable of much continuous exertion (which I do not remember that I ever was) and apt no doubt to look haggard if over-fatigued—but otherwise

I have no ailment and I maintain that I am well, and hope (D.V.) to continue so a while.[12]

This is the passage often pointed to by Brontë enthusiasts and researchers to suggest that Charlotte was in love with Smith, and that she feared his feelings for her might be compromised by the rumors of her sickliness. And it's very possible that they were, and he was dissuaded from developing stronger feelings for her as a result. The woman Smith eventually chose to marry he claimed to have fallen in love with at first sight; she was young, and rosy-cheeked, and for Charlotte's sake I hope you will join me in despising her.

Even if they were never romantically attached, Charlotte was sufficiently invested in their relationship that receiving news of his engagement in 1853 led to a very brief and frosty acknowledgment, and then a chillier silence, until she wrote back to him with news of her own engagement the following year.

I returned from my silent retreat calm and collected. I had eaten a significant quantity of yogurt, peanut butter, and tofu. I had learned to sit still. I felt like I'd had a breakthrough. The torch I carried wasn't *out*, but it had dimmed enough that I could see beyond it. I had to live my life as though Eric were going to be permanently unavailable, and I had to really mean it, not just attempt to work reverse-psychology on the universe. Eric could stay locked in his unhappy relationship, since apparently it suited him, and I would eventually find a partner willing and eager to be with me. Then I would condescend to invite Eric to our wedding and make him die a little inside at how happy and radiant I was. This was Plan A, a significant improvement over Plan B, which was dying abandoned and alone in a forest.

My first day back at work, Eric asked me to lunch, and confessed he actually *had* broken up with his girlfriend while I was away. My newfound serenity wobbled but didn't falter—if we were going to be together, I didn't want him on the rebound. I wanted him for keeps. We existed in sort of a limbo for a few weeks—socializing occasionally outside of work, texting daily, but not constantly. It was exasperating. If he wasn't ready to address this lingering tension by my last day in the office, I planned to acknowledge myself defeated and move on.

On the Monday of my last week at LightBulb he came out to Brooklyn with me after work. We sat on my couch, fidgeted with the red corduroy cushions, and watched the sunlight slant through the windows. I remember putting my toes into the beam that was heating up the hardwood floor where Gracie was sleeping. I was ready to surrender.

"Even when you really want something to happen," I said, "if it's not the best thing for the person you care about, you don't get to just demand it, right? Sometimes you just have to let go. I guess I'm ready." It was weird to be having this conversation face to face. We rarely talked about anything serious out loud, least of all our relationship. I was used to having time to revise or think better of what I was about to say. There was a certain temptation to take out my phone and just text him. My sentiments had sounded so much more poignant in my head. We sat through a long pause while I wiped away a noble tear or two, expecting him to nod and admit he just wasn't ready, although he liked me a lot, it was too soon, and he'd given it a lot of thought but just couldn't in good conscience—

"Wait, are you talking about us?" Eric said. I closed my eyes and exhaled in a very un-Zen huff. Every conversation we'd had for months, no matter how innocuous, was secretly about the Long Term Potential Of Us. How did he not get it? When I nodded, he gave me a hug and suggested we go get some dinner. We walked to Bogota, my favorite restaurant in Park Slope, and continued our circular conversation around "what this *is* exactly." I have no patience for circular conversation. It makes me want to cut to the heart of things, but as the great Diana Ross and a few dozen others have vainly tried to warn me, you can't hurry love. No, you just have to wait. Finally I put down my fork and said, "Listen, we're already here. This is dating. We just haven't kissed yet. The question is, do you want to be here or not? Because I'd understand if you didn't, but I can't keep going on as if you *might* if the truth is you *don't*." I speared a plantain and avoided eye contact while Eric worked out what I had said. He smiled (finally, one thing that's better in person), and said, "I do. I want to be here."

I believe that I blushed. After dinner we got gelato and walked back to my apartment. I invited him up to the roof to "see the view of Manhattan." I assumed anyone who'd ever

dated anyone with a roof, or stairs, or a collection of etchings
knew that a visit to see them was a flagrant transparency, but
later Eric would profess he had no idea why I wanted to go
upstairs. It was to make out, obviously. Maybe the reason
Charlotte could never get things going with George Smith
was the Smith & Elder offices didn't have a rooftop with a
view.

I led him to the waist-high wall at the front of the building and perched up on it with a dexterity that my teenage
self would have applauded. Behind me was Lower Manhattan's skyline and the Williamsburg Savings Bank Tower
clock, with its red neon hands. They seldom both worked at
the same time, but that night they were glowing in tandem.
He got nervous I'd fall, so I slid down to face him. Eric is
almost exactly my height, so I was looking straight into his
eyes. I don't think we'd ever stood this close together unless the elevator was particularly crowded. His eyes were so
blue. I could see individual curls in his dark hair, lit by the
streetlights on Fourth Avenue. His hands were surprisingly
smooth and soft as he slid them into mine. I had a split second to regret the whole idea because we were about to ruin
everything when *finally* he kissed me. We kissed for a while,
until I broke away giggling. I couldn't stop, silly and suddenly shy, despite all my brazenness.

The next day at work we sheepishly said hello over the cube
wall and sat down. I felt like my cheeks were in some shade
of red all day; my coworkers *had* to be aware of the magnetic
waves ebbing through the office. That afternoon, an earthquake shook Manhattan. So maybe the magnetic waves had

nothing to do with us. Our offices were on the top floor of a sturdy Rector Street building, and yet the whole floor swayed. The entire staff either chanced it in the elevators or bolted down all twenty-six flights of interior stairs to reconvene in Battery Park. I may have allowed a moment of smugness— Jane Eyre only got a lightning-struck tree after her first kiss, I got a whole *earthquake*—but then I remembered that it wasn't a *good* omen.* It was, however, another one I chose to ignore. Work abandoned, Eric and I walked all the way up Broadway, soaking in that peculiar feeling of camaraderie New York City gets whenever something drastic happens to us all at once. We parted ways at Union Square with a squeeze of the hand and a kiss on the cheek.

The lesson I *should* have learned from that shaky beginning was that Eric would take action when it felt like now or never, regardless of whether he was actually ready, and it would lead to unpleasant aftershocks every time. As you might have expected, there were some complications in leaping into a serious relationship with a man just out of an existing (and, I would find out later, still largely unresolved) domestic situation who wasn't aware that I already saw our relationship as serious. He didn't want to hurt me, but being with him meant compromises. It meant being patient when he took forever to make plans, and being gracious when

---

*I have a strange track record with omens. My first date with a girl coincided with a tornado touching down in Brooklyn just blocks away from us; my first day teaching, I was almost late because of a track fire; friends suggested I get married in a bunker to reduce the risk of a tidal wave.

plans had to be canceled at the last minute, and being accepting when he refused to make plans at all. I was required to access reservoirs of chill I'd never known before. Whatever grace and acceptance I had learned at the silent retreat had totally evaporated two weeks into our long-awaited relationship. It hurt that we were exchanging our easy everyday banter for tense, testy exchanges when my impatience met his reluctance. I was ready to be in love, and instead we were perpetually in transition.

Eric was candid with me, but just like I'd predicted when I was a teenager, when Mr. Rochester offered a vision of paradise set sometime in the future in exchange for my dignity and self-respect in the moment, I took it and ran. Believing I'd done my due diligence (when I'd only taken the bare minimum dosage of *Jane Eyre*), I swallowed my expectations and eagerly signed up for what Eric had to offer—his hesitancy, his conflicted loyalties, his history of not communicating honestly when it was painful to do so. I imagined I would shape it into what I really wanted later.

Come to think of it, Eric didn't attempt to lure me to a villa on the Mediterranean. I wasn't even invited to his actual apartment, because it was still the contested home of his shared-custody dog. But it wasn't all bad. Our first real date post-kiss, post-quake was a visit to the Museum of the City of New York and a walk down Central Park West. Our third date was *The Elegance of the Hedgehog* and a stroll around Midtown East. We fell into a rhythm—he would come to my apartment after work, we'd make out for a while, have dinner, and he'd go home. If I tried to make plans on the weekend, he was noncommittal and evasive. A smarter woman than I would have backed off immediately, busied herself with schoolwork, and attempted to date other people.

Or, if I'd really wanted to do it up right, I could have thrown myself on the mercy of my aunt and uncle in White Plains, set off in the dark of night on the New Jersey Turnpike. This hypothetical smarter woman would have let Eric take his time with no hard feelings. Or the hard feelings would have won out, so she could stop wondering when he would call and what he would say and when he would want to see her. But I was no smarter than I'd ever been. Dumber, in fact, because for the first time I was outright rejecting the counsel of *Jane Eyre*, who is always full of wisdom and self-respect. When her romantic idol fell drastically short of her standards, Jane walked away. When my love interest showed the same frailty, I shortened my measuring stick. I asked for less, denied I had standards at all. Jane was also still speaking directly to me, by the way, or at least trying to:

Meantime, let me ask myself one question—Which is better?—To have surrendered to temptation; listened to passion; made no painful effort—no struggle;—but to have sunk down in the silken snare; fallen asleep on the flowers covering it; wakened in a southern clime, amongst the luxuries of a pleasure villa: to have been now living in France, Mr. Rochester's mistress; delirious with his love half my time—for he would—oh, yes, he would have loved me well for a while. He *did* love me—no one will ever love me so again. . . . He was fond and proud of me—it is what no man besides will ever be.—But where am I wandering, and what am I saying, and above all, feeling? Whether is it better, I ask, to be a slave in a fool's paradise at Marseilles— fevered with delusive bliss one hour—suffocating with the bitterest tears of remorse and shame the next—or to be a village-schoolmistress, free and honest, in a breezy mountain nook in the healthy heart of England?[13]

The answer is obvious, right? Unqualified surrender, silken snare all the way. A fool's paradise is still paradise when you don't know the difference. Freedom and honesty is all very well, but being loved wins in a landslide, every time. I was too thrilled to have Eric in my life, to have him squeeze my hand back when I squeezed his. I was too afraid. I couldn't step back and protect either of us from the effects of surging ahead too quickly.

Over the next six months we had the equivalent of three good ones together. Some weekends he would make the long train ride from Inwood to not-quite-Park-Slope and we'd go for long walks, sharing a sense of discovery and a love of Brooklyn architecture. We'd force each other to watch movies we knew the other would hate just to get distracted into fooling around halfway through. He got us tickets to Labapalooza, a series of experimental puppet vignettes at St. Ann's Warehouse, and we lit up at the unexpected, the tiny and adorable, the strange.

He took me to a screening of a Ben Katchor cartoon with live musical accompaniment, an ode to the New York Public Library. He convinced me to try sushi for the first time.

Sushi is a lot like love, I thought, insufferably. You look for ingredients you recognize and try not to be scared by the ones you haven't seen before. (And when in doubt, cover it in a slice of ginger?) I started eating sushi so often I actually worried about mercury poisoning.

I wanted to tell Eric I loved him after about two weeks, but I managed to hold off for a whole month—and then I told him in every language I knew except English. When I finally told him in a language he understood, he smiled and whispered back that he loved me too. But a few hours later he sat up on my bed abruptly. "I feel like I'm cheating on both of you," he said, and gathered his things to leave. There would be stretches where he'd be fighting with his ex, or caught up in his obligations to their demanding dog (who was diabetic as well as emotionally unstable), or just distracted, and I'd struggle to feel connected. It was like a switch went on and off—sometimes he was warm, and open, and generous. He got us theater tickets to *Priscilla, Queen of the Desert*, for my birthday and didn't blame me when it turned out to be terrible. We hid notes to each other in coat pockets, surprised one another with little gifts. Other times I had to pry any proof he cared out of the locked box of his closed hand; he met me with silence when I tried to talk about the future, whether it was "ours" or "two weeks from now." I was still convinced that if we could just get through this part, what came next would be everything I'd ever wanted.

Right after Christmas, which I spent in Arkansas with relatives and he spent in New Jersey with his older brother's family, we broke up. I'd urged him to get some therapy, and the therapist had naturally pinpointed the turmoil he felt about our relationship. This prompted him to text me, "My therapist says it sounds like I need more time before jumping into a relationship—what do you think?"—essentially, trying to get me to do the work of breaking up with myself. Communicating over text message again while I was traveling had allowed him to finally voice his need for space, however obliquely. I was in shock. I had bent over backward to accommodate him and assured him I had no emotional needs whatsoever! How did that not work?! Seldom has a terrible decision backfired so predictably. When I got back to New York, he came over for the ritual torture of getting his things back. I gave him the little trinkets I'd picked up as Christmas presents. He brought nothing for me. We sat side by side on the same couch; he couldn't even look at me. I curled into myself and didn't get up when he left.

After a month of misery, not eating, not sleeping, and not writing, I gave in to that selfish feeling Jane Eyre had so stalwartly resisted, and called him to suggest we get back together. Not because anything had actually improved, but because I was just determined to stick it out this time. That's not what I told him, naturally—the story I fed him was that I was finally ready to let things be relaxed and casual, like he needed. *So* casual. My roommate and my coworkers all observed that it sounded like he wasn't ready, my mother asked what I was thinking, and even my ordinarily support- ive brother asked why on earth this was a good idea. But I knew how *Jane Eyre* ended already—with a sweet, happy re- union. Why spend a year banished to a metaphorical village school with only a frosty St. John Rivers to talk to if I didn't have to? Eric and I went to dinner together at the Mermaid Inn on the Lower East Side. Things almost felt normal despite the lingering pit in my stomach and Eric's noticeably monosyllabic conversation. After dinner, the little plastic fortune-telling fish they bring with the check curled right up in my hand ("Ready for love!"), but Eric's just laid there in his palm, flat and dormant ("Cold fish!"). Nevertheless, as we walked uptown on Second Avenue, I cheerily put my arm through his.

"I'm so glad we're back—aren't you glad we're back?" I chirped. Eric looked down and away from me.

"Well . . ." he trailed off.

Despite that palpable flag on the play, I barreled ahead. Even though he *still* wouldn't make plans more than a day or two in advance, I still wasn't invited to his apartment, and he wasn't comfortable staying over at mine. He showed no sign of letting me peek around the edges of his impressive emotional barriers. I knew what Jane Eyre would tell me to do (she would point out this guy bore no resemblance to *her* Rochester, first of all—and Edward Fairfax had *real estate*— and then she would talk about one's moral fiber). I didn't want to hear it, so in exasperation I picked up *The Tenant of Wildfell Hall*. Better the devil that nobody you know has ever read before than the one you have memorized.

Is that not how that goes?

Helen Graham
and Branwell Brontë

*In taking leave of the work, we cannot but express our deep regret
that a book in many respects eminently calculated to advance the
cause most powerfully wrought out, should be rendered unfit for the
perusal of the very class of persons to whom it would be most useful,
(namely, imaginative girls likely to risk their happiness on the
forlorn hope of marrying and reforming a captivating rake,) owing
to the profane expressions, inconceivably coarse language, and
revolving scenes and descriptions by which its pages are disfigured.*

—Unsigned review of *The Tenant of Wildfell Hall*,
Sharpe's London Magazine, August 1848[1]

What the pearl-clutching society set felt about *Wuthering Heights* (alarm, discomfort, the general inadvisability of discussing it in public), Charlotte Brontë felt about *The Tenant of Wildfell Hall*, Anne's second novel. When Smith, Elder & Co. offered to reprint her sisters' novels in 1850, Charlotte gave *Wuthering Heights* and *Agnes Grey* each a revised introduction and a diligent copyedit to excise the typos T. C. Newby had left behind. But she refused to produce a new edition of *Tenant*—that's how uncomfortable it made her. Charlotte, writing to her publishers, said of *Tenant* and Anne,

> Nothing less congruous with the writer's nature could be conceived. . . . She had, in the course of her life, been called on to contemplate, near at hand and for a long time, the terrible effects of talents misused and faculties abused; hers was naturally a sensitive, reserved, and dejected nature; what she saw sank very deeply into her mind; it did her harm. She brooded over it till she believed it to be a duty to reproduce every detail (of course with fictitious characters, incidents, and situations) as a warning to others. She hated her work, but would pursue it. . . . She must be honest; she must not varnish, soften, or conceal.[2]

She insisted Anne should never even have attempted it in the first place. This could be attributed to her defensiveness against the charges of "coarseness" perennially leveled at the sisters, or to the fact that for all they were sisters, Charlotte just didn't appreciate Anne's earnest honesty. But I think the real reason was closer to home. So close to home it lived in the Parsonage and slept in Patrick's bedroom. The reason was Branwell.

The Tenant of Wildfell Hall is essentially the story of fallout from one man's brutal and abusive alcoholic existence. The short version: Robert Huntingdon, the villain of the piece, abuses and terrorizes his wife, Helen, until she runs away to a remote village to take up residence in the aforementioned Wildfell Hall, and falls in love with a local farmer, Gilbert Markham. But before they can confess their feelings for one another, Helen receives word that Huntingdon is at death's door, and she returns to his side to offer him the opportunity for redemption.

At times it's difficult to see the characters of *The Tenant of Wildfell Hall* as individuals and not as allegories for Vice and Duty, but what it lacks in subtlety the novel makes up with candor. There are other contemporary novels about abusive marriages, drunken husbands, and suffering wives—Charles Dickens had been writing for twenty years already when *Tenant* was published—but for anyone accustomed to a certain literary propriety, the openness with which Anne Brontë writes of Huntingdon's sins and Helen's despair is searing. There's a moral here, and it's fully intentional and very brave.

One of the Brontës' worst-kept secrets was Branwell Brontë's unmanageable opium addiction and alcoholism, fueled by his professional disappointments, his romantic rejection, and a lifetime of family indulgence. By 1839, he had already been an unsuccessful portrait painter, a mediocre poet, and a regular at the Black Bull pub, so when Patrick and Branwell spotted an advertisement in the *Leeds Intelligencer* seeking a tutor with the Postlethwaite family at Broughton-in-Furness, they hastily developed a curriculum and Branwell applied immediately. He secured the position but found himself abruptly dismissed after six months; for years the reason was a mystery—Had he devoted too much time to his own scribbling? Had he just been too hungover, too many times? In the most recent edition of her landmark Brontë biography, Juliet Barker dug until she brought the truth to light: Branwell was fired for fathering an illegitimate child with a local woman, most likely Agnes Riley, the twenty-one-year-old daughter of a farmer in Sunny Bank. The child died before she turned two, however, and her mother later married and emigrated to Australia. After being fired from the Postlethwaites, Branwell wrote a poem, "Epistle from a Father on Earth to his Child in her Grave," and threw himself into translations of Horace's *Odes*.[3]

In 1840, Branwell was able to secure a position as the assistant clerk-in-charge at a new railway station near Halifax, which kept him physically busy and offered him all the diversions and entertainment of a new railway hub town, such as lectures, concerts, and visitors. He eventually lost the job over some discrepancy in the bookkeeping, but by then Anne had become the governess to the Robinsons at Thorp Green, and in 1843 Branwell was hired on as tutor to the eldest son, Edmund. He was fired two years later. After that, his drinking progressed quickly and was accompanied by opium use. When Branwell returned home from the Robinsons in disgrace, Charlotte's patience with him was worn out; by the time *Tenant* was published and he was in the final stages of his addiction, she was absolutely disgusted with him.

Early biographers of the Brontës attempted to smooth over Branwell's tarnished reputation in various implausible ways, but now it's generally accepted, on the strength of letters he sent to friends and the behavior of Mrs. Robinson after her husband's death, that Branwell's illicit romance was real. I know I should be sympathetic to Branwell, but I find it very difficult. He's pitiable, sure, but I struggle to get past my irritation that his wounded ego got in the way of his sisters' creativity for even a minute.

After the release of *Poems* in 1846, Mr. Robinson died; Branwell claimed in a letter to his friend J. B. Leyland that Robinson's will stipulated his widow would lose her inheritance if she ever saw Branwell again. Though undoubtedly Branwell (and his sisters and everybody else in the village he complained to) believed this was the case, it's more likely Mrs. Robinson knew that if she remarried, she'd lose executorship of her husband's estate. She had no intention of taking on a second husband with negligible prospects and downgrading her standard of living, so she sent first her coachman and then her husband's doctor to assure Branwell that while she, too, was prostrate with grief, they must be forever divided. In reality, Robinson's will was revised shortly before his death to disinherit his eldest daughter, who had run off with an actor. There is no mention of Branwell or constraint on Mrs. Robinson. During the next two years, Mrs. Robinson sent Branwell various sums of money; whether you believe it was to sustain him or to silence him depends on the optimism of your worldview.

As his physical condition worsened from alcoholism and opium addiction, Branwell was prone to fainting fits and destructive outbursts; Charlotte refused to invite visitors to the Parsonage when he was home, and toward the end of his life Branwell shared a room with his father to ensure he wouldn't set the house on fire while everyone slept.

In my eyes, *Tenant* is the work of a fearless heart. Yes, it's moralizing, and yes, it's unwieldy, but the woman who wrote it was not without power, fire, or originality, as Charlotte once described Anne. *The Tenant of Wildfell Hall* was indubitably Anne's attempt to save other young people from the pitfalls that had destroyed her only brother. In a preface to the second edition, Anne wrote that the book's rougher characters were taken from life, and "if I have warned one rash youth from following in their steps, or prevented one thoughtless girl from falling into the very natural error of my heroine, the book has not been written in vain."[4]

And to Anne's credit, it worked. Eventually, she got me to do what even *Jane Eyre* couldn't, which was open my eyes to the reality I was actually living in, not the one in my imagination. Between researching Branwell's life and death and churning through *The Tenant of Wildfell Hall*, I was in for a dose of aversion therapy. There is no romance, capital-R or otherwise, in *Tenant*. Only emotional squalor, abuse, untrustworthy young men, and conniving village girls looking for husbands. The novel struck a sympathetic nerve with me for another important reason—the same reason I should really be more charitable toward Branwell. I'm an alcoholic too.

I had my first beer at a college party in my freshman year. Alcoholism (and recovery) runs in my family so I'd always been wary of drinking, but I was determined not to spend the *next* four years being different and weird all over again. I joined the line for the keg and when my red plastic cup was filled, I gulped the tepid bitter contents. I immediately felt like a smaller version of me floating inside of myself. It was like sliding the driver's seat back from the wheel of a car and finding an amazing amount of legroom. Somehow the party became more bearable. The noise was less overwhelming. I wasn't afraid of the people around me. The lag time between thinking and speaking (to make sure I wouldn't sound like an idiot) was cut short in favor of talking loudly and confidently, if incoherently. My friends were funnier—more importantly, they thought *I* was funnier—and they seemed much happier to have me around. I don't think I ever turned down a drink after that, no matter how drunk I was already. The appeal of distancing myself from the anxieties and discomfort of my everyday brain was too enticing. I found I didn't mind the atrocious hangovers I always got, because finally, I had something unmistakable in common with my peers and a shared vocabulary with which to discuss it.

I even felt validated by the rich history of drunk writers in great literature, the ones who say things like "Write drunk, edit sober," and die after demanding one more shot from the barkeep. Once I became a critic for the school paper, I would go to a movie or a play, take copious notes, get drunk when I got home, bang out a first draft, and edit through the foggy headache I had the next morning. Formerly compulsively early, I became chronically late for work, I blew off my friends, I missed deadlines. My semester in India? The flip side of rooftop bars and elegant gimlets at the discotheque was spending a month of independent study cooped up in my shared hotel room drinking Kingfisher and ordering pizza. *Pizza.* I could have gone anywhere, seen anything on that once-in-a-lifetime trip, but I stayed in and drank room temperature beer instead. I spent a lot of nights on the bathroom floor during that first summer in New York, too. This was not just drinking the way any college student might drink—I drank as though it were the only way to stay ahead of a massive boulder rolling after me. There was nothing wacky, or funny, or safe about it. I hope it is the only time of my life where I have more in common with Branwell than with Charlotte.

Three years later, during my senior year, I was desperately trying to quit. I would swear off for a year, a month, a week at a time, but a binge and a blackout were never more than a drinking opportunity away. I scheduled all my classes and work shifts for afternoon and evening, to accommodate morning recuperation time. All my "friends" were drinking buddies, and very few of them cared to spend time with me if we weren't getting drunk (which I found out after I got mono and *actually* couldn't drink for a month, when everyone vanished). I was an anxious, fearful torpedo with no healthy mechanism to diffuse all that panic. I kept every hour of the day scheduled and accounted for, striving to maintain the semblance of control. In my lowest moments I even felt beyond the reach of the Brontës; aside from *Tenant*, the only alcohol abuse in their work is John Reed's off-screen debauchery and suicide, Rochester's much-repented youth, and Hindley and Heathcliff's mutual self-destruction. I hid the extent of my guilt from family and friends as best I could. They found out anyway—as I neared my twenty-first birthday, my brother asked my dad, "Is Miranda going to start drinking now?" and Dad replied, "She's been drinking. We just hope she's not going to kill herself with it."

Getting mono brought me close to the end, but what really put me over the edge was sexual assault. I'd met up with my former fellow intern, the free-wheeling Bianca, in New York for fall break, resolving only to have a drink or two so we could go somewhere and catch up properly, which somehow became drink after drink at bar after bar. I would later find out that having mono had compromised my liver function, but at the time I hardly even noticed, because my only goal, once I was drinking, was to drink until I passed out anyway. Somewhere in there we met a foreign journalist named Juan, and I blacked out. The handful of snapshots I have left from that night were enough to send me shaking to the ER for a rape kit, a morning-after pill, and a series of appointments at the counseling center back in Ithaca. The counselor who took me on helped me process the trauma of the assault (I couldn't stand to be touched for weeks, and was convinced I was somehow at fault) and began the work of helping me understand my own drinking. When I found myself slumped on her couch for our weekly appointment after another unintentional black-out night, she referred me to an alcohol counselor, who brought in a guest speaker, who offered to take me to a twelve-step meeting.

I got sober just four months after my twenty-first birthday, clinging to the twelve steps like a life raft. I needed safety, I needed structure, and I needed friends who saw me for who I was. And for the first time, I actually found them. They helped me handle the routines of daily life without becoming overwhelmed—simple, basic things, like getting a headlight fixed or going to the grocery store. That's not an exaggeration—I once called my sponsor from the cereal aisle, immobilized. My father was relieved I'd put on the brakes, and my former drinking buddies soon disappeared from my peripheral vision. I stumbled across the finish line to graduation, thanks in large part to the people I met in the program.

Once I moved to New York, as hard as it is to be a sober twenty-something in the land of the happy hour, meetings and sober parties became my home base, my anchor. The anxiety and feeling of being lost took time to abate, but I knew I never had to be lonely in the city unless I wanted to be. Dating was harder—I needed people who would be both understanding about my sobriety and sensitive to the trauma of sexual assault. Even once I was willing to be touched again, it felt like an excruciating hurdle, a terrible dream I had to relive before I could feel comfortable getting close to someone new.

By the time I started fixating on Eric, I had two home groups—one near my apartment in Brooklyn that I attended Saturday mornings and before work a few times a week, and one near the office at lunchtime. I had recently celebrated my fourth sober anniversary, and had started to chafe under the program's suggestions and slogans. I didn't want to check in with a sponsor anymore, now that I didn't feel like I was in constant danger of going out and getting drunk. I resisted the steps about making things right and staying humble—I thought I knew what I was doing and could manage on my own. It's not uncommon for people to drift away from the program between the five- and ten-year marks; some learn to navigate sobriety on their own, others go out and start drinking again, others drift back in as "old-timers." I knew I should stick around and help people who were newer to sobriety, but I was feeling too defiant to be a good sponsor to anyone seriously interested in the twelve steps. I also didn't want to listen to the advice of more clear-eyed friends in the program who had made their share of destructive relationship decisions, both drunk and sober.

Eric wasn't unsupportive of my sobriety, by any means (just like he was warm and loving when I told him about the sexual assault), but when I was confronted with a choice between an hour in a basement meeting or a romantic walk around lower Manhattan . . . well, I made it to fewer meetings. Then, I wanted my Saturdays free so we could spend them strolling from one flea market to another in Park Slope and Fort Greene, walking Gracie, drinking smug smoothies, and occasionally having passive-aggressive spats because I wanted him to just clean out his damn apartment and invite me over already, while he continued to protest he couldn't rush things. As I lost touch with the program that had brought me so far from the scared, hapless twenty-one-year-old I had been, there was no solid ground to replace it, only the slippery embrace of this headlong infatuation. Fortunately, Anne Brontë had me covered.

The enigmatic Helen Graham, the aforementioned tenant of Wildfell Hall, fascinates the local populace of the small village where the novel is set, especially a local gentleman farmer, Gilbert Markham. Who can blame him—she is beautiful, mysterious, and one of the earliest literary characters to explicitly bring up gender inequality in polite literary society. She's also concealing the existence of an estranged raging alcoholic husband from her neighbors.

Gilbert attempts to court Mrs. Graham and is at first rebuffed (because he's nosy and irritating), but gradually they become friendly. He bides his time until he can make one of the more awkward literary proposals in existence. No proposal where the man assures his beloved that he wants to marry her despite the neighborhood slander, while she tries frantically to retrieve her hand from his grasp, can be said to have gone well. Afterward, Gilbert is loitering on the grounds when he sees her walking affectionately with her landlord, Mr. Lawrence. Convinced he has uncovered a secret romance, Gilbert resolves never to see her again.

If Gilbert had been a lovestruck literary heroine, his only option would have been to fret and pine in solitude, maybe catch a consumption or squeeze a scorpion. Being the rugged, arrogant man that he is, when he crosses paths with Mr. Lawrence a few days later, he assaults him with a whip and leaves him bleeding and semiconscious in the road. It was after this development that my sympathy for Gilbert finally passed the point of no return. I believe I would rather endure a week of St. John Rivers lecturing me about the frivolity of my disposition and habits than read any more about Gilbert Markham.

In response to Gilbert's jealous accusations (and, probably, to get him to leave), Helen presents him with her diary, which we get to read over his shoulder. Helen's diary begins when she first falls in love with the handsome, devilish Arthur Huntingdon, the sort of man who dances elegantly, socializes superficially, and flatters to provoke compliments for himself. Helen defends his faults to her aunt and guardian by placing her own good sense and judgment at Huntingdon's disposal (because who is easier to reform than a self-assured sociopath with no personal boundaries or sense of decorum?). She intends to be Jiminy Cricket to his Pinocchio, flouting her aunt's gentle urging to reconsider. Since I had intended to smooth over any number of Eric's faults with my own virtues, this is about when I started feeling sheepish. The talking-to Helen was getting from her aunt sounded an awful lot like the one I'd gotten from my mother, to which I had petulantly closed my ears. Mrs. Maxwell makes one last attempt to persuade Helen that Huntingdon is bad news. Helen responds with Bible passages that promise a sinner can be delivered from Hell once he has paid his debt, which we can all agree bodes well.

Only a few weeks into our reunion, Eric thought our reasons for breaking up were all resolved and everything was fine. This was mostly my fault since I'd assured him everything *was* fine in order to get us back together. I was spending a good deal of my energy on an elaborate performance art piece I liked to call "Being The Cool Girlfriend." But beneath all the masquerading, I wanted to be wooed a little, or at least to be with someone who appreciated *my* wooing. I wanted a partner who made time for me, showed up promptly, and never made me wonder if they cared. Eric wanted someone to casually date while he sorted through the detritus of his last relationship. Though I have no patience for anyone who is habitually late or discourteous, I bore his inevitable rescheduling with the patience of a bodhisattva. Most of the time.

Unfortunately, Helen discovers within a few weeks of their marriage that Huntingdon is selfish, frivolous, and demanding, as predicted by her aunt and literally everyone else. Like, "Stop reading—those books are taking your attention away from *me*," levels of demanding. Imagine if Belle from *Beauty and the Beast* had actually married Gaston, and he then developed a drinking problem. Or, as one delightful critic put it in the *North American Review*, he becomes "as fiendlike as a very limited stock of brains will allow."[5] It's downhill from there.

This is the beginning of Anne Brontë's critique of the institution of marriage, or at least of young women who enter it convinced their job is to ameliorate all their husbands' faults. *Tenant* contains several other indictments of the paucity of women's options. Helen's gentle friend Millicent finds herself engaged to one of Huntingdon's friends because he is rich and her mother is enthusiastic. Millicent is soon pregnant and utterly miserable. Later in the novel, Helen's neighbor Esther Hargrave comes home dejected from her first London season because her mother only cares about finding her a wealthy spouse; Helen encourages her to stand up to the familial pressure: "You might as well sell yourself to slavery at once, as marry a man you dislike. If your mother and brother are unkind to you, you may leave them, but remember you are bound to your husband for life."[6] Keep in mind this is 1848, more than a hundred years before Betty Friedan, thirty years before the campaign for British suffrage got serious, and we are hearing literary women candidly acknowledge that marriage, their main feminine concern, leaves women worse off. Sociological studies that reach the same conclusion today receive significant social resistance—most of us are romantics at heart, and want to believe that marriage will fulfill us, keep us from being lonely, or lighten our burdens. And Anne Brontë isn't having it. Where Charlotte foments my wildest romantic notions, Anne is that friend who takes you to brunch and tells you to get a cat and just stop pining.

Everything that Jane Eyre resists at Rochester's hands—being dressed up like "a painted butterfly," being shown off in London despite her preference for domesticity—Helen suffers with Huntingdon. And when he has finished dragging her around the city's drawing rooms, he sends her home to Grassdale Manor while he continues to do whatever a dissipated gentleman does in London without his wife's supervision.

This was like having a mirror held up to my own naïveté—I still thought that after two people got married, they would have fewer problems than they'd had while dating. At least, I imagined, anything that didn't stay the same would get easier. Like the foolish Caroline Helstone before me, I thought when you love, you marry. That's just what happens. I had no sense of moderation, and I wasn't exactly an expert on serious long-term relationships. James and I had only been in the same state at the same time for about a year, all told, though we'd been "together" for three. Then there had been a five-year dry spell of terrible dates that went nowhere. The Preeti Infatuation had lasted longer than any of the entanglements that had followed, but you can't call it a relationship if one of the partners doesn't know she's in it. Or so I've been told by an exasperated therapist or two. After I'd thought Anne Brontë was on my side, with all those "he's not that bad!" rationalizations, it was becoming clear this was a cautionary tale, not an aspirational model.

One evening after dinner, Helen catches Huntingdon flirting with the unladylike Annabella Lowborough, even going so far as to sneak a kiss to her hand in a room full of guests (which, for the 1820s, is basically as egregious as you could get in a drawing room during a dinner party). The diary abruptly leaps forward two months to Helen's announcement that she has become a mother, then picks up a full year later with Helen's ruminations on how to spare her son from the sins of his father. By this point Huntingdon is regularly throwing lavish drunken parties, physically abusing Helen, and having a full-blown affair.

Finally, five years into this disaster of a marriage, Helen is ready to make her bid for freedom. She begins selling her paintings, with the help of her maid, Rachel. One uncharacteristically sober night Huntingdon finds her diary and discovers her plan. He burns her painting supplies, steals the money she has saved, then confiscates her jewelry and her remaining canvases. The competition for Worst Brontë Husband between this guy and Heathcliff is pretty fierce; Heathcliff might have an early lead because his debauchery spans multiple generations—but Huntingdon has no tortured backstory and thus absolutely no reason to mistreat everyone in his path. The final straw for Helen is when Huntingdon brings his new mistress to Grassdale to be young Arthur's governess. Helen escapes to Wildfell Hall and adopts her mother's last name, Graham. Here's where we learn that Helen's maiden name, just by the by, was Lawrence. Enjoy a moment of satisfaction as you imagine Gilbert, reading this diary, realizing the man he beat over the head and left for dead is not the paramour, but the beloved, heroic, lifesaving *brother* of the woman he loves.*

By the way, when we meet Gilbert Markham, he's midway through a letter to his brother-in-law, Halford. The entire novel is essentially a pre-Victorian version of *How I Met Your Mother*, replacing "Your Mother" with "Your Wife's Sister-in-Law." The "letter" has fifty-three chapters. Though

---

*Good work, Gilbert.

I accept Helen's diary without question, I have a continual problem with this epistolary device. Can you imagine receiving a letter that was three hundred pages long and featured hand-copied pages from a total stranger's diary? I very much want to appreciate Anne Brontë's experiment in multiple perspectives, but my pragmatism cannot help but focus on how *long* it would take to copy one's wife's diary by hand to send to one's brother-in-law, and wonder that Gilbert didn't just go for a simpler, "We met when she moved in down the lane." Why hadn't he ever told Halford the whole story over Christmas dinner some year? I might have appreciated the gesture more if Gilbert had recorded the events in his own diary or, I don't know, *written a novel* instead. Wouldn't Halford have written back after the first chapter, "This letter cost me fifty pounds. Why can't you tell a story like a normal person?"

But then, Anne was hardly the first to strain the bounds of credulity this way. Austen wrote *Lady Susan* in letters (recently reborn as *Love and Friendship*); Mary Shelley did the same with *Frankenstein*; Bram Stoker used letters to soften the torridness of Dracula's behavior a few decades later. It gives authors distance from, and plausible deniability for, their characters' behavior; it's not something the author is responsible for, they're just describing what someone *else* did! And yes, there's something literarily interesting about Anne Brontë's choice to nest a story about an alcoholic and an abused mother within the more socially acceptable hands of a male outsider. Society had a hard enough time with the idea of a woman *doing* what Helen (or Cathy Earnshaw before her) did, let alone a woman writing about it unapologetically.

Maybe to preserve Helen's moral high ground, she couldn't be allowed to articulate romantic feelings for a man who wasn't her husband, despite the fact that her husband was an absolute snake.

Counter to Charlotte Brontë's later claims that her sisters were just innocents, born of the wild moors with no idea their imaginary tales would strike the reading public as *unseemly*, both Anne and Emily went to great lengths to put space between themselves and their characters, and, on Anne's part, to introduce us to them in a way that would earn them our sympathies. Why would they have done that if they weren't fully aware of the transgressive nature of these imaginary people? Anne plays with chronology, with reader expectations, and with multiple voices. This is not the work of a lucky amateur. *Jane Eyre*, *Agnes Grey*, and *Villette* are all anchored by the first person perspective of lone narrators (who bear passing resemblances to the authors themselves). In *Tenant*, it's hard to tell who the first person is even supposed to *be*. That strikes me as sneaky and subversive, and I like it. If the cost of this literary subterfuge is a (completely implausible!) letter-writing device, I suppose I must accept it.

After I had avoided *Tenant* for so long, Branwell's sorry state and Huntingdon's dissolution had a surprising effect on me. By then I'd been sober for going on five years, but I had to confront the fact that I wasn't "fixed." My impulsive decision-making—anything to avoid the pain of confrontation or loss or being disliked—was still causing me problems. I might talk about being tired of Eric's evasiveness or his emotional baggage, but I maintained our destructive status quo long after it started to hurt. It was my choice to see him every single time he suggested it, and to continually pepper him with invitations in return, even when he turned them down or avoided committing to a time or place. Once we actually made it to that agreed-upon place, he still maintained this wall I couldn't get through. I was still, somehow, convinced things would be easy instead of labored if I could just get to the other side. And here I found Anne Brontë doing her best to disabuse me of that whole idea.

Unfortunately we have nearly caught up to the "present," where Gilbert waits like a squishy worm on a rain-soaked sidewalk. He reads this harrowing tale of a woman's degradation and liberation, and his main takeaway is "joy unspeakable that my adored Helen was all I wished to think her." The fact that Helen's not having an affair with her landlord + she's actually married + her husband is a monster = Virtue? Gilbert belongs in an Austen novel married to an unpleasant younger sister that his parents chose for her dowry, and if not for Helen, that is basically what would have happened to him. The idea that Helen returns Gilbert's warm feelings remains *utterly inexplicable*. But. Love him she does. Then, after returning her diary (without mentioning he'd copied the entire thing into a letter), he ungracefully apologizes to Frederick Lawrence. Not that there is a very graceful way to say, "Sorry I whipped you and left you for dead in the road—I thought you were your sister's boyfriend." Possibly my favorite research discovery on this entire quest was a series of critics making exactly the same complaints about Gilbert. Charles Kingsley, in his review for *Fraser's*, said,

We cannot see any reason why Gilbert Markham, though no doubt highly attractive to young ladies of his own calibre,* should excite such passionate love in Helen, with all her bitter experiences of life, her painting, and her poetry, her deep readings and deep thoughts—absolutely no reason at all except for the last one in the world, which either the author or she would have wished, namely, that there was no other man in the way for her to fall in love with.[7]

The next we hear of Helen, neighborhood gossip Eliza Milford is exultantly telling Gilbert that Helen has returned to her husband. At first Gilbert fears she has been kidnapped, but Lawrence informs him that Helen's sense of duty compelled her to go to her beastly husband's side. Though Huntingdon is not immediately near death from his hunting injury, he is delirious and presumably suffering from alcohol withdrawal. He has become raving, swollen, monstrous, and beyond saving in any eyes but Helen's.

Eric and I weren't in much better shape—we had been wounded by one disappointment after another, and had transformed into something I didn't recognize. Were things going to get better, so I could look back at this painful time with a nostalgic twinge? Or was this relationship the worst idea I'd ever had? I found myself behaving a bit like Huntingdon—lashing out at my sponsor, ignoring calls and texts, blowing off my best friend for Eric's last-minute offers to hang out, even bailing on walks with my beloved Gracie if

---

*One can only assume he had in mind the wretched older Eliot sister from *Persuasion*.

there was a chance to see him after work instead. Evacuating a sinking ship is harder than it looks, especially when you're the captain who insisted on boarding the thing in the first place.

Huntingdon and Helen had remained locked in a bizarre battle of wills too. She gives him occasional "death is coming, get your house in order" admonishments, while he wonders frantically if he is actually going to die or can put off reformation a while longer. Huntingdon accuses Helen of only helping him so that she may go to Heaven while he goes to Hell; Helen mildly suggests he might mend his ways and *not* go to Hell. Huntingdon first rejects the whole idea of Hell, then earnestly implores Helen to save him from it. We'd had some madness and bad blood here and there in the other Brontë works, but mostly, even at their worst, people were just uncouth. I had never seen the late stages of alcoholism so chillingly documented. Was this what would have awaited me? Anne's literary world was darker than the others because her personal life had become darker. I was accustomed to turning to the Brontës for inspiration and comfort, and here I'd been dragged into the falling house of Usher. It was *grim*.

My next thought was bewilderment—Why did Helen stay so long with Huntingdon once she knew what he was capable of? Why, having escaped, did she return to supervise the throes of his grisly demise? I think it's partly because Anne Brontë believed in redemption (as did Charlotte and Jane, and as do I) and wouldn't give up—not on her brother and not on Huntingdon. Plus, she was still committed to fully illustrating the lack of options available to unhappily married women with no independent means. I didn't particularly care for Helen's brand of prim duty, so as I read Huntingdon's long, drawn-out death scene, I was frustrated—*Why doesn't she just leave? Why is this Helen's penance? She doesn't deserve it.* I kept demanding answers. *What is* wrong *with you? Why would you put up with this? Is this how you imagined your life?* I thought angrily. And then I realized. I didn't blame Helen—she had to live with herself, and being by Huntingdon's side was her choice. I wasn't even talking to her. I was talking to myself.

You can imagine my chagrin. I had developed this habit of mentally reviewing all our good moments in my head— that rooftop kiss, our first walk on the Highline as it snaked through Manhattan, the first "I love you" and the sweetness of seeing his feelings for me dawn on his face. We were coming up on six months of promises that it would get better soon. And it wasn't.

Unluckily for Eric, when he canceled our plans or refused to make any, staying in and reading *The Tenant of Wildfell Hall* had finally gotten me mad instead of hurt. We came to our second messy end just days after he canceled our Valentine's Day plans to spend the night at his apartment by texting me *that afternoon* to tell me he was too anxious that his ex would drop by unannounced. I forced myself to be understanding and drowned my sorrows with Gracie, Kate, and full-price Godiva on the couch. The next day he apologized profusely and reissued his invitation. I made my first trip to Inwood to meet his infamous pug and see the unmistakable evidence of a single man living alone in an apartment—he didn't even have a flat sheet, just a fitted one, two pillows, and a smaller-than-full-size bed under a duvet sorely in need of washing. We spent an uneasy evening together; he kept taking phone calls and I sat there waiting for him to come back so we could eat the unromantic takeout we'd ordered.

The next weekend I was still lounging in my living room in my shabbiest pajamas, having moved on to the discounted Russell Stover, when he canceled our Sorry-Again-I'll-Make-It-Up-To-You plans. We were supposed to have a leisurely afternoon and a nice Really, I'm Sorry dinner, but "something came up." With a pit already in my stomach, I asked him what was going on.

He texted back that he was at Ikea with his ex. The person he was supposed to be establishing appropriate boundaries with. He was helping her pick out and transport furniture to her new apartment. She hadn't even finished moving out of their old one. I didn't know I had the power to stop time, but apparently I, in moments of dire need, can force everything to pause so I can be flooded with a *Usual Suspects* montage of my own. It was a barrage of every single broken date, blown-off plan, failed attempt to stand up for myself, and flaky noncommittal exchange we'd ever had. I folded down the corner of *Tenant* (if Huntingdon was *really* dying, I wanted to enjoy it) and used both hands to text him back. Yes, it would have been better to save the confrontation for when we could talk in person, but this felt unpleasantly appropriate. We imploded for the last time as we had exploded in the beginning, in texts of four hundred characters or fewer. I may have wished him a nice life but I probably didn't mean it.

Immature as it was, it was the closest I'd ever come to getting angry with him, let alone actually standing up to him. It felt both good and horrible. My endless compromises, my tiptoeing around, all of it was over. Later, when he calmed down and called to talk, I was gentler but stayed steely. I refused to feel guilty. Even in the face of his plaintive questions: "So there's nothing I can do? Nothing I can say?" and his too-little-too-late apologies, I was resolute. My heart and my head were finally in agreement, and there was no way he could overrule both of us. He wrote me a beautiful letter the next day, with every loving apology I could have hoped to hear, as if releasing what had been stored up during weeks of insisting he was doing the best he could and I just needed to expect less. It was a last-ditch effort to avert consequences that had been a long time in coming. I wish I still had it, but my sentimentality had been more or less burned out of me, and I deleted it from my email a few days afterward.

And so, as a Brontë novel had guided me into my first significant relationship in five years, another Brontë novel spat me unceremoniously back out. *The Tenant of Wildfell Hall*'s message to young women about not letting their affections be won too easily had finally gotten through. I only wished I'd listened the first time when Helen's aunt said, "Keep both heart and hand in your own possession, till you see good reason to part with them. . . . [T]hough in single life your joys may not be very many, your sorrows, at least, will not be more than you can bear."[8] I took my broken heart to a meeting and threw myself on the mercy of my friends at the diner afterward.

It all works out for Helen Graham née Huntingdon née Lawrence, by the way. After Huntingdon's painful death (not painful enough, you might argue), Gilbert waits a respectful period of time before writing to Helen. She doesn't reply, but the neighborhood gossip tells him she's to be married. Gilbert races to Grassdale to prevent the marriage, only to find that Helen's brother, his former friend and assault victim, is marrying Esther Hargrave, Helen's neighbor. Helen is safe at Staningley with her aunt. At last, since Gilbert's too intimidated by the fortune that Helen has come into since they last saw one another, Helen actually proposes to *him*. They are married and live happily ever after.

How much better would *Tenant* have been if told entirely by Helen herself? It would have helped to explain what on earth made Gilbert lovable. Even entrusted to the hands of a milquetoasty protagonist, *Tenant* turned out to be the most salacious of the Brontë canon. And it did as much to zap my romantic yearnings as *Jane Eyre* had ever done to encourage them. *Romance is all well and good for some people*, I told myself firmly as I rid my apartment of any evidence Eric had ever been there, *but I am finished with it*. The only creature whose love I could really be sure of was Gracie, whose canine affections never wavered. She sat on my bed and watched as I rode the tidal wave of righteous anger until it ebbed away, leaving me with a garbage bag full of mementos and a laundry bag full of linens that still smelled like Eric's aftershave. When at last I fell back on my freshly made bed and cried some more, she stretched out along my side like a sixty-pound bolster pillow with a rough warm tongue and sympathetic eyes. Kate treated me to dinner and let me talk through the whole miserable saga again, earning a whole new stack of long-suffering roommate points. For all my maneuvering and all his unreadiness, I'd really believed Eric and I could be together, because why else would we suit one another so well? Nobody else had ever matched wits with me like he had, had interests and experience I valued to recommend him, and still admired me too. Nobody else had ever seen the real me without running for the hills. And none of it had been enough.

BRANWELL Brontë's last months on Earth were miserable. His last letters to his friend J. B. Leyland in 1848 are about debts and drinking and coughing, "intolerable mental wretchedness and corporeal weakness."[9] His final note to his friend John Brown in late August is pitiful, particularly in contrast to the swaggering, bold writer he'd been in better days.

Dear John,
    I shall feel very much obliged to you if [you] can contrive to get me Five pence worth of Gin in a proper measure
    Should it be speedily got I could perhaps take it from you or Billy at the lane ~~it~~ top or, what would be quite as well, sent out for to you.
    I anxiously ask the favor because I know the ~~favour~~ good it would do me.
    <u>Punctualy</u> at Half past Nine in the morning you will be paid the 5d out of a shilling given me then.*

---

*I suspect the shilling was an allowance given him by his father or his sister.

His life had become so small, and so miserable, like many an alcoholic before and since. I do feel sorry for Branwell, it turns out. Intensely sorry. I think there's no way he was unaware of his sisters' publishing; no way at all he remained ignorant of the fact that they excluded him, collaborated, and succeeded where he only failed and failed and failed. I can't even imagine the shame and guilt of not being able to contribute to the family that had grown up expecting to depend on him—and the self-loathing and resentment that followed. As irritated as I am by Charlotte's self-deprecation, Branwell's ego certainly didn't do him any favors. No matter how fun he was to drink with or how well he got along with the ladies, he never finished a novel (that we know of—and I feel like Charlotte would have made sure we knew). He lived on empty promises and unfulfilled aspirations. And that, along with the drinks he took to soothe the pain, is how he died. His beloved Mrs. Robinson remarried a man with money and property two months later. Upon his death, Charlotte was prostrate for five days, then wrote to W. S. Williams:

> The removal of our only brother must necessarily be regarded by us rather in the light of a mercy than a chastisement. . . . It has been our lot to see him take a wrong bent; to hope, expect, wait his return to the right path; to know the sickness of hope deferred, the dismay of prayer baffled, to experience despair at last; and now to behold the sudden early obscure close of what might have been a noble career. . . .
>
> [N]othing remains of him but a memory of errors and sufferings.[10]

I've read every one of Charlotte Brontë's published letters. She practically never mentioned his name again.

ORDINARILY at times like this I would have turned to *Jane Eyre* for comfort, but I was so humiliated I couldn't even look Charlotte in the face. She would know that I'd reaped exactly what I'd sown. She might punish my heresy somehow, rescind Jane and Rochester's happy ending maybe, or send her off with St. John, and I couldn't endure it.

Besides, sometimes in moments of intense sorrow holding up a book and remembering to turn the pages is beyond our capacity as humans. Good books require us to activate our imaginations and transport ourselves somewhere else. When changing clothes or showering seems like too much work, there's no way we have enough energy to travel through space and time. The best we can do is give our red and weeping eyes something pretty to stare at. That is why Netflix was invented, and with it, the literary miniseries.

Wandering the Moors

A representation of Jane Eyre at a Minor Theater would no doubt be a rather afflicting spectacle to the author of that work. I suppose all would be wofully exaggerated and painfully vulgarized by the actors and actresses on such a stage. What—I cannot help asking myself—would they make of Mr. Rochester? And the picture my fancy conjures up by way of reply is a somewhat humiliating one. What would they make of Jane Eyre? I see something very pert and very affected as an answer to that query.

—Charlotte Brontë (as Currer Bell) to
W. S. Williams, February 5, 1848[1]

Just like it had during my isolated, anxious college days, the prospect of holing up with a small screen and a large pair of headphones promised relief and comfort in this time of trial. There are more than thirty TV, film, radio, and stage adaptations (including a seriously misguided Broadway musical) of *Jane Eyre*, and around a dozen of *Wuthering Heights*. There's at least one *Tenant of Wildfell Hall*, and an *Agnes Grey*. And I have watched nearly all of them. Nobody has gotten to *Shirley* or *Villette* yet—I'm not sure which is more daunting, the enlivening of Caroline Helstone or the defrosting of Lucy

Snowe (more on her later). I recently saw a Bristol Old Vic production of *Jane Eyre*, directed by Sally Cookson, which was filmed on stage and broadcast to movie theaters around the world. It managed to incorporate a variety of contemporary music on a bare bones stage, making no effort to convey the lushness of the book's setting and intent instead on capturing the story's energy. Everything about it was lean, though Jane and Rochester had a definite spark, and most of the actors played multiple roles (except for Madeleine Worrall as Jane). It demanded versatility and nuance from the entire cast, and its deconstructed feel was a stark contrast to the approach most stage and film adaptations take.

The first theatrical version of *Jane Eyre* was staged during Charlotte's lifetime; W. S. Williams wrote to her to ask if she'd like to come to London for it, and while she admitted she'd like to go, she declined (as much from dread at the prospect of seeing Mr. Rochester brought to life imperfectly as to keep her anonymity intact, since neither Smith nor Williams knew Currer Bell's true identity at that point). She encouraged Williams to attend so he could report back to her, but confessed her concerns that he would find it terrible: "One can endure being disgusted with one's own work, but that a friend should share the repugnance is unpleasant."[2] She, like everyone who loves *Jane Eyre*, doubted that any theater company would be able to do justice to Rochester's and Jane's peculiarities. According to Patsy Stoneman, who rounded up reviews and scripts from every known stage production to write *Jane Eyre on Stage*, this particular version had the following "distinctive features": Brocklehurst was played as comedic relief, Rochester is portrayed as a philanthropist who takes Jane in when she is thrown out of Lowood, John Reed plots to marry Jane, and it is Jane who insists that Rochester save his wife from the fire and then refuses to marry him "out of respect."[3] Evidently, Charlotte was quite right to stay away from this unrecognizable farce.

Aside from improbable plot revision or the addition of cheesy music, a ham actor is the worst thing that can happen to Edward Fairfax Rochester. He needs to be funny but also glowering, tightly wound but also relaxed in his sarcasm, affectionate but clearly emotionally damaged. Striking, but unhandsome at first. One of the earliest versions featured Colin Clive, from the *Frankenstein* movies, and the fabulously blonde and beautiful Virginia Bruce. It is ludicrous. The Orson Welles version? By the time he finished chewing up the scenery you may have forgotten Jane entirely. Joan Fontaine is amazing at being Joan Fontaine, but when it comes to plain, moral, upright Jane, she's on the wrong planet.

In the 1970s, the BBC made a version starring George C. Scott and Susannah York. I can't account for who thought casting General Patton was a good idea, nor for the ridiculous oversized dimensions of Mrs. Fairfax's bonnet, but they evidently forgot to tell Scott that Rochester was British. He resolutely retains his American accent and is thus impossible to take seriously. York has some of Jane's solemnity but is also blonde, which is as antithetical to Jane Eyre as the white carriage and purple cushions Rochester attempts to foist upon her.

Do not talk to me about Timothy Dalton. Never speak
of Timothy Dalton or the 1983 crime against literature in
which he participated. Ever. Mr. Rochester cannot be pretty
or delicate or posh. He can't. Everyone else in every other
pre-Victorian screen adaptation can, if you like, but not him.
Zelah Clarke, the Jane who suffered his Rochester imper-
sonation, was actually quite good.

I'm told people feel strongly about the Charlotte Gainsbourg version, which came out in 1996. Franco Zeffirelli's cin-
ematography is beautiful, the adaptation is clean and precise,
but Gainsbourg is up against William Hurt's terrible accent
and his inappropriately blond hair. In their proposal scene?
He goes in for the pivotal romantic encounter of my young
life and winds up planting a kiss somewhere to the left of her
actual mouth while she grimaces. He missed her mouth! I
want to be transported by an otherworldly passion. Not mired
in imprecise face rubbing and uncomfortable close-talking.

Ciaran Hinds attempted Rochester in 1997, opposite Sa-
mantha Morton. Hinds, aka the impeccable Captain Wentworth from 1995's *Persuasion*, has a perfect voice, but they
gave him a horrendous mustache, in flagrant defiance of
Charlotte's actual character description. Morton, whom you
may remember from *In America* or *Minority Report*, has the
clear, brilliant eyes you want in a competent Jane, though I
think her demeanor too polished—she's too refined to feel as
uncomfortable as Jane must feel around people who've been
bred amidst expensive things.

For my money there are only two adaptations worth seeing: the Cary Joji Fukunaga film and the Susanna White
miniseries. I love them. Even when I'm not miserable, I watch

them as often as I reread the books. When I am laid low by the perfidy of base humanity, I watch them back-to-back, and with occasional rewinding for the most important scenes.

Fukunaga's Jane is Mia Wasikowska, alongside Michael Fassbender as Rochester. Visually, the film is subtle and exquisitely textured. There are lace patterns everywhere—in curtains, carriage seats, veils, drapery, embroidery. There's a visual cue of Jane lacing and unlacing, dressing and undressing. When the Lowood teachers strip her finely made Gateshead dress away, when she later tears off her wedding gown, the motion is reminiscent, the implication—"I was never worthy of this in the first place"—identical. From stone masonry to cravat knots, this film is made out of its details.

In moments, it feels like Fukunaga was trying to sprinkle a little modern psychology on Miss Eyre and her Edward. For the first time in cinematic rendering, we see the effects of child abuse and neglect on a young woman who cannot see the love waiting before her, who cannot access the passion we are repeatedly told that she has (and that we finally see in her artwork—none of the other productions featured her art so clearly) or the anger she is entitled to. The one facet Wasikowska doesn't really represent is Jane's mischievous streak, but this adaptation feels so serious, there's not really a place for her levity.

Moira Buffini's screenplay cleverly takes the novel's three parts and arranges them for suspense rather than strict linear fidelity. We meet Jane when she is wandering the moors after fleeing from Thornfield, and get the rest through flashbacks. Wasikowska, though too ethereally pretty for plainness, makes her naïveté totally believable in the face of Rochester's obvious schemes. Fassbender is . . . well, Fassbender is next to perfect. That jaw. That gravelly voice. Those eyes. Their chemistry is as intense as my fevered adolescent brain could have wished. The casting of Jamie Bell, despite the fact that he's wearing Arthur Bell Nicholls's muttonchops, even makes St. John Rivers hard to resist.

In choosing what to cut and what to revise, Buffini chose to interpret, rather than adapt. She trimmed out unnecessary Reed and Rivers scenes, nearly erased Lowood, and, worst of all, truncated Jane and Rochester's reconciliation, one of the most adorable scenes in literature. This is what's supposed to happen:

When Jane Eyre returns to Rochester, she arrives without telling him she's coming. As she approaches Ferndean, his manor house, the door opens and Edward steps outside. The ruin of Thornfield has left him maimed—he is blind and his right hand has been amputated. Their first meeting since the day they were supposed to be married, more than a year ago, and Jane Eyre seizes the opportunity to play "Guess Who" with the wounded love of her life. Her first act upon being reunited with him is to ask for a snack and then start fixing his hair. Jane's easy, teasing bedside manner is so delightful, her confidence even more charming when we remember the timid, mistreated girl she was. She keeps things firmly in the realm of the practical, dismissing his morbid talk of ghosts and loneliness by taunting him with the mystery of where she has been and who she has stayed with.

Jane draws out his jealousy, evading his questions, until at last she tells him all about the Rivers family, admits that

St. John proposed to her, and confesses that the only wife she wants to be is Rochester's. Relieved and grateful, Rochester confesses that a few nights previously he'd called out to her, at the same moment that she heard "Jane, Jane, Jane," borne on the wind, and actually heard her reply, "I am coming, wait for me"! Then they embrace and we must remember to hydrate ourselves.

But in the Fukunaga film, instead of jollying Rochester out of his sadness for a few moments, Jane walks straight up to him. When he asks if he is dreaming, she simply says, "Awaken, then." And that's it. Fade to black. It leaves one feeling like Wile E. Coyote running off the edge of a cliff holding up a "Really?!" sign. Buffini and Fukunaga's *Jane Eyre* is as beautiful and airy as a snowflake, but it is a little bloodless.

The adaptation that got the most repeat viewings during my Great Mourning of 2012 is the five-hour BBC production from 2006, starring Ruth Wilson and Toby Stephens. I feel more confident in saying Susanna White's directorial choices are the work of a fan, not an interpreter. *Jane Eyre*'s dark and broody buildings are appropriately dark and broody, with repeated accents of red—Gateshead's red room has crimson hangings and wallpaper, a red sash flutters from Bertha Rochester's tower window, Jane ties a red kerchief at her throat. That last piece is actually a literal representation of something Rochester says to Jane when he's likening her to a gray bird—that there are red feathers hiding under that drab exterior. Screenwriter Sandy Welch incorporated more dialogue directly drawn from the book than any other version (which makes the proposal the most stirring), and she also uses flashbacks to return us to Thornfield after Jane has fled, boosting the momentum of that dreary Millcote section. And because White had five hours to play with, her adaptation is more faithful than any other; nearly every scene in the novel is represented somehow, including a fully fledged reunion and a really compelling, literarily *important* scene where Rochester tries to persuade Jane to stay at Thornfield by gently reclining her onto his bed. In a novel with very little acknowledgment of physical contact, you become Very Aware that your hero has finally gotten a hand on your heroine's collarbone amid actual honest-to-God kissing.

Stephens is my favorite Rochester because he's more annoyed at the world than genuinely forbidding, and he pulls off the sarcasm the best. Wilson's Jane has unusual features and the right sort of bright, broad-set eyes for Rochester to find so striking. She performs all of Jane's uncertainty, her strong opinions, and her more selfish feelings, but quietly, with introspective thoughtfulness. I want to live in this version. I know it sounds crazy but hear me out. I'll be Adele, I'll be Leah the maid, I'll be one of the Rivers sisters and come for an extended visit, just please, let me in.

Wuthering Heights has been adapted for film, TV, radio, and stage, too. And the usual suspects turn up to do scene-chewing turns as Heathcliff—Laurence Olivier (entirely too civilized), Charlton Heston (too gruff), Richard Burton (too Shakespearean), Ian McShane (too macho), Robert Cavanah (too gentle), Mike Vogel (too pretty), and Timothy Dalton again (are you kidding me?).

A 2011 adaptation ventured forth James Howson, a black actor from Yorkshire, as Heathcliff—justified by the fact that Heathcliff's looks are sometimes referred to as dark or compared to a gypsy in the novel. In one of Charlotte's letters she even calls him "black," but whether that was physical description or problematic characterization is up for debate. I think there is plenty to be gained by casting diversely across race, gender, and type in this day and age. I mean, *Hamilton*.

The lineup of Cathys is also populated with marquee favorites: Juliet Binoche is the biggest name. She seems impossibly well behaved for a time-honored literary hoyden, especially opposite Ralph Fiennes, who is compelling, but way too elegant and aquiline for a ne'er-do-well of unknown parentage. Even his *Voldemort* was elegant—Heathcliff needs the ruffian factor turned up to eleven. In the Olivier adaptation, Merle Oberon's arched manner matches Olivier's sleek demeanor, and everyone overacts all over the place; they also brought in a much larger supporting cast than the book calls for. I don't know how you justify a choice like that when the book's world consists of eight people—it undermines the sense of inescapable insularity to populate it with a ballroom full of strangers. Angela Scoular and her perfect 1970s hair took a turn; Orla Brady showed Cathy's elegance, if not her wildness. In case you wondered what *Wuthering Heights* would look like if cross-pollinated with *The OC*, in 2003 Erika Christensen gave us a glimpse into a modern surfer adaptation. But nobody succeeded in making Cathy seem like a human being, instead of a vehicle for every teenager's romantic desperation, until the BBC knocked it out of the park in 2009.

Directed by Coky Giedroyc and adapted by Peter Bowker, this *Wuthering Heights* is the only one that has managed to produce a proper Heathcliff: Tom Hardy, whose pout makes me understand what all the fuss is about. He and his Cathy, Charlotte Riley, are so made for one another they got married in real life.* Also, they have a love scene out on the moors, which feels so appropriate and necessary I'm shocked most other adaptations don't add it. Edgar Linton is played without spine or blood by Andrew Lincoln; for once, sticking by Heathcliff is a total no-brainer, regardless of how well furnished the Linton parlor is. The broader time span of the miniseries again allows the creators to temper the mania of *Wuthering Heights* by unfolding it gradually, interspersed with luscious location shots (cramming all that drama into under two hours never fails to make it seem ludicrous). Years seem to pass in the interval between Heathcliff's storming out and Heathcliff's storming back, between commencing his abuse of Hareton and deciding to force young Catherine to marry sickly Linton. It usually feels like minutes. I still loathe the story and everyone in it, but this version is very satisfying.

Watching all these adaptations brings up lots of big-picture questions about adaptation and reinterpretation. Why, with all the world's novels and plays and short stories, do *Jane Eyre* and *Wuthering Heights* keep turning up in remakes, in French, in Italian, in Japanese? Filmmakers and moviegoers seem fixated on these stories, their universal appeal fueled by the ferocity of the emotions they contain.

---

* See, the Brontës are contagious. Much like consumption.

Everybody loves passion. Everybody loves fate and its cruel mysteries. Everybody loves a woman ahead of her time who resists society's constrictions. Everybody loves a redemption story, whether it comes to our hero directly or unfolds in the next generation. Everybody loves an underdog—the plain governess who gets the man of her dreams *and* her self-respect, the orphan boy striving for legitimacy and revenge. People seem very fond of crinolines, corsets, and cravats, too, regardless of their historical accuracy.

And for all the critics who grumbled that none of the Bells' men or women could really exist anywhere (despite how often they also praised the Brontës' character development), modern audiences continue to relate to the Heathcliffs and Rochesters, Janes and Cathys. We recognize them instinctively as facets of ourselves, even if they're facets we only wish we had. Every decade has its own style to impose upon these imperfect templates—there's something for every palate. The purists want to see their stories rendered absolutely, painstakingly correctly. The revisionists want a modern interpretation that smooths over the implausible leaps in the original source material or breathes fresh air into the claustrophobic hallways. Which one of these counts as "faithful"? The one that tries to render Charlotte's vision exactly, or the one that tries to re-create the sensation her original readers might have felt? What would Charlotte have thought of the racy bedroom scene between Toby Stephens and Ruth Wilson? (Probably a bit more appreciation than Jane Austen might have felt for Colin Firth's infamous *Pride and Prejudice* pond scene.)

Since I know no adaptation will actually bring my vision to life, I also have a soft spot for iterations that throw conventionality out the window and go for whimsy. When I was in high school, my dad introduced me to a series by Jasper Fforde that begins with *The Eyre Affair*, set in an alternate universe where Shakespeare is a religion and people see Richard III the way my friends and I used to dress up for the midnight *Rocky Horror Picture Show*. Fforde's protagonist, Thursday Next, is a literary detective tasked with solving crimes, usually involving forgery and stolen manuscripts; *The Eyre Affair* requires her to pursue a criminal mastermind *inside Jane Eyre*. In Thursday's world, *Jane Eyre* ends with Jane sailing off to India with St. John, and Rochester surviving unscathed, but miserable. Thursday fixes it by starting a fire at Thornfield and calling to Jane outside her window (finally, a plausible explanation for that moment!).

These books bring my oldest literary acquaintances to life with exciting new personalities that are both true to their on-the-page identities and allowed to blossom in unexpected ways. Over the course of the series, Miss Havisham conducts anger management group therapy for the residents of *Wuthering Heights*, Mrs. Tiggy-Winkle takes in ironing, and Marianne Dashwood's always trying to bum cigarettes. Fforde intuitively understands the way books come alive when you love them: What wouldn't I give to be able to burrow all the way into *Jane Eyre* and pay rent at the little Millcote inn the way Thursday does in *The Eyre Affair*.

But since Thursday's book-jumping technology wasn't available, I could only take solace in watching one Brontë adaptation after another while the takeout containers piled up on my kitchen counter. Reading the books, *I* have to feel Jane's and Rochester's and Cathy's and Heathcliff's feelings. Watching the films, I get to watch *other people* having all the feelings. It takes the weight off my shoulders, moves the drama outside of my head and onto a screen, so I can get some distance.

Now that I had watched *Jane Eyre* three times in twenty-four hours, I could see the real moral of the story again: when the object of Jane's affection turned out to have a mad wife in the attic (as good a metaphor for unwieldy emotional baggage as any), Jane packed up and left. She didn't bargain, she didn't explain, she didn't compromise. She had to become independent and prove her self-worth, Rochester had to become penitent (and ditch the mad wife and lose a hand and an eye), and only *then* could they be together.

What I'd tried to do with Eric was skip straight to the tearful, teasing reunion without allowing him to do whatever symbolic burning his house down he needed to do to start fresh. Assuming he even *wanted* to start again, and hadn't just been succumbing to the peer pressure of my enthusiasm. In short, I twisted the gospel of Brontë into something warped and selfish, and this current misery was the price I had to pay, along with my Chinese takeout tab. I would probably die alone, with only Gracie the Fifth by my side. Unless . . . perhaps . . . maybe . . . it didn't have to be as miserable as all that. I got up, disposed of all the Styrofoam containers that had once held my feelings in the form of steamed dumplings and chicken with broccoli, washed my face, and opened the curtains. My life needed a new script.

It was time for *Villette.*

M. Paul Emanuel

I had a letter the other day announcing that a lady of some note who had always determined that whenever she married, her elect should be the counterpart of Mr. Knightley in Miss Austen's Emma—*had now changed her mind and vowed that she would either find the duplicate of Professor Emanuel or remain for ever single!!!*

—Charlotte Brontë to W. S. Williams,
March 23, 1853[1]

The first time I attempted *Villette*, I was too young. I was twelve, and impatient, and I anticipated some kind of *Jane Eyre* sequel. *Villette* just doesn't have the same kind of magic. If *Jane Eyre* is a chocolate milkshake (which I suppose is debatable), *Shirley* is some cocktail that prominently features bitters, and *Villette* is an *affogato*—an acquired taste of maturity with a late-breaking jolt of caffeine. The protagonist, a young teacher named Lucy Snowe, had Jane's intelligence but none of her fervor. *Villette* felt like any other period novel that you might skim or be forced through in English class. But now, older, wiser, and bleary-eyed from days spent watching *Jane Eyre* and *Wuthering Heights* and *Jane Eyre* again, I pulled *Villette* from the shelf and sank into it: a scoop of miserable ice cream finally willing to melt on a bed of bitter coffee.

Lucy Snowe, a young Englishwoman, is driven by unemployment and misfortune to seek a position as a teacher in the city of Villette (a stand-in for Brussels). The novel begins in flashback, with Lucy recalling a childhood visit to her godmother's house, where she first encountered a little sprite with precocious manners named Polly Home. Lucy's godmother, Mrs. Bretton, has a son she calls Graham, whose teasingly formal attentions to little Polly succeed in bringing her out of her shell. We then speed forward eight years to find Lucy working as a companion to a sickly lady in her neighborhood. When Lucy's employer dies, she takes herself and the fifteen pounds she has saved to London, and then across the English Channel, meeting the spoiled Ginevra Fanshawe en route. Ginevra is a student at a family-run *pensionnat*, Madame Beck's, and recommends Lucy seek work there.

Lucy arrives late at night, without a friend in the world, and knocks at the *pensionnat*'s door. Though at first Madame Beck is unsure of her, Lucy's future is secured by the recommendation of a teacher named Paul Emanuel, who gives Lucy the once-over and hires her on the spot. Despite lacking references, luggage, and fluency in French, Lucy becomes the nanny to Madame Beck's children. After some time, she is abruptly promoted to teach English to some sixty pupils—and not studious, well-behaved British children, but infamous "*Labassecouriennes*, round, blunt, abrupt, and somewhat rebellious Belgian schoolgirls." Lucy is terrified, and as she surveys her class, knowing that if she fails to secure their respect she will be unceremoniously ejected from the *pensionnat*, as her predecessors have been, she thinks, "Then first did I begin rightly to see the wide difference that lies between the novelist's and poet's ideal 'jeune fille' and the said 'jeune fille' as she really is."

I taught my first writing class of Columbia University undergraduates not long after reading *Villette*—having prepared myself by teaching high school creative-writing seminars and workshops for two summers, taking two pedagogy classes, and gaining an appreciation of the essay as a form, coming as it does from the French for "to try." Exactly one minute before the start of class, I walked in, set down the briefcase I'd brought as a shield, wrote my name on the board, straightened my tailored armor, and turned to face fourteen nervous faces. Greeting a brand-new class is a unique terror. My Aunt Bobbie, a longtime elementary school teacher, only smiles once during the first two weeks so her students will take her seriously. My grandmother was perpetually sharp and short with her fourth graders, but allowed them to eventually earn *her* respect. Barb always began by posing open-ended questions and passing out articles for us to glance over. Alan Ziegler, my favorite pedagogy teacher, liked to start by pretending he'd forgotten his lesson plan and needed us to get things started. Lucy Snowe commenced her first day as a *maîtresse* by reading the most disruptive student's English composition aloud before tearing it contemptuously in half, then speedily locking the class troublemaker in a broom closet.

But other than that, much of our teaching experience is similar. Lucy Snowe and I both enjoy the feeling of "polishing [our] faculties and whetting them to a keen edge with constant use." We are no strangers to lying awake trying to

decide how best to capture the interest or overcome the resistance of our students. Where Lucy's students needed to be
given easy assignments and then mocked heartily, mine were
very sensitive to sarcasm (which is unfortunate, as it is my
primary love language) and excessively grade-conscious.

Three years later, I finally feel confident enough to act like
a human being on the first day, instead of a robot. I can admit
to making mistakes, to being worried, to failing—and failing
hard. I've taught Columbia's overachievers, future medical
professionals at a community college who just want to get
through the class, high-achieving underprivileged teenagers
applying to college, and most *Villette*-like of all, conserva-
tive religious students at an all-girls school. I brought them
essays by Mindy Kaling and Jamaica Kincaid to supplement
the staid, trite readings they were assigned by the department. I wanted to give them a writer's toolbox, to give them
a sense of agency, a growing understanding of their own process. Many wanted mechanical tricks that would get As instead. We found ways to compromise.

COMPARED to *The Professor*, Charlotte's first attempt to
process her experiences in Brussels, we can tell we're in the
hands of a much more accomplished writer in *Villette*. Where
The Professor was snide and spiteful, *Villette* is more seasoned
and deliberate. The quirky, rude, and clever characters don't
seem merely the products of a resentful brain. The passage of
time had rendered Charlotte much more judicious toward
Constantin Heger's wife, if the portrayal of Madame Beck as

eccentric but powerful is any indication. We also get to know the characters of *Villette* much more slowly—in *Jane Eyre*, we grow up with Jane and know her nearly as well as we know ourselves; in *Shirley*, Narrator-Charlotte tells us exactly who everyone is and what they're all about. But in *Villette*, we only see what Lucy sees (which sometimes she doesn't even describe to us, because Charlotte Brontë is a dreadful tease who loves a plot twist), and we mostly learn about her through the reactions of others. It takes a few successive readings to realize that Lucy is as unreliable as any narrator can be.

Though Lucy is a quiet sort of person, she is not without passion, which she works hard to subdue. I read Lucy's determination to repress her more lively instincts as the latest evolution of Charlotte's feelings about the position of unmarried working-class women in the world. If life is necessarily bound up in service to others, why get excited about anything unsustainable or unachievable? But at the same time, even Lucy's faculties were not immune to the awakening of childhood excitement—during a thunderstorm, for example, or the annual school theatrical performance—and she wrestles with a longing for something to "lead [her] upwards and onwards." It's exactly the same sort of sentiment Jane expressed on the roof of Thornfield, before meeting Mr. Rochester. I cannot stop comparing Lucy and Jane—Lucy Snowe seems like Charlotte's attempt to work out a more realistic life for Jane Eyre: one where there was no outlet for her feelings, no compassionate listener, where her passion wasn't rewarded by a fairy-tale ending, only the continual daily struggle to master her nature, which probably much more closely mirrored Charlotte's actual life experience.

Lucy finds herself drawn into an intrigue—Madame Beck's pet physician, Dr. John, is in love with a *pensionnat* student who is a profligate flirt. He enlists Lucy's help to "protect" the delicate object of his affections, who turns out to be the unrepentant Ginevra Fanshawe. Life at the *pensionnat* is next enlivened by a fête for Madame Beck's birthday featuring a celebration along with a play performed by the students, which is directed by M. Paul Emanuel.

Let me just remind you of how Charlotte described Constantin Heger in a letter to Ellen Nussey:

He is professor of Rhetoric a man of power but as to mind very choleric & irritable in temperament—a little, black, ugly being with a face that varies in expression, sometimes he borrows the lineaments of an insane Tom-cat—sometimes those of a delirious Hyena—occasionally—but very seldom he discards these perilous attractions and assumes an air not above a hundred degrees removed from what you would call mild & gentleman-like . . . [2]

And now, M. Paul Emanuel:

A dark little man he certainly was; pungent and austere. Even to me he seemed a harsh apparition, with his close-shorn, black head, his broad, sallow brow, his thin cheek, his wide and quivering nostril, his thorough glance, and hurried bearing. Irritable he was; one heard that, as he apostrophized with vehemence the awkward squad under his orders.[3]

Just try to tell me the Brontës didn't write from life, after that. *Finally*, I thought, repulsed, *a Brontë narrative that
won't make me fall in love.*

Charlotte wrote *Villette* at a time when she felt utterly
alone in the world; she had achieved the literary success
she'd dreamt of as a child, but I doubt she ever imagined
she'd be enjoying fame by herself. After the deaths of her
siblings, and the publication of *Shirley*, Charlotte began to
cautiously enjoy her newfound access to London's literary
scene. She visited George Smith several times between 1851
and 1853, and was introduced to William Makepeace Thackeray, to Harriet Martineau, to Elizabeth Gaskell, to room-
fuls of people, eager to know her. And though she found
herself lonely and depressed whenever she landed back in
quiet, isolated Haworth, she was never really able to navigate the London society world comfortably. She might be a
spitfire on paper, but in person she wanted to be accepted as
a lady. She was shy and easily exhausted; London's constant
pressure to see and be seen, speak and be spoken to, wore on
her introverted disposition.

While it's tempting for me to wish she'd had a different
response, if she'd spent more time in town her letters would
all be of the terse, logistical variety. We'd have no record
of her silliness with George Smith, her thoughtful literary
exchanges with W. S. Williams, or her first meeting with
Thackeray in 1850, of which she wrote to Ellen,

He made a morning-call and sat above two hours—
Mr Smith only was in the room the whole time. He

described it afterwards as a queer scene, and I suppose it was. The giant sat before me—I was moved to speak to him of some of his short-comings (literary of course) one by one the faults came into my mind and one by one I brought them out and sought some explanation or defence—He did defend himself like a great Turk and heathen—that is to say, the excuses were often worse than the crime itself. The matter ended in decent amity—if all be well I am to dine at his house this evening.[4]

For all her protestations of being shy and retiring, she voluntarily chastised one of the reigning great novelists and got invited to his house for dinner afterward. Thackeray's daughter later wrote of seeing Miss Brontë there—she reported that Charlotte was retiring and taken aback when asked a question in front of the whole party.

Back home in Haworth, Charlotte continued to isolate herself, turning down invitations from old friends and new ones, berating herself for not producing new work. After George Henry Lewes gave *Jane Eyre* a strong review, Charlotte wrote to thank him, and they corresponded briefly. She wrote him,

Let it suffice to answer that I am on the worst terms with myself—alternating between a lively indignation and a brooding contempt, and that if anybody would take out a patent for a new invention enabling distressed authors to command their mood and to compel to obedience their refractory faculties—I should regard that individual as the first benefactor of his race.[5]

W. S. Williams had the best strategy for dealing with Charlotte in a recalcitrant, self-pitying mode—he would send her a box of books from Cornhill and then ask her opinion; it passed the time, engaged her mind, and, best of all, populated her letters with thoughtful, brusque literary criticism. She ruminated on the appeal of Honoré de Balzac and wrote of George Sand approvingly, and for a while writing seemed to come more easily afterward. What she needed most, though, was her sisters, restored to health, and her brother, restored to sanity. And there was no hope of regaining them. If *Jane Eyre*'s overriding theme is Love, and *Shirley*'s is Independence, *Villette* is driven by the Search for Family. Charlotte took her intelligent but isolated heroine, set her adrift, and went about making her a new family from scratch.

Still, while I'm sympathetic to Charlotte, who clearly found intense social interactions as bewildering and exhausting as I do, I'm also a bit frustrated with her for not taking her life into her own hands once she had the freedom to do so. She could have set up her own house in London and only visited with people she felt like seeing, thus assuring herself "something like social cheerfulness" and also protecting her introverted sensibilities. But she wouldn't leave her father behind—Patrick Brontë's happiness and comfort were ultimately her highest priority, even though a consequence of keeping him company was that her own life became very small.

As it would be with any friend, it's hard to hear from Charlotte when she's so depressed. And again, my frustration likely stems from the fact that the weighty feeling of not being able to get out of bed, put pen to paper (or fingers to keys), is a familiar one—I've dealt with chronic bouts of depression since I was a teenager. I dealt with it as I read *Villette*. The world had become a heavy and cheerless place, no matter what sunlit reality actually existed. When I'm depressed, my brain tells vicious lies that demoralize and discourage me, sapping value and vitality out of everything. Even though I was in grad school meeting exciting people and taking classes that lit little fires all over my imagination, the world was bleak. I was living in a city thousands dream of visiting, and I was wasting it, day after day, feeling like the walls were crumbling thanks to the confluence of brain chemistry and heartache.

Meanwhile, in *Villette*, after all the students and professors depart for their summer vacations, Lucy is left alone at the *pensionnat* with only a handful of servants. She finds both the lack of occupation and the isolation painful, but at last begins to explore Villette and the surrounding countryside. One afternoon, in particularly low spirits, Lucy finds herself drawn inside a Catholic church. As she kneels with the congregation, something compels her to take confession (as Charlotte did at her lowest, loneliest point in Brussels).

The simple act of pouring her heart out to the French priest relieves some of Lucy's heaviness, but then she actually faints from the distress of the experience. When she comes to, she's confused to find elements of her godmother's home around her. Now the importance of the opening chapters becomes clear—Dr. John is John Graham Bretton, son of Lucy's godmother, and it's a small world after all. Now we learn that Lucy has known for several chapters who Dr. John really is—she just didn't bother to remind him (or us!) that they'd met.

The Brettons take Lucy to a concert; when Dr. John returns her to the *pensionnat* and promises to write, she is flooded with eagerness to hear from him—her childhood friendship has been transformed to tenderer feelings as she's watched him around the *pensionnat* for the past few months. Fortunately, Reason is there to give her a talking-to:

> Reason still whispered me, laying on my shoulder a withered hand, and frostily touching my ear with the chill blue lips of eld.
>
> "If," muttered she, "if he should write, what then? Do you meditate pleasure in replying? Ah, fool! I warn you! Brief be your answer. Hope no delight of heart—no indulgence of intellect: grant no expansion to feeling—give holiday to no single faculty: dally with no friendly exchange: foster no genial intercommunion . . ."
>
> "But I have talked to Graham and you did not chide," I pleaded.
>
> "No," said she, "I needed not. Talk for you is good discipline. You converse imperfectly. While you speak, there can be no oblivion of inferiority—no encouragement to delusion: pain, privation, penury stamp your language."
>
> "But," I again broke in, "where the bodily presence is weak and the speech contemptible, surely there cannot be error in making written language the medium of better utterance than faltering lips can achieve?"
>
> Reason only answered, "At your peril you cherish that idea, or suffer its influence to animate any writing of yours!"
>
> "But if I feel, may I never express?"
>
> "Never!" declared Reason.[6]

Essentially, Lucy hoped to become more appealing to Dr. John by writing more eloquently than she speaks, much like I used text and email to conceal the depth of my unhappiness. Where was Reason with her tough love when *I* was making written language the medium for my faltering lips to better their utterance, hmm? *Nowhere.* If I'd had Reason making threats at my elbow, instead of a little voice saying, "This is a great idea!," I wouldn't have given in to the temptation of sending Eric the occasional faux work email, or worse, an "I miss you" text in response to his "Thinking of you." I'd attempted to convince myself he had never really thought of me as relationship material—as a pleasant rebound, a quick fall fling—but never with the intensity I'd felt for him. Regardless of whether it was true, it was necessary for self-preservation.

On another visit to the theater, Dr. John and Lucy are thrown back into the orbit of the Home family from the first chapter—little Polly (now seventeen and quite grown up) and her father—who are now known as the de Bassompierres, and, *twist*, are also Ginevra Fanshawe's wealthy relations. Dr. John, freed from Ginevra's ensnarement, finds himself falling in love with Polly. For a few chapters it seems like we're supposed to get invested in their love story—Lucy shrugs off her feelings for Dr. John and positions herself as a sisterly adviser, knowing that he and Polly, both good-looking and young, are meant to be happy together.

Still, something else is going on. Like Lucy herself, I had not thought much about M. Paul Emanuel at all after our first introduction. He's depicted as a "bitter little despot," and Ginevra calls him bearish, meddling, and repellent. But

now he begins to come into focus. He's been making enig-
matical overtures of friendship to Lucy, addressing her as
"little sister" and seeking her out in private moments. At first
Lucy finds herself caught between the enjoyment of teasing
him and being irritated by his "spiteful, acrid, savage" ways
when provoked. During an evening in the common study
area, he takes a seat near her, interrupting her reading:

> He asked, by-and-by, if I would not rather run to my com-
> panions than sit there? I said, no; I felt content to be where
> he was. . . . Again, he inquired whether, if he were to leave
> Villette, and go far away, I should be sorry . . .
>
> "*Petite soeur*," said he; "how long could you remember
> me if we were separated?"
>
> "That, Monsieur, I can never tell, because I do not know
> how long it will be before I shall cease to remember every-
> thing earthly."
>
> "If I were to go beyond seas for two—three—five years,
> should you welcome me on my return?"*
>
> "Monsieur, how could I live in the interval?"[7]

Would it shock you to learn M. Paul has a tragic backstory of thwarted love, and is secretly a good, charitable,
and warmhearted man? M. Paul may be more a resident of
Brussels than a descendent of Zamorna, but this scene is
Jane's and Rochester's with the intensity dialed down. Charlotte chose the last name "Snowe" deliberately—she wanted

---

*I begin to feel less ridiculous about my middle school flirting habits.

a frosty, chilly protagonist, Jane's opposite. But all it took to awaken her long-repressed inner fire was learning more about M. Paul; Lucy is suddenly all too aware of his virtues and his strength of character. He's the type of man who provides for elderly family members and paupers, and the *pensionnat*'s little dog loves him best. She bemoans the fact to herself, "Forget him? Ah! they took a sage plan to make me forget him. . . . They showed me how good he was; they made of my dear little man a stainless little hero."

Charlotte, provoking woman that she is, also reveals to us that M. Emanuel has been in the habit of going through Lucy's desk and leaving behind bonbons and books (occasionally defaced by the removal of particularly heretical pages). Unlike in *Jane Eyre*, where the burgeoning romance is signaled by everything short of a song-and-dance number, M. Paul's passion for Lucy is nearly impossible to detect, even once you know the man better. Just as in *Shirley*, there has been a whole *thing* going on here right under our noses that another writer would have made the meat and potatoes of her story, but Miss Brontë didn't even see fit to serve us outright. Lucy could not be a less reliable narrator if she went on vacation in the middle of the novel and neglected to show up for work the next day:

M. Emanuel had been very kind to me of late days; he had been growing hourly better and kinder. It was now a month since we had settled the theological difference,* and

---

*They have apparently resolved the centuries-old dispute between Catholics and Protestants—What was *in* those bonbons?!

in all that time there had been no quarrel. . . . [H]e had
come oftener, he had talked with me more than before; he
had spent hours with me, with temper soothed, with eye
content, with manner home-like and mild. Kind subjects
of conversation had grown between us; he had inquired
into my plans of life, and I had communicated them. . . .
[T]he mutual understanding was settling and fixing; feelings of union and hope made themselves profoundly felt in
the heart; affection and deep esteem and dawning trust had
each fastened its bond.[8]

But it cannot last—M. Paul is leaving Villette for a long
sea voyage, a turn of events that at first seems random, but
on rereading appears to be engineered by Madame Beck
(who secretly wants to marry M. Paul) and M. Paul's priest,
Père Silas (who doesn't want M. Paul to marry a Protestant).

M. Paul sneaks a message to Lucy that he wishes to speak
to her; she slips out of the *pensionnat* and finds herself in the
midst of a town festival, where, of course, she sees everybody she knows, including M. Paul and a pretty ward of his,
named for the departed nun who broke his heart (source of
his tragic mystique). This leads Lucy to reconsider her faith
in M. Paul's feelings for her, while Charlotte delivers us a
patented Heroine Accepts Romantic Rejection Based On
Knee-Jerk Assumptions inner monologue.

Lucy slinks home in the night armed with two companions, "Freedom" and "Renovation" (in the revitalized-self
sense, not in the sense of household repair), that will help
her be brave enough to face life without M. Paul. She tests
them out the next day:

They had boasted their strength loudly when they reclaimed me from love and its bondage, but upon my demanding deeds, not words, some evidence of better comfort, some experience of a relieved life—Freedom excused himself, as for the present impoverished and disabled to assist; and Renovation never spoke; he had died in the night suddenly.[9]

The way Charlotte Brontë exists in this tug-of-war between the grandiose and the dryly funny always amazes and delights me. The mixing of the earnest and the sarcastic, the noble and the exasperated. Our heroine is about to arise from her fainting couch and conquer the world when—whoops, sorry, Freedom is too poor and sickly and Renovation is dead. You're on your own, kid.

I was similarly occupied with my own hourly torment, and hoped to be free of it very soon. I had crammed all the knowledge of how well I knew Eric and how much I'd wanted him into a box and put it on a shelf. There was nothing to be gained by maintaining this obsession. I'd already given it a year of my life. He couldn't possibly have been as funny and warm and good with dogs and generous as I remembered. He literally couldn't make room for me, despite promising that he wanted to. There was nothing there—and could be nothing.

At last, on the day M. Paul is supposed to leave, he bursts into Lucy's classroom; he takes her hand, pushes back her bonnet (*mon dieu!*) and is about to speak—when Madame Beck intrudes, remonstrating with him and fussing over Lucy. M. Paul takes Lucy on a walk into the countryside, where he takes her hand and says, "All these weary days, I have not for one hour forgotten you." Then I am *pretty* sure they kiss, or else I have no idea what Charlotte meant by, "He stopped, and gave me a short, strong answer; an answer which silenced, subdued, yet profoundly satisfied." I've yet to have one myself that silenced or subdued, however satisfying it may have been, so it must have been a hell of a kiss.

Since his voyage to Guadalupe is to last three years,* M. Paul asks Lucy what she will do in the interim; she's been saving to open her own school and intends to continue teaching. Just then he stops in front of a clean, white doorstep, produces a key, and shows her into the vestibule of her very own *pensionnat*. Flabbergasted, she asks how and why and what and *how*, and laughingly he explains that he has been arranging this for her, that he even has pupils lined up, and that's why he's been so distant the last few weeks. And then, "For the moment of utmost mutiny, he reserved the one deep spell of peace. These words caressed my ear: 'Lucy, take my love. One day share my life. Be my dearest, first on earth.'"[10]

And the next day, he is gone, and I am as forlorn as Lucy is. It shouldn't be touching—none of it should. Their relationship isn't heated or breathless, demonstrative or vividly romantic—I don't even really know what's going *on* half the time. But somehow, it is profoundly moving. Especially that line, "All these weary days, I have not for one hour forgotten you." Charlotte Brontë doesn't so much develop M. Paul's

---

*BUT WHY THOUGH?

character as pan back until we can see all of it clearly—he's
the same man he has always been, and Lucy knows it:

> Once—unknown, and unloved, I held him harsh and
> strange; the low stature, the wiry make, the angles, the
> darkness, the manner, displeased me. Now, penetrated with
> his influence, and living by his affection, having his worth
> by intellect, and his goodness by heart—I preferred him be-
> fore all humanity.[11]

In giving me Lucy Snowe, letting me accompany her on
this search for self, by indulging her unrequited affection for
Dr. John, then sneaking M. Paul Emanuel onto the scene
and letting us grow to love his prickliness and his absurdity
and his generosity, she unlocked what I had been trying to
keep trapped underneath layers of resentment and hurt. All
my boasts of independence and self-sufficiency were worth
no more than Lucy's because of one simple fact. I was still in
love with Eric.

And then, as I began to demand some suggestion of how
my own personal prolonged unanswered question was to be
resolved, Charlotte Brontë resolutely refuses to give it to me.
Ignoring the fact that her readers are likely thirsting for a romantic conclusion to this odd nesting doll of a tale, Lucy un-
dertakes her three years of work. Charlotte brings us nearly
to the day of Lucy's reunion with M. Paul. But then there's
this storm:

> That storm roared frenzied, for seven days. It did not cease
> till the Atlantic was strewn with wrecks: it did not lull till

the deeps had gorged their full of sustenance. Not till the destroying angel of tempest had achieved his perfect work, would he fold the wings whose waft was thunder—the tremor of whose plumes was storm. . . .

. . . There is enough said. Trouble no quiet, kind heart; leave sunny imaginations hope. Let it be theirs to conceive the delight of joy born again fresh out of great terror, the rapture of rescue from peril, the wondrous reprieve from dread, the fruition of return. Let them picture union and a happy succeeding life.[12]

I remember closing *Villette*'s back cover and immediately bursting into tears.

If I could have dinner with one historical figure on Earth, it would be Charlotte. I'd take her somewhere really nice, tell her to order whatever she likes, and then put my hands flat on the table and look her dead in the eye. "Charlotte," I'd say, "We need to talk. This girl starts out with no family, no friends, no work, and nearly no money—because of you. You gave her work, friends, a purpose, a home, and love, and just when you should be diving into the homestretch to tell me what to do with *my* life, there is *probably* a shipwreck that *maybe* destroys Lucy's happiness!? You won't tell me what exactly happened to M. Paul and Lucy Snowe because you don't want to *trouble my heart*? This is not how we literature!" Imaginary-Dinner-Date-Charlotte would appreciate this mode of address because, let's recall, this is how she treated Thackeray. I'm sure her response would be even further cynicism about the comparative benefits of shipwreck over marriage. In fact, this ending to *Villette* actually *was* Charlotte's gentler approach. She acidly remarked to George Smith in a letter,

> It was designed that every reader should settle the catastrophe for himself, according to the quality of his disposition, the tender or remorseless impulse of his nature. Drowning and Matrimony are the fearful alternatives. . . . The Merciful . . . will of course choose the former and milder doom—drown him to put him out of pain. The cruel-hearted will on the contrary pitilessly impale him on the second horn of the dilemma—marrying him without ruth or compunction to that—person—that—that—individual—"Lucy Snowe."[13]

You're damn right I'm marrying him "without ruth or compunction" to Lucy Snowe, because they are perfect together and when two people get along so well they make total strangers cry at the thought of their separation. They are supposed to be together! That is how this goes! I'm not crying, you're crying! All these weary days, he has not *for one hour* forgotten her, *Charlotte*!!

Critical attitudes toward the Brontës had shifted since Charlotte's revealing introductions to the reissued editions of *Wuthering Heights* and *Agnes Grey*. Rather than being appalled by the very narrative ground the sisters chose to tread, critics had become so sympathetic and condescending that all their commentary was offered as humble suggestions to the woman who couldn't be expected to write lucidly on account of her great personal tragedy. But even the maudlin press corps was irritated by this ambiguously tragic ending. My favorite is the critic from the *Examiner* who said,

It was in the power of the disposing author of the book to close her story with a charming satisfying picture, which she really does elaborately paint—she daubs her brush across it, and upon the last page spoils it all for no artistic purpose whatsoever, and to the sure vexation of all lookers-on. In the next edition of *Villette* we should like very much to see the last page altered.[14]

The *Athenaeum* saw *Villette* the most clearly: "A burning heart glows throughout it, and one brilliantly distinct character keeps it alive."[15] They were probably referring to M. Paul, but you and I both know the burning heart in *Villette* belongs to Charlotte.

ULTIMATELY, M. Paul Emanuel and Lucy's thwarted love shows us what love can grow to be, how it becomes deeper and larger over time, and contains a multitude of sweet and less savory feelings. Outside of thunderstruck-at-first-sight sorts of tales, that's how it works for almost everyone. Nobody in the Brontë canon succumbs to a just-add-water flavor of romance anyway—even Cathy and Heathcliff only became so recklessly entwined because they got to know each other so well as children.

As I read *Villette*, I felt like Charlotte had pried open a door in my heart to make room for an imperfect man with only a few larger-than-life qualities to recommend him. I was furious, because once she'd cleared a space for M. Paul, all my feelings for Eric rushed in alongside him. The Mr. Rochesters of this world are big and bold and decisive, and they catch us up in their wake and leave us giddy. But the Paul Emanuels see us. They don't have a fantasy of us that we have to dispel, they help us become our ideals. They are supportive, and irritatingly insightful. Eric and M. Paul have a lot in common: they are brusque, and clever, and imperfect, and terrible at first impressions, but dear and warm and oh how I loved him.

Back before our little apocalypse, Eric and I had planned to go to a comics symposium weekend at Columbia together. With my heart newly softened I thought we might attempt to go as friends. We spent a whole day sitting together, never fumbling for things to say. It was hard not to remember what had been so good about our partnership. It was impossible not to miss him. On the way home that afternoon, I felt deflated and bruised. We'd tentatively discussed going back for the second day of the symposium, but I emailed him to say it probably wasn't a good idea. The previous day had been too difficult. "Let's meet up anyway," he said. "I'd like to see you."

The next day we took a walk on the Brooklyn Promenade. I felt like I was peering out at him from behind a locked screen door. He was sorry. I was sorry. I wished I hadn't pushed, he wished he hadn't dragged his feet. We both hoped to be able to behave better in the future. We hugged, and found neither of us wanted to let go. "I mean, I literally don't want to move my face away from your face," he said. "What would be different, if we tried again?" I asked. "I would do everything differently," he replied. "I made a mistake." Though it's one of the more romantic moments of my life, I can't recall much else.

Eric asked for a few days to think it over. (. . . *but this was your idea*, I thought uncharitably). For once I didn't try to rush him, because even I wasn't completely certain that getting back together was the right step. I felt the warring impulses too—I actually gave it some thought instead of just waiting impatiently by the phone. Should I believe him? Were we setting ourselves up to fall apart again? Would we even last a few months this time? Was he really ready? Was *I* ready? Would things actually be different? Was Charlotte right—was a shipwreck actually more merciful?

My feelings were still strong, but not as impetuous and insistent as they'd been before. I had lost my demanding "we will be together come hell or high water because I say so" attitude. But if, with all the disappointment and disillusion-ment and turbulence, I would *still* rather be with him than with anybody else, there was nothing to do but try again. A few days later, on Friday the 13th—let's not dwell on it—we met up for a walk on Riverside Drive. He didn't want me to give up when things got difficult (*Why would they get dif-ficult? I thought you said you were ready*, I did not say aloud) and wanted to be sure we could hash things out in person instead of imploding over text. I reserved my right to bail if everything was terrible, but I knew it couldn't all be dreamy walks on the High Line and sharing sundaes. I was ready to do the work, as long as it meant I could stop dancing around pretending to be casual.

"And not that this means we really have to make it this time . . . " he began.

"But yes, it does," I said. I was impatient and he was talking in inexplicable circles again. I still hated inexplicable circles. If he was in, I was in. If he was out, I was already gone. Why was this taking so long? Eventually, he got me to sit still. He took my hand. We kissed and made up, again.

A few weeks into our refurbished relationship, Eric's father died—he'd been diagnosed with cancer the previous October, and after we'd broken up, I had lost track of how quickly his condition had been deteriorating. I felt out of my depth in Eric's grief, which was complicated by family and father-son dynamics I wasn't privy to. I did my best to show up when he needed me, to make sure he ate and slept and had room to talk if he wanted. It made him vulnerable. It made me feel needed. It drew us together.

That spring we began taking trips—to DC to meet my family and tour the monuments, to Rehoboth Beach for ice cream and beachy arcades, to Philadelphia for ghost tours. We traveled well together, and these long weekends seemed like proof he was setting aside time for us. And besides our compatible road-trip dynamics, this time we had something more important: Eric's willingness to let me in.

I had a drawer in his apartment before I even asked for one. Months went by without me wondering if he wanted to hang out that weekend. He didn't leave me guessing; he didn't make me ask to be reassured. He told me how he felt, unprompted, and often gave me cards and little gestures of thoughtfulness. He lost that wary, cagey feeling. I don't know what he'd been reading, but something had pried open a door in his heart too. A year after our reconciliation, with all of Manhattan as the backdrop, I moved into Eric's In-wood apartment. His ex moved out of state and took the pug with her (for which I owe her a debt of gratitude). We adopted a beagle/collie puppy and named her Roxy. I was stuck with the ugly couch I had made him pick out, but it seemed like a small price to pay for at last fully inhabiting one another's lives.

That October, we made a trip up to Portland, Maine, for the wedding of my college roommate. There's a fence on a dock in Old Port where couples put locks to celebrate their love, like a tiny New England version of the bridges in Paris (where the practice has recently been banned). Eric ran to CVS and purchased a lock and a Sharpie. We left our best and brightest hopes for the future padlocked alongside dozens of others, looking out over the harbor. Leslie's wedding took place on an island off the coast; her family and friends crowded around holding candles while her brother officiated a ceremony in English and French. After a reception of good food and live music at the island's inn, we took a romantic ferry ride back across Casco Bay under a big beautiful full moon. Eric held me close and whispered in my ear.

"I want you to be my wife," he said. "Will you marry me?"

Before I had half done, he held both my hands, he consulted my eyes with a most piercing glance: there was something in his face which tended neither to calm nor to put me down; . . . he gathered me near his heart. I was full of faults; he took them and me all home.

—*Villette*, Chapter XLI

Arthur

Faultless my husband is not—faultless no human being is; but as you well know—I did not expect perfection.

—Charlotte Brontë to Margaret Wooler,
August 22, 1854[1]

Of all the crossovers I wanted to see between the Brontës' literature and their lives, the one I most hoped for was Charlotte ending up in a blissful marriage with someone she loved as much as ever Jane loved Rochester. I wanted *Jane Eyre* to have become autobiography after the fact, essentially, as much for Charlotte as for myself. What I never anticipated was Charlotte becoming the wife of a safe, rational St. John type.

By the time she accepted Arthur Bell Nicholls, Charlotte's expectations for marriage had become very practical. In a letter announcing her engagement, she wrote to Elizabeth Gaskell,

Things have progressed I don't know how. It is of no use going into detail. After various visits and as the result of perseverance in one quarter and a gradual change of feeling in others, I find myself what people call engaged. . . . He is to become a resident in this house. I believe it is expected that I shall change my name in the course of summer—perhaps in July.[2]

She wanted someone she could respect, and someone to keep her father company, and Nicholls suited. He had been Patrick Brontë's curate for many years. He was never terribly popular with the parish, but he was efficient and performed his duties well. By 1846, rumors were already flying about his feelings for Charlotte—Ellen Nussey got firmly rebuffed in a letter for having the audacity to ask about them—but he didn't propose until 1852. Initially Charlotte rejected him largely on the basis of her father's objections (Patrick thought Nicholls wasn't important enough, or able to support Charlotte, which is especially surprising since Charlotte was doing a dandy job of supporting herself), but she also had reservations about his "odd" and "brooding" temperament.

In response, Nicholls sulked and moped around the pulpit so dramatically that Charlotte was touched by the depth of his attachment and began to reconsider. Elizabeth Gaskell did her best to find him other opportunities through her network of friends. He even found a job to take him away from Haworth, but Charlotte and Nicholls corresponded secretly for months. At last Patrick was persuaded by Nicholls's willingness to come live at the Parsonage with them. I'm more puzzled by Patrick's attitude than Charlotte's. His daughter was nearing forty: Who did Patrick think would magically come along and be good enough? Thackeray? Wellington?

Before they were married, Charlotte seemed to find Arthur as puzzling as he was endearing. He wrote her that he was ill, leading her to worry in a letter to Ellen that she'd chosen a partner with serious health issues; by her next letter, he'd arrived in Haworth to visit, prompting her to tartly observe, "When people are really going to die—they don't come a distance of some fifty miles to tell you so." She continued, "Man is indeed an amazing piece of mechanism when you see—so to speak—the full weakness—of what he calls—his strength. There is not a female child above the age of eight but might rebuke him for the spoilt petulance of his willful nonsense."[3] However much Charlotte had grown and softened, there was some vinegar in her yet.

Any time I get deeply interested in an author, I go see if their correspondence has been preserved—Arthur Conan Doyle, Jane Austen, Virginia Woolf, P. G. Wodehouse, Mark Twain, Dawn Powell—and I devour it. Discovering that dozens of Charlotte's letters had survived in the hands of her school friends and her publishers was like finding out that Christmas was not only arriving early, but every day in small doses, like an Advent calendar. Letter-writing Charlotte is opinionated and ambitious, though sometimes depressed, and frequently annoyed by the scarcity of options available to women of her class. And this is silly, but her letters also assure me of a gratifying piece of trivia: she knew my name. She signed one of her letters to Ellen Nussey "Caliban," which means she read *The Tempest*, which means we would have had at least one small spark for conversation, had we ever met.

In addition to this encouragement, and the appealing daily snapshots of life in the early mid-nineteenth century, the letters Charlotte wrote to Ellen have one strong advantage over her more literary writing. With Ellen, she talked about love. Without Ellen's guardianship, I wouldn't know what Charlotte's voice sounded like when she was young, eager, tired, or grouchy. Charlotte's letters to Elizabeth Gaskell and W. S. Williams are written by a writer, a thinker, someone aware, however distantly, of a public presence in the world. The letters to Ellen, though they were frequently passed between family members, are more private, free from the constraints of professionalism. Without these letters, we'd have no hard proof of how she felt about romantic attachment, or that when Ellen's brother Henry, a minister, proposed marriage to Charlotte in 1839, he was kindly but firmly rejected:

> I have no personal repugnance to the idea of a union with you—but I feel convinced that mine is not the sort of disposition calculated to form the happiness of a man like you. . . . I am not the serious, grave, cool-headed individual you suppose—you would think me romantic and eccentric—you would say I was satirical and severe—however I scorn deceit and I will never for the sake of attaining the distinction of matrimony and escaping the stigma of an old maid* take a worthy man whom I am conscious I cannot render happy.[4]

Eat your heart out, Lizzie Bennet. Charlotte would afterward add, in a letter to Ellen,

---

*Charlotte was then twenty-three.

I asked myself two questions—Do I love Henry Nussey as much as a woman ought to love her husband? Am I the person best qualified to make him happy—?—Alas Ellen my Conscience answered "<u>no</u>" to both these questions. . . . I had not, and never could have that intense attachment which would make me willing to die for him—and if ever I marry it must be in that light of adoration that I will regard my Husband ten to one I shall never have the chance again but *n'importe*.[5]

These were all actually fairly radical thoughts for the eldest of three grown daughters to be having; Charlotte may talk about her duties as a wife, but I think she was also fully aware that Henry Nussey could not have made *her* happy; nor could the social obligations of the marriage he was offering her. Regardless of what Charlotte settled for later in life, she was once as passionate and headstrong as I, and as certain she would require a life-or-death attachment in order to commit herself to matrimony.

It was also to Ellen that Charlotte addressed her thoughts and rationalizations about George Smith in 1851, demonstrating the maturation (or perhaps deflation) of her romantic ideals. Smith was eight years younger than Charlotte, and she felt herself very provincial by comparison:

Were there no vast barrier of age, fortune &c. there is perhaps enough personal regard to make things possible which are now impossible. If men and women married because they like each others' temper, look, conversation, nature and so on—and if besides, years were more nearly equal—the chance you allude to might be admitted as a chance—but other reasons regulate matrimony—reasons of convenience, of connection., of money.[6]

I think she sounds like she was working very hard not to be in love. The dynamic between Ellen and Charlotte is also marked by the disparity in their intellects and interests, which Charlotte never interpreted as a fault of Ellen's, but as a sign of her own deficiency in what was good and proper for a young woman to value. Charlotte is pretty much my ideal woman, so it sometimes feels bizarre to me that she should look up to Ellen so ardently. Then I remember, it probably looked to Charlotte like Ellen was doing everything right, and was happy doing it. Ellen wasn't chafing at the hand life had dealt her. She didn't need to escape from reality for hours at a time to scribble secret stories. Ellen had brothers who were not drunk and disorderly, who could help support her if need be. She had access to a more sustained education, and she never had to go to work. She probably got bored, truth be told, but felt free enough to travel occasionally among the relations that lived nearby. While it's possible she was being disingenuous, I get the sense that Charlotte really thought her own ambition and creative energy made her deficient, or even broken. Charlotte felt so *exactly like I felt*, and still feel, if I'm honest—as though everyone else found it easy to be who they were supposed to be.

Ellen is the source of the vast majority of Charlotte's surviving letters, despite explicitly promising Nicholls she'd destroy them. She became the main custodian of Charlotte's legacy, and she talked about her famous friend to anyone who would listen until she died at the ripe age of eighty. Friendship, like love, is a skill that has to be practiced, and the lesson of Charlotte's staunch loyalty to Ellen is that the effort is worth it. So figure out who the Ellen in your life is, and try to stay on good terms.

THERE'S a certain temptation to leap straight from getting engaged to being married, skimming over the messy, lonely year and a half in between. I could just tell you that eventually, I wrote us into *Jane Eyre,* and not bother to spell out how. But that wouldn't be true. He wouldn't be him, and I wouldn't be me. This would have been a whole different story.

As a young girl I dreamed more about getting into Narnia than walking down the aisle; I wanted a good marriage, not a perfect wedding. Eric's proposal had been emotional and spontaneous—maybe a little *too* spontaneous. He still had some deep-seated reservations about actually getting married, it turned out. He never wanted to talk about it—and not in that cliché "men never plan weddings, they just show up" way. He didn't want to exchange a single word on the subject—not to figure out when, or where, or who to invite. Not to write a ceremony, not to plan a menu, not to make a single decision. I hadn't expected putting together a small, laid-back ceremony would remind me quite so much of pulling teeth. I could have written off Eric's reluctance as typical late-thirties commitment-phobia, but whenever I offered him an out—we could just keep living together, we could go to City Hall, we could elope somewhere else, and believe me, breaking up was still an option—he'd vehemently insist that his hesitance wasn't a reflection of his feelings for me, but a knee-jerk reaction to everything matrimonial.

"Maybe we can suss out what marriage means to *us*, outside of what it means to everyone else," I attempted. "It doesn't mean anything," he replied. "I just proposed because you clearly wanted me to." He apologized, but that sting lingered. Every time I tried to dig deeper I just found another layer of the wall he was building. Drafting our vows—an element that could be entirely reflective of us and what we wanted—left Eric literally curled up on the couch in the fetal position while I took the dog for a walk and bawled. The social script around weddings is not helpful in moments like this. Either everything's a red flag and you should run, or it's all standard pre-wedding jitters, and nothing to take seriously. I felt like I was in one of those nightmares where you wake up in a bull-fighting arena waving a white ball gown you never wanted in the first place, and have to fight your way out clutching a bouquet and glowing radiantly.

To make matters worse, my mother had been diagnosed with breast cancer earlier that year. For months, as my mom prepared for treatments and surgery and recovery, an alarm was going off in my head—"Mom Mom Mom Mom Mom." It only subsided when I set an actual alarm to remind me to check in every other day. In *Shirley*, the daughter gets sick and the mother provides the magic cure, but I wanted to be the one who provided exactly what my mother needed. We'd never had that dynamic before, but suddenly there was an urgency to find it. The anthology launch party that marked the unofficial end of graduate school fell on the same day her chemo started—I can see the tension in our faces in those pictures, the last ones in which my mom had her own hair that we took for a long time. We sat in a midtown restaurant and looked at wig catalogues like everything was normal. I collapsed into Eric's arms afterward.

In addition to the shelter of her ferocious love, I also grew up under my mother's fiercely critical eye. I think she imagined that by making me aware of my faults—my too-loud laugh, a flash of fleshy stomach between my shirt hem and my waistband, my appetite, my affectations—she would enable me to avoid the judgment of outsiders. But by the time my mother realized I was pudgy, awkward, and loud, I already knew. The world makes sure you know. Years later, she is so proud of me that she is in persistent denial I could ever have been unhappy or felt unlovable. She would do anything for me, if I called her in a panic. She once drove eight hours to hear me read for fifteen minutes. During this cancer year, I tried to make sure all of the baggage we carry between us stayed strapped in the trunk—I didn't fight the battles I would usually fight or keep the distance I often keep. I felt vacant and weepy a lot. I couldn't write much; when I did, my feelings about my mom seeped into everything.

I made my presence known any way I could. I came to visit and brought movies to watch on my laptop during

chemo appointments. I tried to be at her disposal, helping around the house, playing whatever she wanted on the
piano, and singing without worrying about how I actually
sounded. When she scheduled a lumpectomy, I met the
family in Baltimore, and did what she would do, which was
stock the hotel room with candy and magazines and lotion
and tissues and place the room service orders afterward. I
texted the extended family with updates. I held her wedding
and engagement rings while they wheeled her in for surgery.
Later, I was the one who stepped forward when the doctor
asked who would help with her drains. Despite a lifetime of
squeamishness, I didn't faint when it came time to empty
them into beakers and measure the contents.*

If this was even one one-thousandth of what Charlotte
Brontë went through as she faced the illness and death of her
brother and sisters, I am in awe that *Shirley* was ever finished,
that she was able to even conceive of *Villette*. Throughout my
mother's year of treatment I clung to Eric, to my books, and
as I hadn't done since I was a little girl, to my mother herself.
It was like a trade-off—my hard-won independence in exchange for the assurance that I was doing everything I could
to make sure she knew I loved her.

Naturally she wanted to help plan the wedding, but despite her proud track record of feminist nonconformity, she
turned out to have a number of traditional ideas. Every alternative element that appealed to me—a private ceremony,

---

*I'm delighted to say she has since made a full recovery, and we are
still trying to figure one another out.

a small dinner with family and friends afterward, a colorful tea-length dress, no bridal shower of any kind—appalled her. She couldn't understand why I would want to go off and get married by myself (even though she and my father eloped); I couldn't believe she thought I should be surrounded by a large group of people during an intimate moment, no matter what's "traditional." Every "mother-daughter moment" that TLC would have me believe was an essential part of being a bride ended in tears; I felt unheard and unseen, she felt unappreciated and excluded.

Eric took my distress as a sign that I would regret not having the big wedding she wanted, instead of a sign I needed his support to stand firm. He didn't believe me when I insisted that eloping was what I wanted, and he withdrew into his own thoughts and feelings. He became less thoughtful and spontaneous, and spent most evenings at his desk in the living room. Some of this was normal "settling down." It can't be all roses and declarations of love under the full moon. At a certain point you have to get work done and clean house and be regular people. But I didn't realize just how abandoned I was feeling until about two weeks before we were supposed to elope. After much coaxing and many roundabout approaches, we had planned a small ceremony in Maine, to be followed a few weeks later by an intimate family dinner in New York.

Eric's twin brother Jason's wife went into labor with their first baby on a Monday morning; Eric called me to tell me the good news; I congratulated him, texted Jason to say I was thrilled, and got on the train back uptown. Back in Inwood, my phone revived as I stepped into the elevator, and I picked up expecting to hear an excited uncle's voice. Instead, the man on the other end bore almost no resemblance to the Eric I thought I knew so well.

He was confused about what train to take to Long Island, but rather than consult a map, ask someone employed by the MTA, or just take a breath and wait for the next train, he was calling to demand I get to a computer and help him figure out what to do. Startled by his urgency, I dropped the dog's leash, got my computer open, and tried to find the hospital's address so I could give him directions. In the back of my mind, I was wondering why he hadn't just done this himself on the phone that he was currently yelling into, which contained the entire Internet. In the few seconds it took for my computer to boot up, Eric's anxiety brewed into a state of agitation I had never seen before, at least not directed at me. It would later turn out he was actually crumpling under the weight of the convergence of his thirty-ninth birthday, our impending wedding, and the idea that since his brother was having a baby, it meant *we* had to have one and his life was over. Our already frantic conversation broke down into inarticulate and almost menacing pieces as his panic became my panic until he finally snapped, *this is useless, thanks for nothing, why did I even bother,* and hung up. In tears, I texted him the name of the train stop that had at last appeared on my browser, and the name of the train he should take to get to it. "Are you screwing with me?" he texted back. It took the better part of an afternoon to even realize why I was so shaken.

Nobody had yelled at me like that since I was a child—maybe since my dad had discovered I'd snuck out of the house and gone to visit the neighbors, worrying my then-pregnant mom. He'd strong-armed me into my room, tossed me on my bed, and hissed in my face. There had been other explosions over the years, the kind that steamroll any response until the only possible reaction is hysterical crying. I had learned to marshal my anger, turn it into reason, present it like a closing argument instead of an instinctive reaction. Hearing Eric on full blast triggered helplessness and fear I never thought I'd feel again. I was due at work shortly afterward, so I cried on the floor of the shower until it was time to pull myself together. Once I got on the train I buried my face in a book and tried to stop shaking; then I felt a tap on my shoulder.

It was my college friend C.J.! We had always flirted but never dated, despite the shared love of jazz and the Marvel Universe that had kept our friendship warm. He was supposed to be in Israel, but some quirk of fate had put him on that train, on that day, to give me a big hug and ask why I looked like I had seen the end of the world. I gave him a slightly defensive version of the truth, and without taking sides or passing judgment, he managed to acknowledge that people lose tempers, and I also had every right to be hurt. He let me vent a little while longer, and then we pulled in at my stop. "Being happy is a choice," he said to me, squeezing my hand. "I know you'll know what to do." It was like a *Jane Jane Jane* moment, calling me back to myself.

The Incident, as I think of it now, brought to light what a fight-or-flight mode Eric had been in since well before we got engaged. Maybe I'd been walking on eggshells since I'd first tentatively begun to bring up marriage, a year before. Maybe since my building in Brooklyn had been put on the market and we talked about moving in together. Maybe since his dad died. Maybe if Eric had been more communicative under duress it wouldn't have happened; maybe if I had been more experienced in relationships or less burdened by childhood baggage, I wouldn't have been so rattled. But I *was* rattled, and scared, and eventually angry. I'd watched my mom navigate the emotional minefield of being married to someone who screamed during arguments—she and my dad had made it work, but it was not what I wanted.

I talked to friends, I talked to counselors, I tried, of course, to talk to Eric himself. The first day, he offered me a brisk apology, and when I was still upset he acknowledged he'd been wrong to lose his temper. He didn't seem to see the crack in our foundation. The next night, armed with the validation of people with more relationship experience, I tried again. It was an uphill battle in the pouring rain. It was apparently very important to him to be in a relationship that allowed him to absolutely lose his shit at the woman he loved, without consequences. I curled up in a ball, clutching Roxy, who was panting with worry, and tried to make sense of it.

Eric had always had tempestuous relationships before, and thought the occasional explosion was normal. The fact that we'd never had a big fight in nearly three years of dating was an anomaly in his eyes, not an ideal. True, I had never gone through significant ups and downs with another person, but I had endured my share of confrontations. There had to be a better way to handle them than abandoning all veneers of civility just to get to the Long Island Medical Center. Besides, my sensitivity was something I hoped he'd recognize and want to protect, not something to brush aside.

"I can't be with someone who screams at me," I finally said, in a moment of courage.

"Then I guess I have a lot of thinking to do," Eric said with contempt, before going to sleep on the couch. When I woke up the next morning, after he had already left for work, it was time to map out my exit strategy. I made an appointment to see a nearby apartment share, emailed movers for a quote, and made plans to crash with Kate in the meantime. The only thing that calmed my nerves was faith in my own competency—if I needed to go, I could go, and it would be okay. *Jane Eyre* 101.

Before leaving for work myself, I packed up the essentials. A few days of clothing, toiletries, food and toys for the dog, my laptop, the teddy bear that had accompanied me around the world, and the battered copy of *Jane Eyre* that had started this whole thing. My plan was to go to work, come home after my shift to break the news to Eric, and then head to sanctuary in Brooklyn.

When I walked in, he was at his desk in the corner, quiet but still defiant. I think he expected to go for round three. He thought the fact that I didn't want to live without him would conquer my sense of self-preservation. He had reckoned without the combined power of the Brontës. I quietly explained that I didn't want to be with someone who tried to diminish my joy in what I loved, who didn't want to protect me where I was vulnerable. Because if I can't go to my partner with my pain, my fears, who can I go to? I wasn't going to try to talk him into being someone he wasn't. I didn't have the answers. I couldn't script my way out of this.

There was a moment of silence.

"So what now?" he said.

A long pause. And then, a moment of truth.

"I think I have to go," I said.

He could have said nothing, and let us shake apart. Or tried to thunder me into staying, which is what Rochester would actually have done. Instead, something remarkable happened. Eric left his desk and joined me on the couch.

He took my hand, and quietly said, "Please, don't go."

In the next few hours, I watched him voluntarily demolish all the walls he'd bricked around himself. I didn't have to say much; he was finally ready to talk. He still didn't know why he was so tangled up about marriage, but he knew full well he'd been an ass—and not just that week, but for months, he'd spent the entire time fending me off as I worked to knit our lives together. He'd been scared and stubborn and arrogant, and he apologized wholeheartedly.

The next few days felt wrapped in cotton—we were each gentle and ginger. I felt bruised; he knew how thin the ice was. We dismantled the tiny wedding, and since all our tickets were nonrefundable, I took two of my closest friends to Maine for a strange weekend of spa treatments and restaurant reservations in the shadow of our phantom nuptials (which I do not recommend). The lock we'd placed on the dock of Old Port was gone—whether it had spontaneously cracked like the Dark Crystal or was removed by the board of tourism to make room for the next batch, I couldn't be sure.

Every day since, I've looked for Eric's concerted efforts to be open, to listen and to reach out to me—the way he did when I fell for him, while we worked side by side. For months after we decided to stay together, I was defensive at the slightest conflict. I am still impatient, always racing ahead, prone to great expectations, and hating to have them thwarted. But I stand up for myself more consistently in matters large and small, whether Eric likes it or not. Eric is still more patient and more cautious than I am, still goofy and sweet in turns. Our solid foundation, six years of friendship, is always there when we reach for it. We jockey for independence and seek out moments of collaboration, usually in good humor. We have to remember to be romantic, and to get away from the city together as often as we can. I always thought "relationships take work" was a cliché that referred to making decisions or compromising on big choices like furniture or apartments. Now I know it's a daily effort to be attentive, to fight the urge to tune out, to apologize for hurt feelings even though you said exactly what you meant, to coordinate making dinner or walking the dog without sighing in exasperation because we *just* did this a day ago. It's just what I hoped for, when we both work at it, and plenty I didn't expect. As Charlotte herself said of matrimony, "it tends to draw you out of, and away from yourself."[7]

WHEN Jane and Rochester finally got married (and let's not forget their first wedding attempt was a *way* bigger disaster than ours), they just slipped down to their local church. Afterward, Jane casually informed the household servants they'd been married. "Huh," they said. Life went on. It was not a fairy tale after all—two people met on a windswept road and decided to keep walking it together.

During the last snow of winter on the first day of spring, Eric and I stood in front of a Justice of the Peace at City Hall—or rather the Marriage Bureau at a federal building a block away. Out front, where enterprising New Yorkers will sell you everything from wedding rings to photography services, stand up as your witness or polish your shoes, I bought pale pink roses for Sally, who was our witness, photographer, and maid of honor all in one; I chose hot pink roses for myself, and a white one for Eric's lapel. I wore a silver bracelet from my mother, blue glass earrings from my Aunt Bobbie, purple ballet flats Sally had brought for me to borrow, and a tea-length black dress.

The whole ceremony took two and a half minutes. We didn't anticipate we'd actually get to say the vows we'd written, so when the officiant asked Eric, "Do you have anything to say to Miranda?" and paused expectantly, we had to wing it. Eric said this was the happiest day of his life. When it was my turn, I went blank, and truthfully said it meant a lot that we'd even made it there that day. When we were first dating, I used to hold my breath before saying "I love you," which Eric said felt like a tiny leap of faith, every time. We agreed to make that leap together, as often as we could. The officiant almost forgot to have me slip Eric's ring onto his finger.

We called my parents to tell them the news. My dad welcomed Eric to the family and put us on speakerphone, my brother gloated that he'd known about it the whole time, and my mother icily congratulated us from across the room. A few weeks later, we made plans to go down to Virginia for a visit—what the Victorians would have called a bridal tour. Mom began planning a small gathering for her best friends that immediately became a formal dinner at a nearby historic house, decorated with large pictures of Eric and me, and featuring a suspiciously white three-tiered cake. It was not a wedding, but it was all the proof my mother needed that had she been allowed to throw me one, it would have been a tremendous success. I do think part of my resistance to a big wedding was a lingering uncertainty that anyone would care to attend, and it was wonderful of my mom to show me that I needn't have worried. It was a beautiful party full of family and friends who've known me practically all of my life. I have no regrets—except to wish I'd brought home more of the cake.

WHEN Charlotte Brontë and Arthur Bell Nicholls were quietly married in 1854, his profession on the marriage license was "clerk"; hers was "spinster." Ellen was fairly antagonistic toward Nicholls, but when Charlotte finally walked down the aisle, Ellen helped her with her bonnet and Miss Wooler gave her away.

Charlotte approached the married chapter of her life with independence and low expectations. Her letters reflect respect, compassion, and appreciation for her husband, if not passion or adoration: "I make no grand discoveries—but I occasionally come on a quiet little nook of character which excites esteem—He is always reliable, truthful, faithful, affectionate; a little unbending perhaps—but still persuadable—and open to kind influence. A man never indeed to be driven—but who may be led."[8] Her higher estimation of Arthur began when she accompanied him to his hometown in Ireland on their honeymoon. Seeing Nicholls through the eyes of his family and his neighbors helped her reexamine his strengths; he was greeted enthusiastically and praised highly wherever they went together. I recall the first time I saw Eric and his brothers all together with their families—particularly the way he played with his nephews and niece. Let's just say it was not ineffectual that even on the day of The Incident, I received a picture of him holding a newborn.

Like Gaskell, who said, "I like his having known . . . all she has gone through . . . and being no person who has just fancied himself in love with her because he was dazzled by her genius," I do appreciate that Arthur knew Charlotte as a writer—and probably loved her well before he knew about her literary fame.[9] After all those years of hiding her literary life from Ellen, it must have been marvelous for Charlotte to know that the man who loved her also loved her work. Talking with Eric about my writing has occasionally been more fraught than discussing how long to stay at either family's Thanksgiving.

An unfortunate (but not unexpected) consequence of Charlotte becoming Mrs. Nicholls was that his clergy duties kept her from writing. Most of the surviving letters written during her marriage feature some form of "Arthur is calling me, I must go," or, "My time is not my own now; Somebody else wants a good portion of it—and says we must do so and so. We do 'so and so' accordingly, and it generally seems the right thing—only I sometimes wish that I could have written the letter as well as taken the walk."[10] If they had lived longer together, I imagine Charlotte would have reclaimed her time eventually. Even without having kids, truly functioning as part of a couple is tricky, for a variety of reasons. My writing thrives when I have several weeks at a time to log four- or five-hour shifts without distractions, until the dog's persistence drags me out into the world to blink at the sun and stretch. If Eric and I get serious about having kids, I know the balancing act will get even more precarious. I'm looking forward to it anyway. Most of the time.

As if it wasn't enough for Arthur to co-opt Charlotte's evenings, he also interfered in her correspondence, particularly with Ellen; Charlotte quoted him as saying "such letters as mine never ought to be kept—they are dangerous as lucifer matches."[11] He even exacted a pledge that Ellen would burn Charlotte's letters, threatening to censor the content if she refused! Instead of giving him a Shirley Keeldar–style dressing down on the rights of women correspondents, Charlotte found it amusing, and said, "It is a man's mode of viewing correspondence—Men's letters are proverbially uninteresting and uncommunicative—I never quite knew before why they made them so. . . . As to my own notes I never thought of attaching importance to them, or considering their fate—till Arthur seemed to reflect on both so seriously."[12] This is the Victorian equivalent of the "you're not

going to tweet that, are you?" conversation we have at our
house regularly before I post something ridiculous Eric has
said online. Maybe Arthur's tone was lighter than comes
across in Charlotte's letters, or maybe she fully intended to
write whatever she wanted regardless, but her laugh-it-off reaction seems odd. Arthur's attitude is at best patronizing and
at worst heretical, at least in the eyes of this fan, who treasures
her ability to snoop in Charlotte's private correspondence. I
have to acknowledge he was also right to be cautious; neither
of them could have imagined how many people would read
Charlotte's letters in the next two hundred years.

The fact is, I do not think I like Arthur Nicholls at all,
even though he was clearly a comfort to Charlotte as her father's health failed, and even more so as her first trimester
of pregnancy left her seriously ill. Nicholls obviously loved
Charlotte very much. The house in Ireland where he re-
treated after Patrick Brontë's death, which he later shared
with his second wife, was full of Charlotte's drawings, her
letters, her books, and even those precious *Young Men's
Magazines*. Many of the Brontëana collections around the
world take their provenance from the auctions of the Nicholls estate.

But first of all, he seems like a bore. Second, his handling
of Charlotte's legacy was exasperating—when he and Patrick
hand-selected Elizabeth Gaskell for Charlotte's biography,
they guaranteed that Charlotte's reputation as a shy, sheltered
girl who grew into a weak and sickly woman would endure
for decades. Nicholls *folded the Branwell portrait in quarters*
and put it on a shelf, and worse yet, agreed to publish *The

Professor without significant revisions after Charlotte's death. Even Charlotte knew *The Professor* was beyond redemption! And it is! Unless maybe I just need to read it again.

I'm frustrated with Charlotte, too—I don't know how to reconcile the wild, romantic young woman, whose *Jane Eyre* reached into my heart and switched the light on, with the practical thirty-nine-year-old bride who just didn't want to be alone anymore. I decided being with Eric was worth the price of his imperfections and that I could trust him to accept mine—but when it came down to it, I would have managed being alone again just fine. Then again, who am I to judge what Charlotte determined would suit her best as she got older? At least she picked a husband she could tease.

I suppose it makes me angry that Charlotte spent the last two years of her life on a man who kept her from her work—whose career she *knew* would keep her too busy to write, and whom she didn't even love, not the way she knew love could be. In her final illness, she wrote to Ellen Nussey, "I want to give you an assurance which I know will comfort you—and that is that I find in my husband the tenderest nurse, the kindest support—the best earthly comfort that ever woman had. His patience never fails and it is tried by sad days and broken nights."[13] That is some consolation. After her death, Nicholls fulfilled his promise to continue caring for Patrick Brontë until his death at the age of eighty-four—he outlived the last of his children by six years.

Charlotte Brontë Nicholls died on March 31, 1855, of "phthisis" associated with tuberculosis. It was exacerbated by hyperemesis gravidarum, the excessive pregnancy-related vomiting and dehydration lately suffered by the Duchess of Cambridge during both of her pregnancies. We can be reasonably sure Charlotte knew she was expecting, because she wrote to Ellen asking about a mutual friend's pregnancy symptoms; she found the similarities reassuring, but in the end her illness was much worse.

It will have to be enough that Charlotte got what she wanted. It doesn't matter that it's not what I wanted for her.

THERE are moments you don't see in literature when authors pan forward ten and twenty years—the dynamic contractions and expansions that mark the days and weeks and months of a life together. It's odd to have to remind myself that in my marriage, the only behavior I can successfully modify is my own. I'm constantly squirreling away parts of myself that don't fit the "couple" version of me. Later I rediscover the art supplies, the romance novels, the Bollywood DVDs, the old radio shows, the video games, and realize how much I missed whatever it is I instinctively hid. Eric doesn't ask me to set these things aside—it wouldn't even occur to him, any more than he'd think to conceal parts of himself. No, I hide these things voluntarily, and then consider myself bereft.

I don't ever want our marriage to become a dilapidated mansion with rooms boarded up or curtains drawn, whole wings abandoned while we crowd into the kitchen to step on one another's toes, or worse, stomp out into the night. I want this marriage, our marriage, to be a *much* kinder ending than a shipwreck. And so far, it is. We have low moments, when we find unexpected corners that jab or rough spots that chafe. I measure our lives with my eyes on the minute hand, while he marks leisurely hours and feels content instead of anxious. I am learning it's okay to be mad; he's learning it's okay to be vulnerable. It's difficult, but I make myself turn toward him to ask for what I need, again and again if necessary. I try to remember he likes it when we go to the store together, that his feelings get hurt sometimes too. I count myself lucky that Eric is a decided romantic, better at big gestures than anyone I've ever known. I never doubt that he is glad we got married.

To celebrate our first wedding anniversary, we returned to the island in Maine where we got engaged. We took the same ferry, visited the same restaurants, and laid the ghost of the canceled elopement to rest. One evening we walked over to the rocky beach where Leslie got married. On the way, we talked through that unpleasant year. It felt like releasing a breath I hadn't realized I was holding. I filled my lungs all the way up for the first time in ages. After everything, I would still choose Eric. I do, in fact, every day. Almost every day. By the end of the day, for sure.

Sometimes I mourn that starry-eyed girl who had such faith that marriage would mean she felt adored and beloved forever; that's a fairy tale nobody could have provided. But I don't feel sad for too long. Instead of a perfect happy ending, or even her favorite weird ones, she has found a partnership worthy of *Shirley,* a healthy sprinkling of caution from *The*

Tenant of Wildfell Hall, and a M. Paul Emanuel of her very own. That shining spark of *Jane Eyre's* passion has survived too, and she prizes it all the more for nearly having lost it.

ONE of Charlotte's final relationship lessons for me is a pragmatic one: when she arrived home after their honeymoon, she wrote to Ellen, "It is a solemn and strange and perilous thing for a woman to become a wife," and signed it "Yours faithfully C ~~Bron~~ Nicholls."[14] I love that. It's like Charlotte's pen didn't want her to forget who she was.

I am about to run out of road, so to speak, on the Brontë life map. It does feel perilous, losing this line along which I've paced my steps so far. It also offers a great many possibilities. If I start a new job, if I relocate for my career, if I have kids, I'll be telling stories Charlotte never got to tell.

Though she will never write another book, and found leading a classroom to be an ordeal rather than a vocation, Charlotte is still a born teacher. After I finished Charlotte's letters, I began to notice her influence in my life in subtle ways. I use lessons I've learned reading and writing about the Brontës in the hope of inspiring my students the way the Brontës inspire me. I have started to appreciate my imperfect friendships differently; I write to my friends more often—a quick check-in message, a "saw this and thought of you" email. I even pick up the phone occasionally to leave Sally long, rambling voicemails. I spearheaded a writing retreat for my grad-school friends, and we have plans to make it a semiannual event. I make an effort to return holiday cards and inquire after family members. I call my parents regularly and try to be as nice to my brother as he is to me. I may not have a large group of people in my constellation, but the ones I do have are loyal, kind, and funny, and I value them immensely.

I finished the last of Charlotte's letters thinking, this is it. This is all there is.

But there was still one place left.

Haworth

Our excitement as we neared Haworth had in it an element of suspense that was really painful, as though we were to meet some long-separated friend, who might have changed in the interval—so clear an image of Haworth had we from print and picture.[1]

—Virginia Woolf, 1904

When I first discussed the possibility of a trip to Haworth with Eric, he was eager to come along. As the trip got closer, he was less sure—he was afraid he'd be in my way, that he'd distract from my experience, that because he didn't love the Brontës as I love the Brontës, I would be less able to immerse myself in Haworth and its history. Possibly he was worried I'd run mad on the moors and leave him stranded without the cultural familiarity to navigate home. "Don't be ridiculous, you're half the point of going," I told him, before making him watch the five-hour BBC *Jane Eyre*. He had the good sense to pretend he liked it very much, whether he did or not.

Thanks to the Brontës, I had begun to learn how to share my life (and what's more, my *actual* life, not merely an elaborate performance of a well-behaved one). He had to be there.

My mission was as simple as it had always been—to get as close to Charlotte Brontë and her family as possible, to see what could only be seen from standing where they stood. We began our trip in London, where we would spend three days before going on to Yorkshire. Fortunately for us, on their first trips to London, Charlotte and Anne were as much tourists as anyone else, flocking to landmarks like St. Paul's and Winchester Cathedral; we got the best of old and new London as we followed their footsteps. As Charlotte later wrote in *Villette*,

> Elation and pleasure were in my heart: to walk alone in London seemed of itself an adventure. . . .
>
> . . . I went wandering whither chance might lead, in a still ecstasy of freedom and enjoyment; and I got—I know not how—I got into the heart of city life. I saw and felt London at last: I got into the Strand; I went up Cornhill; I mixed with the life passing along; I dared the perils of crossings. To do this, and to do it utterly alone, gave me, perhaps an irrational, but a real pleasure. Since those days, I have seen the West End, the parks, the fine squares; but I love the city far better. The city seems so much more in earnest: its business, its rush, its roar, are such serious things, sights, and sounds. The city is getting its living—the West End but enjoying its pleasure. At the West End you may be amused, but in the city you are deeply excited.[2]

We saw where Charlotte and Anne would have stayed in Paternoster Square, where they first met George Smith on Waterloo Place, and we heard the bells she would have heard when we woke up on our first morning there—they drew us straight to St. Paul's Cathedral, just like they did for Lucy Snowe:

> When I awoke, rose, and opened my curtain, I saw the risen sun struggling through fog. Above my head, above the house-tops, co-elevate almost with the clouds, I saw a solemn, orbed mass, dark blue and dim—THE DOME. While I looked, my inner self moved; my spirit shook its always-fettered wings half loose; I had a sudden feeling as if I, who never yet truly lived, were at last about to taste life. . . .
>
> Prodigious was the amount of life I lived that morning. Finding myself before St. Paul's, I went in; I mounted to the dome.[3]

The front steps of St. Paul's are bustling, the steps crowded with tourists and the streets with buses and taxis. Though the dome is an impressive sight from all over London, right at the cathedral's base it becomes hardly noticeable. Once inside, in awe of the cathedral's size and spectacle, the ornate marble and bronze decorations, I stopped by a particularly impressive monument in the nave featuring a man on a horse surrounded by ornamentation and pomp. "I wonder how I'd have to live my life to get this kind of memorial," I said irreverently, before walking around to the side with the subject's name etched into it. It was Lord Wellington. Charlotte's personal hero and secular patron saint.

And then, on the left side of the nave as I approached the altar, there were plaques commemorating World War

I veterans. On one of them, I saw my last name, "Penning-ton," etched in neat capitals. Then I gasped. Four rows above it was "Eyre."

We decided to climb all the way to the topmost gallery of the dome. It was a scary, anxious undertaking, walking up marble steps, then stone steps, and finally ascending nar-row spiral iron staircases, teetering between the inner dome and the outer one. I kept repeating, "If Charlotte could do this, with no arch support and no immune system, so can I." I could imagine the headlines the following day—Brontë Enthusiast Plunges to Death, Punctures Hole in Ceiling of Cathedral That Survived the Blitz.

The climb was worth it. The views from each of the over-looks are breathtaking. As Charlotte (who was notoriously nearsighted) put it in *Villette*,

> I saw thence London, with its river, and its bridges, and its churches; I saw antique Westminster, and the green Tem-ple Gardens, with sun upon them, and a glad, blue sky, of early spring above; and between them and it, not too dense, a cloud of haze.[4]

We made our way back down and ventured out into the city. I fell in love with London immediately—the Thames, the cabs, the bridges, the innumerable "on this spot stood something designed by Christopher Wren that was de-stroyed in the great fire" signs and the quirky alleys every-where. A great many fish and chips were consumed, along with large quantities of fizzy lemonade and tea. After two days of acclimation (and the progression of my terrible fake accent through every act of *My Fair Lady*) we were ready to follow Charlotte back to the Parsonage.

We arrived in Haworth, that "lonely, quiet spot, buried away from the world," the way Charlotte Brontë might have returned to it—a train ride from London to Leeds, then a shorter train ride to Keighley (pronounced, I now know, with a sort of ich-laut, tapping the tongue on the roof of the mouth as you pass over the *gh*). We watched the sun get lower over the beautiful countryside from the train windows, nudging each other to point out church spires and anything that looked like a castle. By the time we alighted at Keighley, it was dark and we could only see the gray stone buildings where they were lit by street lamps, following the narrow road up out of the Worth Valley and into the village of Haworth. We took a cab; the Brontës would have taken a one-horse trap cart, or, horrors, *walked* the remaining four miles. Our cabbie asked if we'd been there before, and when I said no, he asked "Home to see the sisters?" and I said yes. Home to see the sisters. If I stopped to mention every time I cried on this trip, it would double the length of the chapter, so just assume I perpetually had the vapors.

We passed by some of the fearful tourist Brontë-exploitation I'd been afraid of: a Brontë laundromat, an apartment building called "Thornfield," a coffee shop called "Villette," a store called "Eyres and Graces." I thought, "I am coming here to Haworth on my knees—there is no need to sell the Brontës to me," accompanied by a flash of irritation that *anybody* needs to have the Brontës *sold* to them. We passed a railway station, then what looked like an old factory with a "cars for hire" sign on it, and at last turned onto a bumpy, narrow cobblestone road, so steep we were pressed back into our seats. I was surprised the little cab's engine was able to move us upward, the grade was so extreme. "This is Main Street," the cabbie announced, and we peered out our respective windows at the small shops and pubs that lined it.

He pulled over in front of our lodgings, the Apothecary Guest. Next door, Rose and Co., which had been a real apothecary back in the Brontës' day (that sold Branwell real opium), now sold kitschy soaps and candy. We rang the bell, fearful suddenly that we were about to find ourselves in a Poe novel, but Nic, the smiling proprietor, opened the door, took my suitcase, and led us up some narrow stairs. Our room had a copy of Branwell's famous portrait of his sisters on the wall, with Branwell misguidedly painted back in. After a moment of delighting over the old-fashioned lock and key, we ventured back out onto the dark, misty streets of Haworth, heart of Shirley Country and nexus of the Brontë universe. I would have knelt to kiss the cobblestones, but it occurred to me that for all it was two hundred years later, public hygiene probably wasn't quite improved enough for that.

In 2012, Daphne Merkin wrote for the *New York Times Magazine* that "there is always the hope that whatever led the Brontës to pull great books out of themselves might work again if one only entrusted oneself to the same brooding surroundings."[5] Even the most pragmatic of earlier visitors, who commented rather harshly on the manners of their tour guides, were unable to resist mentally reviving the sisters. We just can't help ourselves. In 1861, American Charles Hale visited during the renovation of the Parsonage, following the departure of Arthur Bell Nicholls. He pilfered Patrick Brontë's bellpull, and purchased a window sash from Charlotte's bedroom and purloined some of the panes. He wanted pieces of the Parsonage to frame other pieces of the Parsonage. But this is grisly souvenir-seeking; this is not the act of a man on pilgrimage.[6]

Many have written about what readers and writers seek when they visit the homes of their heroines and heroes. Virginia Woolf's first piece of published writing was a recollection of a visit to Haworth in 1904, in which she remarked it was better to stay home and read the books themselves than to undertake sentimental journeys to famous doorsteps.[7] I both understand and object to her argument. Of course we get a jolt of contact when we read the Brontës' work, no matter where we are, and certainly, we are deluded about the power of place. But that doesn't mean there's nothing to it. We want to feel close to them. To imagine they feel close to us. To sense their presence. We think we'll know them better, we'll see the work more clearly, we'll become touched by greatness ourselves. Perhaps we just want to say, "Thank you, thank you for what you did and I'm sorry about the consumption and so, so grateful for your life and your work." And what's wrong with the sentimental journey anyway— not just for the Brontë-seekers, but for devotees of any author who has touched readers deeply?

We passed the Black Bull on our left, where Branwell used to regale his fans and neighbors with drunken exploits, glanced down to the White Lion on our right, then turned left at the Kings Arms and realized we were facing the side of the Haworth church. A few steps farther and we were standing alongside the graveyard, which meant the illuminated building up ahead could only be the Parsonage. *That* Parsonage. My eyes filled with urgent tears and then I sobbed. Three days of imagining "Charlotte Brontë visited near here and would have seen this, not precisely these buildings, but definitely something similar to this" in London gave way to a true and absolute certainty that "she was here, she walked here, she saw this. This is all real. This is where she is."

The Parsonage faces the church, with the graveyard spread in between and crawling around to the left. A stone wall runs the length of the graveyard and encloses a small front lawn; an iron gate admits visitors, and over it hangs an ironwork sign of a woman at a desk, writing. Behind the Parsonage is the ticket office and the inevitable gift shop, and beyond are the moors, invisible in the darkness. We stood quietly for a few more minutes. The house seemed smaller than I had imagined, though it was at least as big as my childhood home, which only ever had to contain two children. I imagined teleporting through the walls, and being alone with the Brontë relics I knew were there.

We walked back down the darkened lane. My eyes were still streaming. It felt exactly right. Gloomy and still and so beautiful. I could see why Elizabeth Gaskell had given into the impulse of mythmaking. The damp grass and dead leaves of the graveyard made a more picturesque backdrop for the Brontës' Gothic tales than the daffodils impudently nodding in barrels below the church windows. Much of Haworth shuts down on weeknights, since the tourist traffic is less active in the off-season, so we felt lucky to find a restaurant that was still open for a late dinner. Afterward, back in our bedroom, as I was imagining how it would be to knock on the Parsonage door and take Charlotte Brontë's tiny hand into my own, the adrenaline wore off and I fell asleep.

WHEN we woke up the next morning, Eric was decidedly unwell. He'd complained of a sore throat in London but we had both chalked it up to plane germs and London fog. My vision of the morning's events (a triumphant return to the Parsonage, where the ghosts of the Brontë sisters would offer me tea in the dining room and keep me company while I researched, answering all my questions with wit and good humor) had to be set aside. I set off in pursuit of over-the-counter remedies, and when the Rose & Co. apothecary was no help (damn you kitschy soaps!), I hiked all the way down the impossibly steep hill in a misting rain to the nearest grocery.

I tried to balance concern for Eric's health with frustration over the way this once-in-a-lifetime trip was being disrupted and the physical discomfort of seriously, the steepest hill ever. Suddenly I felt calm descend. What could bring me closer to the Brontës of Haworth than having my creative fulfillment compromised by the illness of a loved one? Now I, too, would experience the straight-up inconvenience of

Yorkshire-induced ailments. I might even have the opportunity to triumph over adversity before, regretfully, succumbing
to the sore throat and body aches my beloved was currently
enduring. Would they bury me in Haworth!? Would I win
some sort of most dedicated tourist award? Could this even
make me an honorary sister? Things were looking up.

At last, the hill conquered (it was a million times worse
to ascend, by the way), and Eric dosed with ibuprofen and
breakfast, he felt well enough to come with me to the Parsonage. A breathless, jumpy feeling overtook me as we got
our tickets and walked to the front of the building. Running
narration dogged my every step. *I am in Charlotte Brontë's
yard. I am on her steps. That is her door. She heard those hinges
squeak. This was her foyer. This is it, this is her floor. This wall I
am not supposed to be touching was her wall. Her skirt brushed
this doorway.* I gazed into the Brontës' dining room, decorated as it would have been in the 1850s, after Charlotte put
red curtains over the windows and hung portraits of Thackeray and Wellington on the walls. I ran my eyes over the
blur of Patrick's study, the kitchen, Arthur Nicholls' study.
Then up the stairs (*she stepped on this step and held the bannis-
ter maybe here or maybe here*), passing the grandfather clock
on the landing. I glanced into the servants' bedroom, then
Patrick's bedroom, outfitted to match a sketch Branwell
had done in which Death loomed over him in bed;* then
the nursery, which had been made smaller when Charlotte
expanded the master bedroom next door. There are pencil
sketches and doodles on the wall that may have been done

---

*What a drama queen.

by the Brontë children. Branwell's studio was renovated by the curate who came after the Brontës, and now contains an exhibition of Brontëana.

Finally I stepped into the room that Patrick and Maria had shared, where Charlotte and Arthur had slept after their marriage, and where Charlotte had finally died. It wasn't furnished like a bedroom; instead, it held display cases of trinkets and treasures, personal items that had touched Charlotte's hands. The ceiling was low and the wooden floor creaked as I stepped gingerly around the room. The central case held a silk dress on a mannequin, so if you glanced out of the corner of your eye it looked like one of the sisters was standing there, headless. Charlotte's wedding bonnet sat beside it, doing nothing to dispel the illusion. Her botanical pictures lined the walls. Pamphlets from the Great Exhibition, which she'd visited several times, and Aunt Elizabeth Branwell's glasses, and pairs of impossibly tiny lace gloves were dimly illuminated under glass. And I felt nothing.

For the first time since setting foot in Haworth I didn't have an emotional reaction. Maybe I'd done too much research—I recognized nearly everything from pictures I'd seen. For a while that headless silk dress had been my cell phone's wallpaper. Or maybe the exhibits made the bedroom feel too far removed from its previous life. Other people, the Reverend Wade and his family and subsequent caretakers, slept and woke and lived in it after Charlotte did, and now it felt the most like a museum of any room in the house. The dining room, I fancied, held more of Charlotte's creative energy, or the kitchen that, though renovated, still looked as though the Brontës might have just stepped out of it.

I was shown into the research library (which meant cross-
ing the velvet rope and getting to walk through the Brontës'
kitchen!), where the library and collections officer had laid
out some of the Brontës' own books for me. I slipped on a
pair of white cotton gloves and dove into their copy of Goldsmith's *Geography*. Charlotte signed her name twice on its
inside cover and filled the flyleaves with sketches and doodles. She, or Emily or Anne, added their place names to the
index (Gondal, and perhaps Glass Town?).

I was filled with love and affection for her. This is the
whole point of primary research—to be surprised and delighted by things you can only discover in person. *Geography*
showed me how she came to learn about far-off places, and

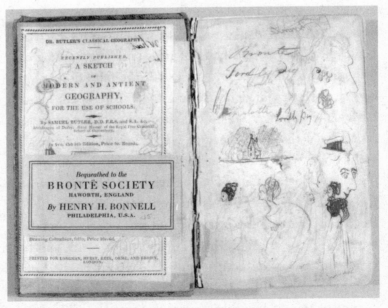

Figure 14.1: Doodles in the flyleaf of Goldsmith's *Geography*.
PHOTO COURTESY OF THE BRONTË PARSONAGE MUSEUM.

how she felt she could know them despite not having traveled there. In addition to short narrative descriptions, the book features illustrations of cities and clothing, invokes poets to describe the scenery when appropriate, and includes editorial observations to enliven what might otherwise have been a fairly dry recounting of people and places. It makes total sense she and her siblings would have been interested in establishing their own countries and making games out of historical figures—these were their toys.

Why does Charlotte Brontë come to life in the pages of a little geography book she doodled on and not in the very room she died in? Virginia Woolf said, referring to the clothing on display, that it was because "the natural fate of such things is to die before the body that wore them, and because these, trifling and transient though they are, have survived, Charlotte Brontë the woman comes to life, and one forgets the chiefly memorable fact that she was a great writer."[8] When Charlotte doodled in that little book, and Anne annotated its index, they gave it pieces of themselves that still endure, not as Great Writers, but as curious, engaged young girls. I'm touching something Charlotte touched, bracing it with my hands where she might have held it, as she sketched a fine lady in a long gown. Nobody has repapered over the book or moved its furnishings around. They didn't have to reconstruct it from their best period estimates. It was already here. Charlotte drew her thoughts and when I look at them, I see what she was thinking, and thus she is alive again for a moment.

When I stand where she stood, hold what she held, and hear things she might have heard (the gusting wind on the moors, for example) I can almost forget there are no living reminders of Charlotte Brontë left. Or that none of us have the luxury of leaving our actual selves behind, outside the pages of our books or the canvas of our artwork. People left graffiti on the staircase of St. Paul's to make their mark, so we know they were there. And sometimes that's as permanent a memento as we can hope for.

For the preservation of Haworth we have the hard work of the Brontë Society to thank. It was formed in 1893 and immediately became responsible for obtaining and preserving every scrap of Brontëana that it could get. Its first president was the Right Honorable Earl (later Marquess) of Crewe, Robert Offley Ashburton Crewe-Milnes.[9] The collection became the largest in the world upon the sudden death of collector and publisher Henry Houston Bonnell, who bequeathed to the museum his extensive collection of Brontë manuscripts, letters, first editions, and personal effects in 1926.

There is an amazing body of scholarly work in the Society's transactions, essays, research, and transcriptions of first-person accounts. My favorites are the narratives from early visitors to Haworth, who came to visit while Arthur Nicholls and Patrick Brontë were still alive. *Everyone* talks about those hills. The lucky ones sat in the Haworth church to hear Patrick or Arthur preach, and a few were invited into the Parsonage to talk to Patrick afterward. Their accounts of the village's grimness and its surroundings are generally pretty dramatic, though some do acknowledge it was pretty in summer. People seem to have the hardest time believing the Brontë children could ever have been cheerful. Even though I get to see Brontë relics too, how jealous I am of all the early Brontë fanatics who got to hear stories directly and handle all the mementos themselves, sitting in the kitchens and parlors of neighbors. They got to speak with maids at the Black Bull and sextons to whom Branwell owed money, and shopkeepers who sold the Brontës their paper.

When I'd absorbed as much Brontë communion as I could take for one day, I went back to the guesthouse to check on Eric. He felt like his throat was closing up and it was becoming difficult to swallow. I spoke with our host, feeling fairly confident leeches weren't still Haworth's best option for medicine, and he directed us to a "surgery" just around the corner. I felt worried until I realized "surgery" is the British word for clinic. The doctor there sent us to a specialist at the Bradford Royal Infirmary because he was afraid Eric's throat ailment was quinsy. This was hard to hear, but it felt great to say it in my fake British accent, because we don't have "Royal Infirmaries" in America and nobody gets quinsy (KWIN-zay) anymore. I felt a pit of dread in my stomach when he told us to look for the "casualty unit," until I found out it was British for "emergency room."

We took a cab to Bradford, the next town over, which is a thriving metropolis compared to quiet, hilly Haworth. I spent a lot of the ride reassuring Eric that quinsy almost never needed surgery (it often does) and that it had absolutely not killed George Washington (it definitely did). On a positive note, we got to see Yorkshire countryside we'd never have seen without a visit to the hospital. A miserable evening on the ENT ward later, Eric was diagnosed with tonsillitis and sent home with antibiotics and baby Tylenol, since the pharmacy was closed and they wanted us to at least have *something* to get through the night with. Bless you, socialized medicine.

OUR second day in Haworth, Eric was still in pain and elected to stay in bed. I had a stroll through the freezing church, which was unlocked and only inhabited by a long-haired black cat, who'd taken up residence on a fifty-pence book table near the entrance. I saw the Brontë memorial marble plaque, which had been preserved from the original church. Even if it was for space reasons, I'm miffed that Branwell gets his own line. Anne is the only missing member, as she was buried at Scarborough.

Charlotte's pew is long gone, and the reconstruction pews aren't nearly as quaint. There were a variety of postcards and photos for sale, surrounded by disheartening pleas for financial support. I dropped a pound coin in the box and petted the cat gingerly; it felt like I quite had Brontë Country to myself for the morning.

Eric's throat was even more swollen when I finished reading Goldsmith's *Geography*, which blithely asserted that calf-sized American elephants could be found in the New World, and Brontë Society *Transactions* for the afternoon, so back to Bradford we went, to see a doctor, who teased us for giving Eric's weight in pounds ("Don't you speak proper English?" he asked dryly. "Is it . . . stones?" I said, tentatively. "Kilograms," he replied, with playful disdain. Even my medical references are from outdated literature). Then he gave Eric steroids to reduce the swelling so the antibiotics could do their work.

It was a characteristically Haworthian day, gray and cloudy with occasional rain. The grimness of the landscape seeped into my imagination and I envisioned the glorious misery of a plane ride home alone to explain that Eric had caught a case of the Brontës and perished on Haworth moor. Amazingly, two hours after taking his first dose of steroids Eric sat up, announced he was hungry, and ate all of our remaining rolls (pronounced *tea cakes*). The next morning he woke up before I did, still ravenous. Modern medicine had worked its magic, the sun had burnt off the fog, and I was quite happy to say goodbye to that particular realm of Brontë overidentification.

MY third day, I dove into the *Blackwoods* magazines, starting with 1825, when Charlotte was nine. These are the magazines on which she and Branwell based their own hand-sewn versions. I found evidence of articles and stories she certainly must have read—the burning of Indian widows; folktales with brownies, fairies, and witches; essays about the life of the Duke of Wellington. There was advice for bachelors and unmarried women, a great deal of satire, poetry, history, dispatches from all over the British Empire, open letters to the editor, political essays, debates on women's rights, and brief installments of novels and plays. The bound-up editions of the actual magazines I got to read aren't the Brontës' own copies, but they live on the bookshelves in the Brontës' dining room. Now that I've read their source material, I can see how precise the Brontës' imitations were, and better appreciate their adoption of so many editorial "voices" at such young ages. At two, my now "usual" quitting time, Eric met me at the Parsonage and we had a quick lunch before the unlikely beauty of a sunny day in Yorkshire beckoned us onto the moors.

Our walk was glorious. The relief at Eric's recovery combined with the splendidness of the weather and the unspeakable wonder of the landscape. If seeing the Brontës' London felt like ringing a little bell inside my ribcage, gazing out on their moors was like striking a gong the size of my whole body. Every Brontë acolyte who's ever come this way has done exactly as we did—crossed the churchyard and turned right into the narrow walled-in lane, reached the moors, and decided whether to make for Top Withens or Stanbury or the Brontë Waterfall. I began as a waterfall skeptic, since it sounded like touristy nonsense, but then I found an account by Ellen Nussey of a day trip to Haworth in which the sisters *did* take her on a long walk. They had idled away the afternoon, in fact, by a waterfall. We walked and exclaimed and walked some more.

I took a sprig of heather to tuck in my journal (an homage to the one Charlotte allegedly carried in to Emily during her last weakening days). There were stone walls and grassy fields all around, and the view stretched down and away for miles and miles. The colors went from ruddy brown to bright green and faded yellow across the landscape. We passed small farmhouses and scattered flocks of sheep, grazing and napping in the sun next to their lambs. When we crossed over the road from Stanbury we came upon a large group of rams munching grass together, staring at us with their keyhole-shaped pupils.

Every time we passed a halfway passable pool of water we wondered if we'd reached the "meeting of the waters," and debated turning back. Eventually we were rewarded for our perseverance when the path became stonier and the stones became steps and the moors bent into a seam, out of which burbled quick-flowing water. If you ever make this journey yourself, just trust me and keep going. When you find it, you'll know. It is not vague or subtle. Just like everything else about the Brontës, their waterfall is emphatic and deliberate and unmistakable. The Brontës would have crossed the stream with stepping stones, but the Brontë Society has placed a bridge there for pilgrims to use. We walked as close to the water's source as we could in unsteady shoes, and I kept an eye out for ghosts. Unfortunately, only another hiker and his two spaniels, presumably mortal, made their presence known.

When I was a kid, visiting relatives in rural Arkansas or woodsy Connecticut, I'd occasionally enjoyed a walk out into the flat grass-filled plains or the hilly forests around their houses. I liked the outdoors as a concept, as a view from a cabin window or from the top of a moderate hill near the parked car that had driven me there. But I had never seen anything like this. The mossy stones, the villages that looked like train-set models, the farmhouses set apart from their neighbors. There was nothing I saw that I did not love immediately. If I could, I would have opened my eyes wider, let them take over my whole face just to see more of West Yorkshire at a time.

The only difficulty in the whole day was the wind, which was always present and at times quite, well, wuthering. But despite that—or more likely because of it—we had a remarkable day that felt like it was sent just for us (the ultimate delusion of pilgrims to well-traveled historical sites). I have never been so sad to leave a place as I was to go back inside after being on those moors. No wonder Emily Brontë sickened to be away from them. No wonder Charlotte devoted whole passages of *Shirley* just to landscape rhapsody. No wonder none of them could be happy cooped up in a city or confined to a nursery caring for someone else's children. They knew what real liberty felt like, and no alternative would ever be worthwhile as long as this awaited them at home.

OUR last two days in Haworth were overcast—ideal for research, as if the moors didn't want me to overdose. The next morning the Parsonage employee at the admissions desk greeted me like a regular. I spent the day immersed in books on the Brontës, their education, and the significance of their artwork. I mined their letters for references to *Blackwoods* and any other publications I would be able to track down back home. It was damp and rainy, but it was also Thursday, so some of the shops that had been closed all week were finally open. Eric and I made the best of it and shopped along Main Street with sodden feet.

Our last morning in Haworth, I started my day in the graveyard. I have always loved cemeteries, never found them scary or ominous. My cat friend, Oscar, who I heard sometimes slips into the Parsonage and tries to lay on the beds, came to say hello. I stopped by the graves of Tabby and the Browns, friends of the family who also worked for the Brontës, who were now buried close to the churchyard wall. Oscar and I wandered around together, noting big families and odd surnames and unusual memorials. Many of the interred would have known the Brontës, and some still have family ties in the village. A man walked by while I stood near the railing at the front and said, "You'd nought have been standing the' las' night—it was slashing down 'ere, and I came by an' back thro' it and wondered why I'd ever gon' out," in a Yorkshire accent so delicious and thick that every word had either half or twice the usual number of syllables. There was actually a time delay while I worked out what he'd said. It made me think of an early visitor to Haworth, who'd said after a similar encounter in 1877, "I . . . could have hugged the good woman for allowing me to hear it in Yorkshire air."[10]

Then I walked down the footpath toward Haworth moor, which we hadn't visited on our perfect day on Penistone Hill. The morning was sunny and clear and cold. I could see the shadows of clouds moving over the fields in the valley. To my left and up the hill were several ewes with their lambs, frolicking on the green or sleeping in the sun. To my right was a row of cottages just waking up, starting the day with this view. The Brontës' ability to evoke the moors so vividly seems all the more impressive when you consider how the scenery brings even the most verbose outsider to an awed sort of stillness. At last, I turned back to the Parsonage, and was pleased to see Oscar padding over to say goodbye. I scratched behind his ears, pulled some leaves from his tail, and watched him saunter off on whatever cat business took him on his way.*

Eventually I had to go inside and take my seat for the last time. I'd saved the best for last—three of the surviving tiny *Young Men's Magazines* handcrafted by Branwell and Charlotte. The librarians had laid them out on a cushion for me. Not facsimiles, not transcriptions, not copies, but the little manuscripts themselves, even smaller than I'd anticipated. I dramatically opened the folder in which they sat, anticlimactically catalogued in plastic bags. I'd expected to be blown away by their intricacy, but for all their imitative fidelity, these tiny paper booklets were clearly made by the hands of children (albeit precocious ones). I pulled on cotton gloves and figured out how to brace them in my fingers so I could read with a magnifying glass and take notes. If it weren't for my gloves, our fingerprints might have lined up in that moment.

The first magazine I opened began with a narrative of walking in a country landscape much like the one we had

---

*Rest in peace, Oscar! He succumbed to advanced feline age just a month or so after our visit.

roamed over a day ago. I transcribed most of the first little book, dated August of 1830, chuckling over the silliness
of Captain Tree and Stumps, marveling at the versatility of
Charlotte's wit and imagination. Upon reaching the end, I
had a brief thrilling moment, wondering if I could possibly
be one of the first people to sit there and puzzle out these
particular tiny manuscript books. Then a reference in my edition of selected juvenilia led me to an entire collection of *The
Early Writing of Charlotte Brontë*, where the magazine I'd just
transcribed and half a dozen more were reprinted. Still. I bet
not many people have sat here and done it by hand, taking
the time to decipher a confusing misspelling or an archaic
turn of phrase. Or maybe everyone who visits does—Would
that really make it less of a miracle?

I found in the end that Eric didn't distract me at all,
though his hospital visits certainly escalated the verisimili-
tude. Without him, I wouldn't have gotten to see the Royal
Infirmary, which was at least as exciting as it was frightening.
I wouldn't have enjoyed the moors so completely, because
I would have been constantly wishing he was there to see
them too. On our trip and in our lives together, he helps me
make room for everything I want to do and see, and keeps
me from rushing through it. He's also good for making sure
I stop and eat occasionally.

Realizing we could get one more full day in London if we
left Haworth early, we packed our things and changed our
train tickets to Friday night, instead of Saturday as initially
planned. Back in London, we got to see Buckingham Palace
deserted under a full moon, and the next morning, St. James's
Park and its daffodils and at least four different species of

ducks. We rode the Eye and basked in its panoramic views, and heard Big Ben toll a final time before we headed to the airport. I researched holiday rentals and tried to figure out how I could ever afford to come back. I imagined taking a room for a month or two to write and visit the moors and pester the librarians with questions about the Brontës' bank balances, thinking, "I could truly be happy here!"

But by the time I took my seat on the plane to New York, I was wondering how true that was—Could I be happy someplace so quiet? Maybe it's the effect of so many childhood moves, but I always want to stay someplace long enough to feel comfortable. It rarely occurs to me that I'd eventually get bored. I'd miss going to movies in the middle of the night, the satisfaction of living somewhere the world thinks of as a global capital. But on the other hand? *I could be Charlotte Brontë's neighbor.* I could walk my dog on the moors with Emily's ghost. As a member of the Brontë Society, I can visit the museum every single day if I want to. I could come to know their dining room better than my own. I could read every single piece of Brontë material in the catalogue—and still not have seen it all, because there are Brontë collections in Austin, in Boston, in Buffalo, and New York. I'm comforted by the knowledge that there are still plenty of Brontë fragments for me to pore over, housed in libraries and even private collections. Charlotte was at work on a novel called *Emma* when she died—Thackeray published it in *Cornhill* with a eulogy he wrote himself a few months later. There may still be undiscovered pieces out there somewhere in Charlotte's tiny, usually precise, but occasionally careless hand.

Since our trip, I've visited the manuscripts at the Morgan Library and Museum downtown, a fitting palatial home for such treasures. One afternoon I went to Columbia University's Rare Book and Manuscript Library to see a box of Mrs. Humphrey Ward's effects—she was a Brontë Society president who wrote introductions for new editions of all the Brontë novels in 1905. A few weeks later at the Strand I found those editions of *Shirley* and *Villette*—it felt like I was enmeshed in a Brontë constellation, as if I had found my place in their orbit.

Sometimes it feels like my whole life has been coherently pointing in this direction. Just as liking led to love and reading one book led to another, being a huge dork led to a life wrapped in literature, art, history, languages. And, finally, to Haworth itself, where I wipe away tears with the back of my hand because this, this is as close as I can get. I know how Charlotte Brontë sounded on paper as a child, as a young girl, as a woman. I know who her hero was and where he is buried. I know what she might have seen when she woke up in London on a morning in March. I know which imaginary places Anne felt were important enough to record in her geography book. I know what her neat, tidy stitches looked like. I've seen the kitchen where Emily studied German and the front door she rarely felt like going through. I've seen the pub where Branwell drank and bragged and drank some more; the corner where he met his friend John to sneak a final dram of gin. I could still go to Brussels, I suppose, and see where the *pensionnat* used to be, or return to Yorkshire to visit the houses of their friends. But I don't know that it's necessary. I know where Charlotte wandered, I know where she married, I know where she died. Perhaps that is enough to tell me what I need to know.

DURING my time at the Parsonage, I only asked to see one letter—from Charlotte's time in Brussels. Charlotte concluded a letter to Ellen with "Good-bye to you dear Nell when I say so—it seems to me that you will hardly hear me—all the waves of the Channel, heaving and roaring between must deaden the sound."[11] On the back, she sketched a cartoon of the two of them. Charlotte is a disproportionate, gnome-like figure, waving under a speech balloon that says "G o o d b y e," and looking across the sea to Ellen, who is graceful in an elegant dress, with a male companion in a top hat (labeled "The Chosen"). A steamship is puffing by in the background. I held onto the letter until my very last moment in the library, imagining Charlotte was waving goodbye to me, too, as I prepared to make my way home with my chosen, not just across the whole Atlantic Ocean, but all the intervening years too.

Before I left, I took one last tour of the museum. And this time, what had been impossible to access on my first harried walk-through sank into me like waves. It wasn't a museum anymore; it was a home. I'd sat in Reverend Wade's former dining room and breathed the house's air, heard its creaks, crossed its kitchen flagstones every morning and afternoon. As I read, Charlotte was writing in the dining

Figure 14.2: Cartoon of Charlotte waving.
Letter to Ellen Nussey, March 6, 1843.
PHOTO COURTESY OF THE BRONTË PARSONAGE MUSEUM.

room, Patrick was smoking in his study, Emily was reading
to Aunt Branwell, Anne was sewing, Branwell was painting
upstairs, and Tabby was making tea. All of this was happening without regard to the passage of time, while I paged
through tiny manuscripts and deciphered magnified pencil-
marks. The chimes I heard from the clock on the stairs were
the same tones the Brontës heard every hour—one morning

the clock ran down, and the research librarian had to go get Patrick's keys and wind it. They were still Patrick's keys! School groups and clusters of visitors from all over the world had gathered on the other side of the kitchen wall behind me, and I heard them even through the closed door—they'd asked questions about a cooking implement or how the place was heated, what the Brontës ate or how long they'd lived. Another scholar or two shared the big table in the research library with me from time to time, checking postal records or examining illustrations up close. One thing I'll say for the Parsonage—it is small and solitary, but it is full of life.

And I can take comfort in this: however she may have signed all those hurried letters after her marriage, Charlotte belongs to the readers who love her most. She will forever be Charlotte Brontë. It was not Mrs. Nicholls who insisted "I'm just going to write because I cannot help it," or boldly traveled to Brussels, or wrote *Jane Eyre*.

When we left Haworth, I cried. Our cab to the train station eased to the bottom of the hill, turning onto the main road and steering us back to the present. As it did, a rainbow stretched in front of us, each end buried behind a rise of the moors. We drove toward it all the way to Keighley and never reached it. We never even came close.

Acknowledgments

First, my very heartfelt gratitude to the Research Librarians of the Brontë Parsonage Museum, Ann Dinsdale and Sarah Laycock, who gave my pilgrimage the infusion of resources and knowledge it needed. A particular thank you to Christine Nelson for her time and generosity (and for leaving me speechless with Mary Taylor's copy of *Jane Eyre*), as well as the other estimable librarians of the Morgan Library and Museum in New York City. Thanks also to the staff and stacks of Columbia University's Rare Manuscript and Butler Libraries.

Many thanks to my exuberant agent, Julia Lord; my editor, Stephanie Knapp; and to Julia Campbell, Katherine Streckfus, Susie Pitzen, Trish Wilkinson, Faceout Studio, and the hardworking teams at Seal, Da Capo, and Hachette. This book became real because of your support, your enthusiasm, and your diligence.

Enthusiastic thank yous are owed to the teachers and mentors who nudged me to take myself and my Brontë affinity seriously—Richard Locke, Lis Harris, Rebecca Godfrey (the champion of the anti-heroine), and the warm and wonderful Margo Jefferson. Barbara Adams, you are invaluable as a mentor and a friend. Patricia O'Toole, I can safely say I stuck to it, and it was because of your help. Thank you to Sue Mendelsohn, Jason Ueda, and the rest of the Columbia University Writing Center denizens for their warmth and Jedi insights. A special thank you to Michelle Orange for being the first person to plow all the way through a complete draft, despite our differing opinions on Cathy Earnshaw.

Thank you to Meg, Becca, and Jaime G., who read drafts of this book from its birth as a fourteen-page research essay to its unwieldy newborn-giraffe adolescence. Your eyes, ears, and red pencils were always appreciated, and I miss you. Love to Kate, sharer of apartments and provider of actual home-cooked food; to Sheryl, empathetic listener and relationship role model; and especially to Sally, perpetual cheerleader and all-around best gal. To Leslie, Jaime H., Adrienne, and Betsy, testaments to the power of reconnection. To Molly J., who is a beam of light.

Thank you to my family—my parents, Mark and Lynda, my brother Thomas. Without them, I would not have known where to start, I would not be myself, and I would not have been nearly so well entertained along the way. To my aunts and uncles and cousins and grandparents, I love you and I miss you and I hope there's nothing too embarrassing in here.

For Eric: "There was no harassing restraint, no repressing of glee and vivacity with him; for with him I was at perfect ease, because I knew I suited him. . . . It brought to life and light my whole nature: in his presence I thoroughly lived; and he lived in mine."

And good heavens—there's no way I could finish a book about *this* family without sending out all my love and appreciation to the Brontës themselves. Thank you Patrick, Maria, Aunt Elizabeth, Emily, Anne, and even Branwell. And, of course, endless gratitude to the singular Charlotte Brontë, for teaching me what I needed to know.

Bibliography

All of the Brontë sisters' novels and surviving letters, and many of the contemporary reviews, are in the public domain and accessible through Project Gutenberg, the British Library, The Brontë Parsonage Museum, and other public sites of record.

Allott, Miriam Farris. *The Brontës: The Critical Heritage*. London: Routledge and Kegan Paul, 1974.

Barker, Juliet. *The Brontës*. London: Weidenfeld and Nicolson, 1994.

———. *The Brontës: A Life in Letters*. New York: Overlook Press, 1998.

———. *The Brontës: Wild Genius on the Moors. The Story of a Literary Family*. New York: Pegasus Books, 2012.

Brontë, Charlotte. *The Belgian Essays*. Edited by Sue Lonoff. New Haven, CT: Yale University Press, 1996.

———. *Juvenilia, 1829–1835*. New York: Penguin Books, 1996.

———. *The Letters of Charlotte Brontë: With a Selection of Letters by Family and Friends*. Vol. 1, *1829–1847*. Edited by Margaret Smith. Oxford: Clarendon, 1995.

———. *The Letters of Charlotte Brontë: With a Selection of Letters by Family and Friends*. Vol. 2, *1848–1851*. Edited by Margaret Smith. Oxford: Clarendon, 2000.

———. *The Letters of Charlotte Brontë: With a Selection of Letters by Family and Friends*. Vol. 3, *1852–1855*. Edited by Margaret Smith. Oxford: Clarendon, 2004.

———. *Selected Letters of Charlotte Brontë*. Edited by Margaret Smith. Oxford: Oxford University Press, 2010.

Brontë Society. *Brontë Society Transactions* (1893–2001).

Gaskell, Elizabeth Cleghorn. *The Life of Charlotte Brontë: Author of Jane Eyre, Shirley, Villette, &c,* 2nd ed. London: Smith, Elder, 1857. Project Gutenberg.

Lemon, Charles. *Early Visitors to Haworth: From Ellen Nussey to Virginia Woolf.* Haworth, UK: Brontë Society, 1996.

Miller, Lucasta. *The Brontë Myth.* London: Jonathan Cape, 2001.

Shorter, Clement King. *Charlotte Brontë and Her Circle.* New York: Dodd, Mead, 1896. Project Gutenberg, Kindle ed.

Stoneman, Patsy. *Jane Eyre on Stage, 1848–1898: An Illustrated Edition of Eight Plays with Contextual Notes.* Farnham, UK: Ashgate Publishing, 2007.

Taylor, Mary. *The First Duty of Women.* London: Emily Faithful, 1870. Nineteenth Century Collections Online.

Thormählen, Marianne. *The Brontës and Education.* Cambridge: Cambridge University Press, 2007.

Woolf, Virginia. *The Common Reader: First Series.* San Diego: Harcourt Brace Jovanovich, 1984.

Notes

WALKING INTO THE BRONTËS

1. Miriam Farris Allott, *The Brontës: The Critical Heritage* (London: Routledge and Kegan Paul, 1974), 108.

THE FAMILY

1. Allott, *The Brontës*, 254.

2. Juliet Barker, *The Brontës* (London: Weidenfeld and Nicolson, 1994), revised and updated as *The Brontës: Wild Genius on the Moors. The Story of a Literary Family* (New York: Pegasus Books, 2012).

3. Clement King Shorter, *Charlotte Brontë and Her Circle* (New York: Dodd, Mead, 1896 [Project Gutenberg]), Kindle ed., loc. 706.

4. Barker, *The Brontës* (2012), 110.

5. Charlotte Brontë, *Juvenilia, 1829–1835* (New York: Penguin Books, 1996), 3.

6. Charlotte Brontë, *The Letters of Charlotte Brontë: With a Selection of Letters by Family and Friends*, Vol. 1, *1829–1847*, edited by Margaret Smith (Oxford: Clarendon, 1995), 153.

JANE

1. Charlotte Brontë, *Jane Eyre*, Chapter XII.
2. Allott, *The Brontës*, 98.
3. Charlotte Brontë, *Jane Eyre*, Chapter XXIII.
4. Ibid.
5. Ibid.

A WISH FOR WINGS

1. Brontë, *Letters of Charlotte Brontë*, ed. Smith, 1:266.
2. Ibid., 1:268.
3. Ibid., 1:284.
4. Ibid., 1:285.
5. Charlotte Brontë, *The Belgian Essays*, edited by Sue Lonoff (New Haven, CT: Yale University Press, 1996), 140.
6. Ibid., 362.
7. Ibid., 363–364.
8. Ibid., 360.
9. Brontë, *Letters of Charlotte Brontë*, ed. Smith, 1:300.
10. Ibid., 1:317.
11. Ibid., 1:334.
12. Ibid., 1:340.
13. Ibid., 1:109.
14. Ibid., 1:379.
15. Barker, *The Brontës* (1994), 441.
16. Shorter, *Charlotte Brontë and Her Circle*, loc. 735–736.
17. Brontë, *Letters of Charlotte Brontë*, ed. Smith, 1:435.
18. Elizabeth Cleghorn Gaskell, *The Life of Charlotte Brontë: Author of Jane Eyre, Shirley, Villette, &c.*, 2nd ed. (London : Smith, Elder, 1857 [Project Gutenberg]), 194.
19. Ibid., 210.

MAKING THE ROUNDS

1. Charlotte Brontë, *The Letters of Charlotte Brontë: With a Selection of Letters by Family and Friends*, Vol. 2, 1848–1851, edited by Margaret Smith (Oxford: Clarendon, 2000), 744.
2. Barker, *The Brontës* (1994), 117.
3. Brontë, *Letters of Charlotte Brontë*, ed. Smith, 1:168.
4. Ibid., 1:169.
5. Ibid., 1:239.
6. Allott, *The Brontës*, 62.
7. Ibid., 65.
8. Brontë, *Letters of Charlotte Brontë*, ed. Smith, 1:537.
9. Ibid., 1:539.

10. Allott, *The Brontës*, 67.
11. Ibid., 70.
12. Brontë, *Letters of Charlotte Brontë*, ed. Smith, 2:49.

WEARYING HEIGHTS

1. Allott, *The Brontës*, 229.

CATHY EARNSHAW: ANTI-HEROINE

1. Allott, *The Brontës*, 227.
2. Ibid., 220.
3. Charles Lemon, *Early Visitors to Haworth: From Ellen Nussey to Virginia Woolf* (Haworth, UK: Brontë Society, 1996), 242–243.
4. Emily Brontë, *Wuthering Heights*, Chapter XV.
5. Ibid.
6. *Slings and Arrows*, Season 2, episode 1, directed by Peter Wellington, 2003.
7. Virginia Woolf, *The Common Reader: First Series* (San Diego: Harcourt Brace Jovanovich, 1984), 159.

AGNES GREY

1. Allott, *The Brontës*, 252.
2. Brontë, *Letters of Charlotte Brontë*, ed. Smith, 2:742.
3. Anne Brontë, *Agnes Grey*, Chapter XIV.
4. Charlotte Brontë, *Selected Letters of Charlotte Brontë*, edited by Margaret Smith (Oxford: Oxford University Press, 2007), 31.
5. Anne Brontë, *Agnes Grey*, Chapter VII.
6. Ibid., Chapter XII.
7. Ibid., Chapter XXI.

SHIRLEY AND CAROLINE

1. Lemon, *Early Visitors to Haworth*, 119.
2. Ibid., 117.
3. Charlotte Brontë, *Shirley*, Chapter VII.

4. Ibid.
5. Barker, *The Brontës* (1994), 612.
6. Brontë, *Letters of Charlotte Brontë*, ed. Smith, 1:135.
7. Ibid., 2:81.
8. Ibid., 2:88.
9. Ibid., 2:107.
10. Ibid., 2:439.
11. Ibid., 2:136.
12. Charlotte Brontë, *Shirley*, Chapter XXIII.
13. Brontë, *Letters of Charlotte Brontë*, ed. Smith, 2:195.
14. Ibid., 2:222.
15. Ibid., 2:224.
16. Charlotte Brontë, *Shirley*, Chapter XXIV.
17. Brontë, *Letters of Charlotte Brontë*, ed. Smith, 2:179.
18. Allott, *The Brontës*, 117.
19. Charlotte Brontë, *Shirley*, Chapter XXXVI.

MEETING MR. ROCHESTER

1. Charlotte Brontë, *Jane Eyre*, Chapter XVIII.
2. Ibid., Chapter XV.
3. Ibid.
4. Ibid., Chapter XII.
5. Brontë, *Letters of Charlotte Brontë*, ed. Smith, 1:198.
6. Ibid., 2:112–113.
7. Ibid., 2:655.
8. Ibid., 2:662.
9. Ibid., 2:680.
10. Ibid., 2:492.
11. Ibid., 2:699.
12. Ibid., 2:606.
13. Charlotte Brontë, *Jane Eyre*, Chapter XXXI.

HELEN GRAHAM AND BRANWELL BRONTË

1. Allott, *The Brontës*, 265.
2. Brontë, *Letters of Charlotte Brontë*, ed. Smith, 2:745.

3. Barker, *The Brontës* (2012), 334.
4. Anne Brontë, *The Tenant of Wildfell Hall*, Introduction.
5. Allot, *The Brontës*, 262.
6. Anne Brontë, *Tenant of Wildfell Hall*, Chapter XLI.
7. Allott, *The Brontës*, 272.
8. Anne Brontë, *Tenant of Wildfell Hall*, Chapter XLI.
9. Brontë, *Letters of Charlotte Brontë*, ed. Smith, 2:77.
10. Ibid., 2:82.

WANDERING THE MOORS

1. Brontë, *Letters of Charlotte Brontë*, ed. Smith, 2:139–140.
2. Ibid.
3. Patsy Stoneman, *Jane Eyre on Stage, 1848–1898: An Illustrated Edition of Eight Plays with Contextual Notes* (Farnham, UK: Ashgate Publishing, 2007), 33.

M. PAUL EMANUEL

1. Barker, *The Brontës* (1994), 723.
2. Brontë, *Letters of Charlotte Brontë*, ed. Smith, 1:284.
3. Charlotte Brontë, *Villette*, Chapter XIV.
4. Brontë, *Letters of Charlotte Brontë*, ed. Smith, 2:414.
5. Ibid., 2:516.
6. Charlotte Brontë, *Villette*, Chapter XXI.
7. Ibid., Chapter XXXIII.
8. Ibid., Chapter XXXVIII.
9. Ibid., Chapter XLI.
10. Ibid.
11. Ibid.
12. Ibid., Chapter XLII.
13. Charlotte Brontë, *The Letters of Charlotte Brontë: With a Selection of Letters by Family and Friends*, Vol. 3, *1852–1855*, edited by Margaret Smith (Oxford: Clarendon, 2004), 142.
14. Allott, *The Brontës*, 177.
15. Ibid.

ARTHUR

1. Barker, *The Brontës* (1994), 752.
2. Brontë, *Letters of Charlotte Brontë*, ed. Smith, 3:247.
3. Ibid., 3:265.
4. Barker, *The Brontës* (1994), 302.
5. Ibid.
6. Brontë, *Letters of Charlotte Brontë*, ed. Smith, 2:557.
7. Barker, *The Brontës: A Life in Letters*, 392.
8. Brontë, *Letters of Charlotte Brontë*, ed. Smith, 3:271.
9. Ibid., 3:248.
10. Ibid., 3:286.
11. Ibid., 3:295–297.
12. Ibid., 3:298.
13. Ibid., 3:325.
14. Ibid., 3:284.

HAWORTH

1. Lemon, *Early Visitors to Haworth,* 125.
2. Charlotte Brontë, *Villette*, Chapter VI.
3. Ibid.
4. Ibid.
5. Daphne Merkin, "Life on Moors," *New York Times Magazine,* March 18, 2012, 37–38, 40.
6. Lemon, *Early Visitors to Haworth,* 73–85.
7. Ibid., 124.
8. Ibid., 126.
9. Brontë Society, *Brontë Society Transactions,* Vol. 1 (1895–2001).
10. Lemon, *Early Visitors to Haworth,* 99.
11. Brontë, *Letters of Charlotte Brontë, ed.* Smith, 1:312.

Miranda K. Pennington is a lifelong Brontë enthusiast. She has been a writing consultant and university writing instructor at Columbia University, where she also received her MFA in creative nonfiction. She has spent time working in test prep publishing, working in arts education nonprofits, and teaching academic and creative writing. Her work has appeared on Electric Literature, The Toast, *The American Scholar* online, The Ploughshares Blog, and The Catapult podcast. A proud member of the Cherokee Nation, she was born in Tulsa, Oklahoma and grew up in northern Virginia. This is her first book.